Keeping the Corporate Image:
Public Relations and Business, 1900–1950

**INDUSTRIAL DEVELOPMENT AND
THE SOCIAL FABRIC Vol. 3**

Editor: Glenn Porter, *Director, Regional Economic History Research Center,
Eleutherian Mills—Hagley Foundation, Greenville, Delaware*

INDUSTRIAL DEVELOPMENT AND THE SOCIAL FABRIC

An International Series of Historical Monographs

Series Editor: Glenn Porter

Director, Regional Economic History Research Center,
Eleutherian Mills—Hagley Foundation, Greenville, Delaware

For My Parents

Keeping the Corporate Image:
Public Relations and Business, 1900–1950

by RICHARD S. TEDLOW

Graduate School of Business Administration
Harvard University

 JAI PRESS INC.

Greenwich, Connecticut

Library of Congress Cataloging in Publication Data

Tedlow, Richard S
  Keeping the corporate image.

  (Industrial development and the social fabric;
v. 3)
  Bibliography: p.
  Includes index.
  1. Public relations—United States.
  2. Publicity—United States. 3. Public relations
—Corporations. I. Title. II. Series.
  HM263.T37   659.2′0973   78-13839
  ISBN 0-89232-095-8

ISBN NUMBER: 0-89232-095-8
Library of Congress Catalog Card Number: 78-13839
Manufactured in the United States of America

Contents

List of Tables

Acknowledgments

It is a pleasure to acknowledge the assistance of those who made contributions to this study.

This book began as a doctoral dissertation in American history at Columbia University under the sponsorship of Professor John A. Garraty. I would like to thank Professor Garraty for his support of this rather unorthodox topic and of its (sometimes unorthodox) author. His criticism and that of Professor John W. Chambers II of the Barnard College History Department were most helpful. A number of classmates at Columbia gave portions of the manuscript a sympathetic reading and provided helpful suggestions. These include Professor David Bensman of Baruch College, C.U.N.Y., Professor Estelle B. Freedman of Stanford, and Mr. Michael Merrill, presently of New Guinea.

The *Business History Review* published a slightly altered version of Chapter 3 in 1976. The then editor of the *BHR* and the editor of this series, Professor Glenn Porter, has provided welcome encouragement for this project. Work on Chapter 3 and on the book as a whole was greatly facilitated by a grant-in-aid from the Eleutherian Mills Historical Library in Wilmington, Delaware. I worked at the EMHL for seven pleasant weeks and would like to thank its staff and especially Dr. Richmond D. Williams for their help.

There is no adequate way to express my gratitude to my colleague in the American Studies Department at Brandeis, Professor Stephen J. Whitfield. He read the complete manuscript and proved a constant source of ideas and encouragement. His eye for the piquant anecdote has done much to liven up the text. His assistance has really been immeasurable.

The above-mentioned scholars deserve much credit for the contributions this study makes. Needless to say, the responsibility for its shortcomings is strictly my own.

Various individuals granted me interviews and/or made unpublished material available to me. These include Mr. and Mrs. Edward L. Bernays, Mr. Harold Brayman, Professor Scott R. Cutlip, Mr. Fred Mason, and Mr. John R. McGraw. I would especially like to thank Mr. and Mrs. Bernays, who allowed me to work through the papers at their home during the summer of 1973.

I am fortunate in having many friends who put me up in their homes and who put up with me in general during the four and a half years it took to complete this book. I would like to thank Dr. Robert W. Bucholz, Wendy E. Callahan, Dr. Marybeth Ezaki, Gil Fuchs, Dr. Marvin Stern, and Bob Sussman.

Lastly, I would like to thank my parents. They and I know how completely they have earned the dedication.

Preface

We live in a land suffused with salesmanship. Turn on the television, and we are assaulted by numberless commercials for commodities which we may not previously have even thought to want. Turn to public television, and we find a large percentage of air time devoted to self-promotion, employing some of the tactics of subtle prevarication we had thought reserved to the other channels.[1] Take a drive. If we turn on the radio, it is more of the same. If we leave it off, we will still see bumper stickers and decals, signs and billboards aplenty proclaiming the virtues of everything from the Parrot Jungle to Jesus Christ. Take a walk. If we look down, we may find spray-painted slogans advertising movies. If we look up, we can see airplanes, skywriters, and blimps proclaiming the virtues of tires and restaurants. No wonder a child in Carl Sandburg's *The People, Yes* asks, "Papa, what's the moon supposed to advertise?"[2] Indeed, it is easy to imagine Proctor and Gamble launching an Apollo project of its own in order not to let such a strategically situated site go to waste. Advertising pervades our newspapers and magazines and surrounds our books. Go to the mailbox, and we discover we are on mailing lists time out of mind. Stay at home, leave everything off, and try having a quiet dinner alone. After turning the Fuller Brush man away from the door, we may be lucky enough to receive a phone call featuring a dissertation on the advantages of land in New Hampshire. Even the Central Intelligence Agency, in a move which must have baffled our "adversaries," has instituted an 18-member public relations staff. Explained its new director, "I think we need to sell our product to our customers more, I think we need to expand our service to other customers—including the public."[3]

In our country, almost nothing sounds odd prefixed by the word "sell." Products, of course, are sold. So, too, however, are ideas. In fact, one of our greatest jurists wrote of ideas getting themselves accepted in the marketplace, and the prose of perhaps our greatest philosopher is laced with commercial metaphors.[4] Then there is the selling of human beings. This activity in the most literal sense was smiled upon in large parts of the country for about two centuries, and today a phrase like "to sell myself" raises no eyebrows. The selling of politicians, meanwhile, has become a cliché.

The pages which follow describe and analyze one corner of the American world of salesmanship: corporate public relations. This activity began in America and from here spread to bureaucracies of all kinds both here and in every nation with a relatively free press. Before the reader begins the narrative, I would like to provide him or her with some thoughts on why America should have been the leader in this field as well as in advertising. What is it about American culture that has raised salesmanship to such a high art and encouraged the selling of what in other nations would be considered nonnegotiable?

The key, I believe, lies in faith in public opinion as the arbiter of value and the concomitant rise in media to communicate with the masses.[5] These developments have their roots in colonial times, and there is no better place to begin a discussion of them than with the life of Benjamin Franklin.

Franklin refined advertising by transforming the layout of the copy which appeared in the *Pennsylvania Gazette* and by using remarkably modern sales appeals,[6] but more significant for present purposes were his shrewdly self-conscious efforts to construct a persona acceptable to his peers. Early in life he adopted the

> habit of expressing myself in terms of modest diffidence; never using, when I advanced anything that may possibly be disputed, the words *certainly, undoubtedly,* or any others that give the air of positiveness to an opinion; but rather say, I conceive or apprehend a thing to be so; it appears to me, or *I should think it so and so,* for such and such reasons; or *I imagine it to be so;* or *it is so, if I am not mistaken.* This habit, I believe has been of great advantage to me when I have had occasion to inculcate my opinions, and persuade men into measures that I have been from time to time engag'd in promoting; and, as the chief ends of conversation are to *inform* or to be *informed, to please* or to *persuade,* I wish well-meaning, sensible men would not lessen their power of doing good by a positive, assuming manner, that seldom fails to disgust, tends to create opposition, and to defeat every one of those purposes for which speech was given to us. . . .[7]

In a society in which social mobility was possible to an extent unknown in the Old World, Franklin emphasized the need to look good. His autobiography contains many remarks about personal appearance, and in what has justly become one of its most famous passages, he explained that

> In order to secure my character as a tradesman, I took care not only to be in *reality* industrious and frugal, but to avoid all appearance to the contrary. I drest plainly; I was seen at no places of idle diversion. I never went out a fishing or shooting; a book, indeed, sometimes debauch'd me from my work, but that was seldom, snug, and gave no scandal; and, to show that I was not above my business, I sometimes brought home the paper I purchas'd at the stores thro' the streets on a wheelbarrow.[8]

Reality was not good enough. Appearance was necessary as well, for the public had to be convinced. Franklin, in other words, busied himself with constructing an image. The American with the greatest reputation in the world boasted of trimming his sales to the prejudices of anonymous men. He knew that the public was not to be despised, and this sensitivity was probably part of what endeared him to later generations.

The *Autobiography* is more than a chronicle of how Franklin discovered a style pleasing to his customers, creditors, and fellow Philadelphia merchants. It was also designed to make America pleasing to the world and can be viewed as the summit of a long tradition of promotional literature[9] for that purpose. It would, wrote Benjamin Vaughan, "present a table of the internal circumstances of your country, which will very much tend to invite to it settlers of virtuous and manly minds. And . . . considering the extent of your reputation, I do not know of a more efficacious advertisement than your autobiography would give."[10] By describing how he sold himself, Franklin hoped to help sell the new nation as well.

Public opinion was a central concern to Franklin as it was to many other revolutionary leaders. The sanctity and rectitude of public opinion are so generally accepted in the western democracies today that it is startling to discover the term's checkered past. "In the beginning," as Daniel Boorstin has pointed out, "'opinion' was a synonym for uncertainty—for a notion grounded in personal preference (rather than fact), and hence was thought likely to be the pathway to error."[11] Prior to the last quarter of the eighteenth century, few if any political thinkers expected the citizenry to have anything worth saying to the ruling class about governance. It was only with the decline of royal prerogative and aristocratic power that it was thought proper for the "public" to have an impact on statecraft. "Public opinion," Hans Speier has rightly remarked, "is a phenomenon of middle class civilization."[12] It is not surprising that reverence for it should grow in the middle-class world of the colonies on the eve of the Revolution and flourish with the decline of deference in the nineteenth century.

The concept of public opinion demands not only a modicum of freedom of expression but also a means of disseminating the thoughts expressed. Without this, to state the obvious, all opinion would be private. It is to be expected that a society looking to the expression of public opinion for political legitimacy would seek to refine methods of reaching the public (i.e., mass media), and that is what happened in the United States.

In an oft-quoted reflection, John Adams wrote that "the Revolution was effected before the war commenced. The Revolution was in the minds and hearts of the people. . . ."[13] Adams might have added that it was in the minds and hearts of a class of people who had not theretofore been part of political decision making in any major nation.[14] In the newspapers and pamphlets of the Revolutionary era, patriots reached out to the common man. Of these authors none was more successful than Tom Paine, of whom Eric Foner has written,

> What made Paine unique was that he forged a new political language. He did not simply change the meanings of words, he created a literary style designed to bring his message to the widest possible audience. His rhetoric was clear, simple and straightforward; his arguments rooted in the common experience of a mass readership. Paine helped to extend political discussion beyond the narrow confines of the eighteenth century's "political nation" (the classes actively involved in politics to whom most previous political writing had been addressed).[15]

"Massification" of communication and respect for public opinion thus became part of American discourse from the nation's very beginnings, and it is to these factors which we must attend in discussing persuasion. "[F]ew American politicians," Boorstin notes, "and almost none who survive to be noticed by a later generation, have dared not to praise the wisdom of Public Opinion."[16] Even conservatives adopted democratic rhetoric. Those who slipped, as John Quincy Adams did when he warned Congress against being "palsied by the will of [its] constituents," were supplying the opposition with potent ammunition.[17]

And this was not only true of politicians. As we shall see, conservative businessmen in the twentieth century never doubted that the locus of power lay with public opinion. What is more, they accepted this situation as right and proper. If the public turned against them, as some thought it was tending to during the Progressive era and as many thought it had during the 1930s, it was because the public was being misled. Therefore, it was up to them to set it right through mass communication. Indeed, the necessity for business to "tell its story" has been a constant refrain over the last 75 years. "The Revolt of the Conservatives" during the Great Depression can thus be seen as taking a characteristically Ameri-

can form when it worked through the National Association of M
facturers, the Liberty League, and various trade associations to
the American way of life to the American people,"[18] as opposed to
porting forceful action to take power away from those chosen by the
majority.

The bulk of scholarly writing on public opinion has been concerned
with its impact on politics and government. Yet businessmen have often
viewed themselves as servants of the public. They have claimed that the
public "voted" for them as well as for politicians when it bought their
products. This form of election has meant a great deal, because in this
country few things are endowed with intrinsic value. The public test
must be passed.

Like other elites, businessmen have thirsted for public approval.
Power and wealth have not been enough. They have sought to have their
status rationalized, no easy task in a nation which at least since the 1830s
has offered social equality to the world as its great contribution to civilization. They have tried to "sell" themselves by expending far more effort
than their European and Japanese counterparts in developing a market-
able "creed." This aim has had a tremendous impact on their rhetoric,
their self-image, and, to a degree not easily determined, on their actions
as well. Their methods and purposes and the results they achieved are
what this book is about.

A Note on Definition

Corporate public relations has played a central role in determining
how the public views individual big businesses, industries, and the business system as a whole in the twentieth century and how, in turn, business leaders see the public. An immediate difficulty facing those who
wish to write about it is the problem of definition. There have been
scores, indeed hundreds, of attempts at one.[19] Most of these have one
factor in common—communication. They agree that public relations is a
conduit of information from an organization whose views or activities
are noteworthy (at least in the opinion of the leaders of the organization
in question) to the public through the mass media. Here the agreement
ends. Some commentators have dismissed public relations as
hucksterism or sophistry. Others have viewed it as a somewhat circuitous
form of advertising, involving talk rather than action and with the emphasis on self-promotion. Yet others have had more sophisticated ambitions for the vocation. They believe it consists not only of telling the
public good things about the client but changing the client's actions when
necessary to conform to public demands. The client must not only talk
but also listen and act on what it learns. Their practitioner directs traffic

on the oft-spoken-of "two-way street." He is not only a publicist but also a sort of ombudsman. Public relations is in this view a "management function" with the counselor a top-level adviser to corporate decision makers, not a press agent who merely takes orders.

What I mean by this elusive term will become apparent in the course of the text, but a concise working definition might be helpful at the outset. Public relations is the controlling of news about an individual or organization by planned and organized effort through informing and cultivating the press and through encouraging the corporation itself to alter its policies in accord with perceived public desires. The neatness of this definition may be misleading. There have been and still are people who are nothing more than press agents with no influence on the actions of their clients, who adopt the impressive-sounding title of public relations counselor[20] nonetheless. Despite their choice of title, neither they, nor press agentry, nor publicity as such have been of central concern. This study has focused on those who not only act as press liaisons but also have exerted, or at least tried to exert, influence on policy. There are indeed such people, although their influence has often proved less extensive than they themselves have claimed.

In addition to its specific impact on business and journalism, public relations has had broad cultural implications. Along with the craft itself as a discrete vocation has grown a public relations–mindedness.[21] The essence of public relations–mindedness is giving the consumer, voter, or whomever the truth but the seller's truth, so to speak, rather than the buyer's.[22] The impact of this phenomenon has been clearly visible in language, where protective reaction strike has substituted for attack, incursion for invasion, and news event for publicity stunt. These are obvious examples. Others have become so much a part of our perception that they pass unnoticed, such as life insurance for death insurance or credit card for debt card.

Some of these linguistic manipulations are only a matter of viewing the glass as half full rather than half empty, but others, especially in the first set above, denote an emphasis, becoming ever more pervasive, on image at the expense of reality. Unvarnished truth, transmitted to the public through the dramatic methods of the modern media, might well contribute to disorder which businessmen and other managers of today's large organizations would prefer to avoid. The growth of public relations for business should be seen—along with trade association activity, cooperation in certain circumstances with regulatory agencies and even labor unions, efforts to circumvent the antitrust laws, the rationalization of corporate internal structures, and the overall development of a science of management—as part of an effort to bring order to a social landscape in which landmarks are constantly being obliterated by what Joseph A. Schumpeter has aptly called "the perennial gale."[23]

Notes

1. Les Brown, "Why All Those Fund Appeals on Non-Commercial TV?" *New York Times*, June 5, 1977, Sec. II, p. 29.
2. Carl Sandburg, *The People, Yes* (New York, 1936), p. 8.
3. "An Old Salt Opens Up the Pickle Factory," *Time*, June 20, 1977, p. 23.
4. Oliver Wendell Holmes, Jr., and William James, respectively.
5. Both these phenomena are discussed at length by Lord Bryce, *The American Commonwealth*, Vol. II (London, 1909) pp. 245–374. Bryce held, correctly, that no nation had put itself in the hands of public opinion to the extent that America had.
6. Thomas Fleming, "How It Was in Advertising 1776–1976," *Advertising Age*, April 19, 1976, p. 1, 27ff.
7. *The Autobiography of Benjamin Franklin* (New York, 1976), pp. 27–28. Emphasis in original.
8. Ibid., p. 69.
9. So extensive was this literature and so intensive were allied attempts to sell America during the colonial period that Richard Hofstadter described the effort as "one of the first concerted and sustained advertising campaigns in the history of the modern world." *America at 1750* (New York, 1973), pp. 33–34. It is perhaps worth noting that in this instance advertising was the product of scarcity (specifically the scarcity of labor) rather than the "Institution of Abundance" as David M. Potter called it in his famous essay, *People of Plenty* (Chicago, 1954), pp. 166–188. For an excellent brief discussion of colonial labor recruitment through advertising and activities which we would now call public relations, see Abbot Emerson Smith, *Colonists in Bondage* (New York, 1971), pp. 43–66. See also Albert B. Faust, "Swiss Emigration to the American Colonies in the Eighteenth Century," *American Historical Review*, Vol. 22, No. 1 (October 1916), pp. 21–44, and Erna Risch, "Joseph Crellius, Immigrant Broker," *New England Quarterly*, Vol. 12, No. 2 (June, 1939), pp. 241–267.
10. Franklin, *Autobiography*, pp. 73–74.
11. *Democracy and Its Discontents* (New York, 1975) pp. 12–21.
12. "Historical Development of Public Opinion," in Charles S. Steinberg, ed., *Mass Media and Communication* (New York, 1972), p. 98.
13. Quoted in Bernard Bailyn, *The Ideological Origins of the American Revolution* (Cambridge, Mass., 1967), p. 160.
14. A century later, Lord Bryce could write that "in the United States public opinion is the opinion of the whole nation, with little distinction of social classes." *Commonwealth*, Vol. II, p. 268.
15. *Tom Paine and Revolutionary America* (New York, 1976), p. xvi.
16. *Discontents*, p. 15.
17. Robert V. Remini, *The Election of Andrew Jackson* (Philadelphia, 1963), p. 37.
18. See Chapters 3 and 4. This phrase can be found, for example, in Edward L. Bernays, *Public Relations* (New York, 1952), pp. 335–345.
19. For the most recent major attempt, see Rex F. Harlow, "Building a Public Relations Definition," *Public Relations Review*, Vol. 2, No. 4 (Winter 1976), pp. 34–42.
20. A note on semantics is in order here. There is no convenient noun to describe one who does public relations; no such thing as a public relations-ist or a public relator. Members of the vocation often refer to themselves as practitioners or counselors, and I have used both terms. The former is neutral enough, but

the latter has caused some confusion. Investment advisers and lawyers are also referred to as counselors, and the term public relations counselor was purposely created to give the vocation the prestige of these professions which have standing in law and in the public mind. The use of this word may therefore seem to imply the conclusion that the practice of public relations is deserving of such recognition. I have used it with no such intent but simply for convenience.

21. I do not believe that there was no public relations-mindedness before modern public relations. In the first chapter, in fact, I argue quite the reverse. But it does seem to me that public relations-mindedness has become both more widespread and more deeply ingrained with the growth of the public relations vocation.

22. Thomas Griffith, "Must Business Fight the Press?" *Fortune* (June 1974), p. 204.

23. *Capitalism, Socialism, and Democracy* (New York, 1950), p. 90.

Chapter I

Businessmen and Public Opinion: The Background of Modern Corporate Public Relations

Businessmen went quietly, often secretly, about their tasks.
Thomas C. Cochran, 1951[1]

Arise, ye men of Sandusky! Shake off your apathy! Risk all for her, and I trust she will reward you for your care.
Jay Cooke, 1837[2]

Businessmen . . . are . . . at the same time allured and terrified by the glare of publicity . . . vain perhaps but very unsure of themselves, pathetically responsive to a kind word.
John Maynard Keynes to Franklin D. Roosevelt, February 1, 1938[3]

I

A constantly recurring leitmotif of Matthew Josephson's famed indictment of the business community in the age of enterprise was the secrecy with which the "Robber Barons" conducted their affairs. Commodore Vanderbilt kept his accounts in his head, concealing his business methods even from his own son. Daniel Drew, the "sphinx of the stock market," advised, "Never tell anybody what yer goin' ter do, till ye do it." The California quartet of Huntington, Crocker, Stanford and Hopkins "worked together in silence" and "kept each other's secrets." John D. Rockefeller's early railroad rebate arrangements were "maintained in utter secrecy," and members of the South Improvement Company had to sign an oath to the effect that they would keep secret all their dealings

1

with it. The Carnegie Associates "formed a compact, close-mouthed, loyal brotherhood." And J. Pierpont Morgan is described as "broodingly silent."[4]

These men held their cards close to their vests and did not deign to reply to the ever increasing attacks made upon them and their methods. To Josephson, this deafening silence was an indication of a "supreme contempt" for critics and the public in general. The word "public" appears only twice in his index, once in connection with a statement by J. P. Morgan, "I owe the public nothing," and once for a declaration by William H. Vanderbilt which has symbolized for one hundred years the attitude of his contemporaries, "The public be damned!"[5]

Many aspects of Josephson's work have been disputed, but this emphasis upon secrecy is not one of them. N. S. B. Gras, a stalwart defender of the American business system, has observed that private enterprise grew up "in the shops or stores attached to private homes or out of the pack or saddle bag of a migratory tradesman or . . . in the private booth of an artisan or tradesman at a bazaar." One of the words used to denote trade was *ministerium*, meaning mystery, and the plays performed by guild members at feast days were called mystery plays. There even developed a confusion in the fourteenth century between a trade and a mysterious occupation. This aura of mystery and commitment to the privacy of private enterprise, Gras believed, flourished in nineteenth-century America as well.[6]

In his meticulous study of railroad leaders, Thomas Cochran too recognized the secretive nature of business transactions but ascribed it not to contempt for the public but rather to confusion. Intelligent railroad executives recognized the potential power of public sentiment, warned their employees to be polite and friendly with customers, and went as far as to maintain services, such as dining cars and sleeping facilities, at a loss for the sake of good will. There were, however, elements of railroad management in the rugged era following the Civil War which executives viewed as unavoidable but which they were sure the public would not accept. The bribing of legislators, the manipulation of stocks, and the formation of pools all would be frowned upon if made public.[7] Hence secrecy was the order of the day.

Conservative reformers of the era felt that the stealth of American enterprise was one of its most dangerous attributes and early advocated remedies. Henry Varnum Poor, a railroad builder himself who won renown as the editor of the *American Railway Journal*, saw publicity as a solution to the problems of managerial irresponsibility and lack of incentive which were developing because of the increasing separation of ownership and management in the 1850s. "Full and complete statements of every act must be required," he wrote. "Daylight should be let into every department of service." To this end Poor proposed a plan early in 1858 by which he would mail 600 questions to every road in the nation in order to assemble heretofore unavailable information. He had the backing of some of the leading banking houses of Britain and America, which had been shocked by the revelations of chicanery arising out of the Panic of 1857. This kind of reporting, Poor believed, would make the roads once again accountable to public opinion, but the roads were not anxious to cooperate.[8]

State legislatures picked up the idea of publicity and endowed some railway commissions with the power to investigate and make public important data. The Interstate Commerce Act of 1887 directed roads to make reports according to the specifications of the Interstate Commerce Commission's statistician. As a result of all this activity, American railway reports compared favorably with those of England by the century's close. Whether this in turn led to a "renovated public opinion," which, Charles Francis Adams, Jr. believed, was "the only remedy" to the evils of railroading, is another matter.[9]

It would be wonderfully tidy to show how these economically proficient but socially insensitive moguls were gradually forced to defend themselves in the public forum by making use of the developing profession of public relations counseling. This is the "scenario" constructed by numerous public relations men who have explored their field's past.

Such a sequence is not without some validity, but history is rarely so one-dimensional and it certainly is not in this case. Two stumbling blocks complicate our story: from colonial times successful American businessmen have been notoriously solicitous of public approval and aware of the necessity of keeping the public "with us," and they have been rivaled only by the politician in their proficiency in using publicity to further their enterprises.

When the Puritan merchant Robert Keayne was reprimanded in 1639 for charging what the traffic would bear for his nails rather than a "just" price, he was not as upset by the hefty £200 fine levied against him as he was by being "brought forth into open court as a publique male-factor." It was that which was "the griefe of my soul." Keayne's lengthy will, Bernard Bailyn has observed, was "written under the compulsive need to gain final approval" from his fellow Bostonians.[10]

Keayne's conflict with public opinion was particularly dramatic, and his ability to articulate his feelings vividly has made it a well-known incident. It is fair to say, though, that as merchant classes began to emerge in the colonies from the chrysalis of Calvinism and the Old World social order, businessmen weighed with care their activities and acquisitions against public expectations. Not only could unwonted display or the keeping of bad company result in painful ostracism, it was bad for business. The sensitivity of Franklin, that "arch-exemplar of the capitalist spirit,"[11] to these matters has already been mentioned.

In the early years of the nineteenth century, leading businessmen were objects of public scrutiny and curiosity[12] and felt keenly the influence of public opinion. Boston merchant princes were not lost in the crowd as were their London counterparts. "Their virtues and vices could be closely observed and their characters judged. Men did not live in isolation but in a highly articulated social order which not only set standards but encouraged and enforced right conduct."[13] Some found the conflict between business enterprise and conscience a severe strain and entered into early retirement, as did some Quaker merchants of colonial Philadelphia for similar reasons.[14] William Appleton remained in business late in life not, he said, for the pecuniary gain but rather because his mercantile virtuosity won him the "applause" of his peers.[15]

With the advent of businessmen of the Robber Baron era, it may be objected, this sensitivity to outside approval and duty vanished. As the interests of the leading entrepreneurs turned from the naturally broadening pursuit of foreign trade to the intensive and hectic development of the North American continent, as the essential business type was transmogrified from the cultivated and well-rounded leader of the community to the self-made business drudge "not in business for our health but . . . out for the dollars," did the strictures of public opinion become largely irrelevant or contemptible?[16] How else account for the socially absurd predicament of post-bellum America in which a railroad titan, the son of a semiliterate boor who commanded one of the nation's key railroad systems and a stupendous sum of capital, could with impunity "damn" the public?

It is true that one would have to search hard among a Fiske, Drew, or Vanderbilt to discover the finely tuned sensitivity of a Hone or Appleton. On the other hand, the picture is not as bleak as it appears at first glance. Let us begin with a brief analysis of the "public be damned" statement.

The *New York Times* published the text of the interview in which the statement was made on its front page of October 9, 1882. Questioned by two reporters about the profitability of one of his lines, William H. Vanderbilt observed that it did not pay but he was forced to operate it because of the actions of one of his competitors. "But don't you run it for public benefit?" inquired one reporter. Vanderbilt was quoted as replying:

The public be————. What does the public care for the railroads except to get as much out of them for as small a consideration as possible! I don't take any stock in this silly nonsense about working for anybody's good but our own because we are not. When we make a move we do it because it is in our interest to do so, not because we expect to do somebody else some good. Of course we like to do everything possible for the benefit of humanity in general, but when we do we first see that we are benefitting ourselves. Railroads are not run on sentiment, but on business principles and to pay, and I don't mean to be egotistic when I say that the roads which I have had anything to do with have generally paid pretty well.

When the coarser trimmings are peeled away, we have here an expression of a philosophy of business management widely accepted even among admired railroad men and still vigorously defended today,[17] to wit, that the primary fiduciary responsibility of the business executive is to his firm's stockholders rather than to some undefinable public.[18] What is a good deal more interesting is that immediately upon publication, Vanderbilt denied using the language attributed to him.[19] Although Lee Benson has written that the magnate's epigram was "thoroughly characteristic of him, and one which he had frequently employed before," at least two other historians disagree.[20] Whether he used the words or not, his denial has the force of a retraction. The point is that even the infamous Vanderbilt had enough sensitivity to public opinion to understand that it was a serious mistake for him to flaunt his contempt for it if contempt he felt.

Leading capitalists seemed to accept the criticism and even hatred their activities provoked as occupational hazards, trying at the same time to mitigate their effects by the munificence of their benefactions. More than once, they justified themselves on the grounds of developing resources in an efficient manner and ultimately lowering prices for the public.[21]

These men were, in the words of Edward C. Kirkland, "sensitive to rhetoric."[22] For one industrialist, a Standard Oil executive, public disapprobation brought as much pain as public approval had brought pleasure to an earlier generation:

We are quoted as the representation of all that is evil, hardhearted, oppressive, cruel, (we think unjustly,) but men look askance at us. We are pointed at with contempt, and while some men flatter us, it's only for our money and we scorn them for it and it leads to a further hardness of heart. . . . None of us would choose such a reputation. We all desire a place in the good will, honor and affection of honorable men.[23]

Businessmen, even in these times, were more than mere profit-calculators.[24]

If nineteenth-century businessmen were reluctant to divulge those "secrets in manufactures" and "secrets in trade" which gave them competitive advantages[25] and if they were loath to comply with reformers' schemes for publicity, it does not follow that they were maladroit in the use of publicity for their own purposes. Numerous entrepreneurs were expert in employing it as a competitive weapon, as an aid in battle with the government or angry customers, or as a mechanism to conjure forth an enterprise from the void.

Daniel J. Boorstin has described a type that he believes indigenous to the United States, the booster. This new form of life, *businessman Americanus,* based his career upon developing towns by selecting a site and then frantically trying to attract settlers, merchants, the railroad, etc. His loyalties were intense but volatile, and the success of his venture depended on his ability to persuade others that it would succeed. To that end, the newspaper editors whose publications seemed miraculously to spring up in the midst of these myriad villages were not above "represent[ing] things that had not yet gone through the formality of taking place."[26] One of the foremost manipulators of the press in the pursuit of free publicity was "a hardheaded businessman" named Phineas Taylor Barnum.[27] He and other impresarios managed to attract attention to their intriguing hoaxes and exhibits by staging stunts (or what Boorstin would call "pseudo-events") and exciting bogus controversies.

From the pages of Josephson's own book, one can cite many instances in which these supposedly tiptoeing industrialists and financiers aroused the fascination of the public.[28] The building of the transcontinental transportation system and the industrial plant formed one of the great dramas of the nineteenth century, and businessmen at times found themselves beneficiaries of publicity which the grandiose scale of their efforts naturally attracted. Prior to mid-1867, for instance, the market for Union Pacific securities had been extremely weak. The speed with which the construction of the road progressed, however, made a deep impression upon press and public alike. Some of the newspapers in Chicago reported the progress of the work daily, and as a result the position of Union Pacific stock improved.[29] The world of finance has often been represented as secretive—"the mysteries of Wall Street" is a common phrase—but often the most successful financiers were those who, like Jay Cooke, knew how to arouse public support for their projects.[30]

We are thus confronted, in the period prior to the development of a formal public relations apparatus, with businessmen both shunning and seeking publicity and generally approaching the problem in a haphazard fashion. With the turn of the century, some businesses began to devote increased attention to the political and economic problems caused by their image. By the time America entered World War I, innumerable speeches, articles and pamphlets had been devoted to public relations—a term which in some quarters was supplanting publicity and press agentry.

II

As with so many other problems of modern management, the railroads pioneered in corporate press relations. They had two means at their disposal with which to influence the kind of news printed about them. One was through coaxing reporters. The other, somewhat more direct, was through the purchase of newspapers.

"Deadheading" is newspaper slang for a practice with a long and not always honorable history. It refers to giving gifts to reporters, and in the case of railroads it usually took the form of a free pass, also often given to politicians, ministers, and sundry community leaders along the route. Deadheading dates back to the 1830s and became so commonly accepted that by the 1870s it was hazardous to deny a request for a pass.

Hand in hand with deadheading walked "puffery," the publication of items in the news columns which appear to be normal reportage but which are in fact thinly disguised advertisements. These were expected by advertisers and "deadheadors" as a response for their support. Newspapers also allowed customers to pay them outright for printing articles; as late as 1886, the *New York Times* admitted publishing favorable material about the Bell Telephone Company for $1,200.[31]

These various arrangements were satirized by a Chicago reporter when he published his "schedule of railroad advertising rates":

For the setting forth of virtues (actual or alleged) of presidents, general managers, or directors, $2 per line for the first insertion and $1 each for subsequent insertion. . . .

For complimentary notices of the wives and children of railroad officials, we demand $1.50 per line. We have on hand, ready for immediate use, a splended assortment of this literature. . . .

Poetry will be made to order at $3 per inch agate measure. We are prepared to supply a fine line of heptameter puffs, also a limited number of sonnets and triolets, in exchange for 1,000 mile tickets. Epic poems, containing descriptions of scenery, dining cars, etc., will be published at special rates.[32]

Despite some protestations to the contrary, railroad executives read the newspapers and cared about what appeared in them.[33] As the above rate schedule makes clear, they were interested not only in favorable mention of their roads but of themselves as well.

To further stimulate publicity, businesses began to employ press agents in the late 1860s. A niche for press agentry was created by the development of the "department store" concept of the newspaper. Prior to the penny press, editors had sought, as their audience specialized, differentiated publics. They catered primarily to members of a political party, or to merchants, or to a religion. In 1835, James Gordon Bennett tried to resynthesize newspaper readership, to appeal, that is, to all these groups in a single publication.[34] The result was a dramatic increase in circulation but also a dilemma. With few exceptions, it was and is impossible for a newspaper to have a staff expert in all topics about which its columns might carry information. The press agent's duty was to call to the paper's attention items which in the opinion of his employer were newsworthy but which the editor had overlooked. In 1884, a newspaper trade journal observed that any organization which advertised would also have a man "working the press" for free publicity, and it admitted that "this is to a certain extent a legitimate result of the hurry and bustle of our business life. . . ."[35] Not all journalists, however, bore this imposition with such equanimity. Washington Gladden resigned from the *Independent* because three departments—insurance, finance, and "publisher's notices"—were edited to make pure advertising appear as legitimate copy.[36]

Another indication of the respect executives felt for the power of public opinion and the ability of newpapers to mold it was the number of newspapers they purchased. Once again, here the railroads led the way. Jay Gould, who became influential with the Associated Press in 1881 through his control of Western Union, supplied funds for Whitelaw Reid's purchase of a controlling interest in the New York *Tribune* after Horace Greeley's death. In 1876, Tom Scott of the Pennsylvania bought the New York *World* and that paper too later fell into Gould's hands. Henry Villard, an ex-correspondent himself and one of the most astute of business publicists, bought the New York *World,* also in 1876.[37] "Papers on the financial rocks, indeed, had a way of drifting into portfolios of big-time investors, who recognized the utility of having press spokesmen on their side."[38]

That railroads had an immense impact on the nation is a cliché of American history. By the final quarter of the nineteenth century, their influence "penetrated every cranny of the economy and touched every man's interest" as did no other institution.[39] As a result, dealing with public opinion about them was a complex problem and one which they ultimately failed to solve satisfactorily. But that serious efforts in that direction were essential became progressively more apparent to railroad leaders. Various expedients were experimented with, and in 1906 Alexander J. Cassatt, the president of the Pennsylvania, turned to the man who has rightly been called the father of modern public relations, Ivy Ledbetter Lee.

Lee came to Cassatt's attention because of some work his firm had done to counteract unfavorable articles about the road[40] and also, perhaps, for his efforts in rationalizing the hitherto dreadful public relations of the anthracite coal mine operators. Since the Pennsylvania was an acknowledged leader in railroad management, occupying a position of respect in the business world similar to that enjoyed by General Motors in the 1950s, his retention was an important stride both for his career and his profession.

With considerable boldness, Lee set about to transform the road's traditional policy of secrecy. When an accident occurred and the company commenced as was its custom to black out all news about it, he dramatically departed from standard practice by arranging for reporters to travel to the scene at the railroad's expense and then facilitating the taking of photographs and the gathering of information. At about the same time, an accident took place on the New York Central, whose cover-up went unchallenged from within the company. The result was journalistic criticism for the Central and unwonted praise for the Pennsylvania.[41]

Lee viewed his job as "interpreting the Pennsylvania Railroad to the public and the public to the Pennsylvania Railroad." He wrote that the directors of the road were pursuing a "policy of broad common sense" which consisted of doing as much for the public as possible because they knew that in return the public would reward the road with its patronage. As with his other clients, Lee sought to "humanize" the road. He believed that, in the drive for maximum efficiency, the corporation had become too impersonal. The antidote was the human-interest story. In pamphlets, press releases, and speeches, Lee told the world about the Pennsylvania's contributions to agricultural education, the YMCA, pension plans, college scholarships, and the like. He portrayed his client as "one big happy family" and gained wide publicity for simple, homey stories that illustrated corporate care for the underling.[42]

Lee also showed the Pennsylvania that his ability as a communicator could be put to use to fight for higher freight rates. Locked in a battle with shippers, two other roads joined the Pennsylvania in employing Lee to influence the public in their favor. He proceeded to launch a public relations blitz which included news releases, speeches, leaflets, bulletins, and other types of printed matter directed at the many different publics, such as passengers, stockholders, community leaders, etc., whose opinions might possibly have some effect on the decisions of the Interstate Commerce Commission. Some legislators were outraged by the campaign, Senator LaFollette called it a "monument of shame," but Lee persevered and the roads were awarded their rate increase.[43]

Singly and jointly, other railroads built public relations programs for themselves. An indication of the degree of sophistication these efforts reached is the following description of a campaign which Anderson Pace conducted on behalf of Illinois railroads. Pace's object was to organize a bureau to develop "a better understanding among the railroads of what the public wants and thinks; a better understanding by the public of railroad needs and problems; and a hearty cooperation between the railroads and the people they serve."

Pace first made a survey and discovered that the average citizen wanted better stations and lower rates than those of competitive towns. He also found that "to try to argue with him on any of these subjects is simply to breed more trouble." He tried a different approach:

> We are running advertisements in order to show the public that the railways are not autocrats, always ignoring the public; to seek out overlooked causes of trouble; to get away from the old begging attitude; to win the sympathy of the employees; to put the public in a boosting frame of mind; and to put a premium on courtesy and good service.
>
> We are building mailing lists of farmers, retailers, school teachers, manufacturers, clubs, associations, laboring men and railway employees, for the purpose of following them up through the mails. . . .
>
> Speakers are placed upon programs, and before granges, farmers' institutes, town meetings and gatherings, . . . we are telling the story of the interdependence of farmers, manufacturers, distributors, consumers and the railways. In the case of all associated groups, friends are made.

A large portion of early advertising men were clergymen's sons (as was Ivy Lee as well), and the suggestion has been made that advertising is the secular equivalent of preaching.[44] The fervid enthusiasm of Pace's approach also suggests a religious analogy. He concluded his discussion by declaring that the employee was management's greatest potential public relations ally. "Get him on the side of the railroads, let him be our missionary, and the conversion of the public is over." He understood what later public relations counselors were to learn and what Edward L. Bernays made an article of faith (if such a phrase is permissible) in his strategy: rational disputation may have its place but it is often ineffectual in changing people's minds. Appeal to the emotions was essential. Since the most readily available analogy for such an appeal was the camp meeting of the old-time religion, it is not surprising that this program should have the aura of a revival.

If Pace's description of his work can be trusted, he filled a much broader role than that of the press agent. He used advertising as part of his strategy, he made a survey to find out what people felt, and he "segmented" his publics, appealing to each separately in the appropriate fashion. What is missing is any indication that the roads might take what they found out seriously enough to change in substantive ways their methods of doing business. Pace believed that the average citizen "[u]nfortunately . . . does not understand railway operation, management, finance or regulation." One of the objects of his project was to educate the public, thus facilitating dialogue, but until that education was completed one may safely assume that executives were in no hurry to take the advice of the ignorant.[45]

The idea that both the corporation and public would profit if a counsel for public relations played the role of ombudsman, making possible two-way communication between them and leading to mutual changes not only in attitude but in activity as well had to await Edward L. Bernays for forceful enunciation. Nevertheless, despite some complaints that railroad men paid too little attention to it,[46] public relations by World War I meant more to many of them than merely working the press for free publicity.

Like the railroads, public utilities were in an exposed position vis-à-vis other businesses, the government, and the public. The root of their difficulty lay in providing services to great multitudes of customers who almost immediately regarded these services as a right. Many customers meant many points of friction with the public.[47]

As early as the 1890s, George Harvey did public relations work for street railways in Boston, but in the following decade the Philadelphia Rapid Transit Company, in spite of its abrasive relations with its customers, did not follow the example of the Pennsylvania and hire a public relations man.[48] In the 1910s, articles in the *Electric Railway Journal* indicated that public relations was becoming a major concern. The *Journal* ran a 100-page public relations special in 1914. A commentator in a later issue proposed that a public relations bureau be organized to supply data to refute newspaper allegations while another urged traction companies to use public relations to strike back at the "demagogue and his ilk."[49]

The leading utility in the field was the American Telephone and Telegraph Company. The Bell system grew up under the protection of the patent laws, so it had one strike against it from the beginning because it was a sanctioned monopoly. It was also unable to meet the rapidly increasing demands for its services, thus increasing resentment.[50] With the expiration of the patents, harsh competitive warfare broke out with Bell in most cases emerging the victor. Under the presidency of John E. Hudson, from 1889 to 1901, the company treated competition ruthlessly:

> No effort was made to conciliate the independent companies—to "take them into camp," after the later method. They were merely ignored, and in more than one instance where they were forced to the wall the Bell Company acquired for a song their wires and their telephones, and in truly medieval fashion piled the instruments in the street and burned them. . . . This was not the best way to promote good feeling. . . .[51]

Indeed it was not.

Bell had, in fact, aroused considerable hostility. At length the company's officers realized that the public had to be assuaged. The 1903 annual report spoke of the necessity of providing efficient and courteous service and emphasized that each employee who had direct contact with the customer must be as skillful in dealing with him as in solving technical problems. Also in 1903, AT&T retained the services of the Boston-based Publicity Bureau, the first firm devoted solely to publicity. James Drummond Ellsworth, who handled the account, viewed his job as bringing to the public's attention those "perfectly harmless facts" which the company had concealed out of the entrenched habit of secrecy, an approach which had aroused unwarranted suspicions.[52]

The real beginnings of public relations at Bell dated from the accession of Theodore Newton Vail to the presidency in mid-1907. As an employee of the corporate forerunner of AT&T more than twenty years previously, Vail had recognized the importance of public satisfaction with service.[53] Now he had an opportunity to institute a comprehensive approach to public opinion, and it was an opportunity he did not fail to use.

One of his first moves was to sever relations with the Publicity Bureau. The proximate cause for this action apparently was the Bureau's claiming credit for work it did not do. Perhaps a deeper reason was that Vail realized the importance of public relations and did not want AT&T's handled by an outside firm with other clients and other problems.

With some misgivings, Vail, in 1908, hired Ellsworth, who had resigned from the Publicity Bureau after an argument with its founder and president, George Michaelis. Ellsworth's first title was "Special Agent" but that was deemed inappropriate by legal advisers who feared it might enable him to speak with the authority of the company. He thus began his duties with no title, a yearly salary of $2,000, and general responsibility for advertising and publicity. He quickly gained status, however, and worked well with his chief.[54]

The modern public relations counselor realizes that its chief executive officer can be a company's greatest asset or greatest liability in establishing a reputation. Henry Ford was both, but Vail was a public relations man's dream. He initiated Bell's new policy of "publicity and full disclosure" and understood the necessity of constant repetition of the company's views. Newspapermen found him delightful, and he developed a reputation for honesty with them.[55] As an executive, he should be classed with Charles M. Schwab, whom Glenn Porter has called "a transitional figure to the twentieth-century executive. He spent a lot of time working hand-in-glove with big government, huddling with public relations people and struggling to adjust to the growing public accountability of previously private business activities."[56]

Two aspects of Vail's policy are especially noteworthy. He accepted government regulation because he did not think the company could survive the public's visceral dislike of monopoly without some sort of government control. (Put another way, he was anxious to use the regulatory agencies to shield the company from the public.) Secondly, he recognized the importance of making employees ambassadors to the public. Others also emphasized this, but none were as thorough as AT&T:

> There had been a time when short answers and curt treatment had been expected from telephone employees. A telephone manager had been a person to be approached with awe; a telephone operator was about equally indifferent and impolite. Now, all at once these unpleasant features of the service had disappeared. From the highest managerial position to the girl who answered your call there was human consideration, and the mild answer that turneth away wrath. "The voice with the smile" became famous. . . .[57]

In addition to rails and utilities, some industrial firms established press bureaus and public relations activities during the Progressive period. Standard Oil, the first of the great trusts and one of the early large combinations of capital, bought from thousands of suppliers and sold to millions of customers. It was therefore "singularly exposed to public attack." The company hired Joseph I. C. Clarke, former editor and man about town, to handle press relations in 1906 and opinion is said to have generally improved toward it thereafter.[58]

Selling to numerous consumers was not a prerequisite for interest in public relations. United States Steel, whose formation was greeted with something less than universal mirth, was "big, and therefore conspicuous." Such other nonconsumer manufacturers as Bethlehem Steel and Du Pont established public relations or publicity departments by the end of World War I.[59]

III

Why did public relations begin when it did? Two speculations present themselves. One is that its appearance was a harbinger of a changed attitude and approach by the business community to its social responsibilities. The other is that it arose as a defense for the beleaguered businessman.[60]

By the turn of the century, the "heroic age of American enterprise" seemed to have passed. The great tycoons whose stories make Matthew Josephson such lively reading had died off, retired, or were in their last years. With the exception of Henry Ford, no businessman of the twentieth century attained the eminence of a Carnegie or Rockefeller. As managerial enterprise evolved, public relations has been cited as an indication of a new interest in pleasing the public.[61]

Among certain businessmen, the idea that the corporation owed the public more information than it had been accustomed to dispensing was gaining acceptance. Insofar as the former secretiveness did evince a contempt for the public, the rise of public relations can be viewed as an indication of the lessening of that contempt. It is also true that in some rare instances company policy was affected by the advice of the man in charge of the public relations function. Alan Raucher, a very skeptical student of early public relations, credited James D. Ellsworth with suggesting a pension plan for AT&T which was eventually adopted. Furthermore, it can be argued that "public relations-mindedness" governed the management of U.S. Steel and Ford.[62]

However, public relations was not yet sufficiently widespread on the business scene, "more a portent than a major factor," to use Thomas Cochran's words,[63] to be credited with a part in such a business transformation if indeed one was taking place. The two-way-street idea had been only sketchily enunciated and was probably not taken too seriously at this time. And it is a mistake to suppose that corporate liberalism and public relations always appear together as they did at AT&T. As we shall see, some of its vigorous exponents in the 1930s were quite conservative. The thesis that public relations was called into being to defend business against increasing journalistic and political attacks has the support of numerous scholars. In the early years of this century exposé journalism through the medium of the popularly priced magazine caught fire. Between 1903 and 1912 almost two thousand muckraking articles appeared in these magazines, generously buttressed by editorials and cartoons. The public devoured the revelations, and editors and authors devoted unprecedented amounts of time and money to their investigations.[64]

Not all the important muckrakers were antibusiness. George Kibbe Turner, impressed with the achievements of city manager government, felt that business principles could save the nation, and Ida Tarbell thought that fair and free enterprise brought out the best in men. Burton J. Hendrick, muckraker of insurance and traction, found himself unable to conceal his admiration for the successful financier, thus neatly exhibiting the American ambivalence toward the tough businessman.[65] Nonetheless, the thrust of muckraking was to expose wrongdoing by numerous corporations and industries, and whether or not the author viewed his subject as an aberration from a potentially beneficent form of economic organization or as an example of the ineluctable rottenness of capitalism was a moot question to the managers of the organization being assaulted.

Eric F. Goldman has ascribed to the muckrakers

a critically important role in discovering "publicity" . . . Up to the early 1900's, most Americans, including much of American industry, considered publicity a bad thing. The idea was to operate in secrecy. Then T. R. led in discovering publicity as a political weapon. The muckrakers used publicity as an anti-business weapon and industry, in direct reply to the muckrakers, began to feel that if publicity could be used against them it could be used for them. Hence the birth of the whole public relations industry.[66]

Businessmen saw that damaging revelations could have adverse effects upon sales and could encourage the election and programs of hostile politicians. Indeed, historians have attributed the decline of muckraking in part to the "below the waterline" activities of offended businesses.[67]

The Progressive era was, if nothing else, a period of righteous indignation, an attitude which businessmen fully shared. God-invoking if not always God-fearing, they were not content to sit "helplessly by, inarticulate and frustrated, waiting apprehensively for the next issue of *McClure's* Magazine to come from the presses." When they did try to speak out, too often the results were clumsy and unfortunate. George F. Baer, for example, had to learn the hard way that in an age of aroused public opinion, he needed an expert to help him express himself through "authorized statements."[68]

There is an obvious coincidence in time between the rise of the muckrakers and the beginnings of public relations, and logic as well as some data indicate that one caused the other. Specifically, companies within industries which were subjected to the muckrakers' scrutiny tended to lead the way in establishing press bureaus.

Nevertheless, attributing the rise of corporate public relations exclusively to the goading of muckrakers leaves many problems unsolved. First of all, a vigorous literature critical of big business dated back at least to the Civil War and featured such influential works as "A Chapter of Erie" and *Wealth Against Commonwealth*.[69] Why did not public relations arise to respond to such tracts as these? In fact, as has been seen, there were some press agents during the 1860s, but they did not develop the professional self-consciousness or techniques associated with modern public relations. And why has not public relations diminished in importance with the decline in anti-big-business animus? At the turn of the century, the intensity of public feeling toward big business was such that chastisement of giant enterprises and their managers was an accepted part of political and journalistic discourse. But by 1950, the middle classes had come to view big business as an acceptable component of the national polity. No longer was antitrust a stirring rallying cry.[70] Despite recurrent scandals which would have greatly exercised the muckrakers, business journalism has become steadily more neglected.[71] Yet during this same period public relations became firmly entrenched and very well funded. And lastly, why did nonbusiness institutions which were not particularly scrutinized by the muckrakers, such as universities,[72] churches, charities, and the armed services, follow the lead of business and experiment with press bureaus at this time?

Goldman's line of analysis contains the shortcomings of the school which views the Progressive period as essentially a contest between "the people" and "the interests." What it neglects are developments within the business world itself.

Corporations were growing at an unprecedented rate at the turn of the century. Between 1895 and 1905, 300 separate firms disappeared through mergers every year.[73] Just as railroad leaders had discovered earlier, the managers of giant manufacturing firms were learning that bigness resulted in problems different not only in degree but in kind from those confronting the small entrepreneur. No longer were the key decisions about a local plant being made by a manager living in the plant community. No longer did the manager know all his employees by name, nor was he necessarily on intimate terms with the town's civic leaders. He may not have even known the doctors, the lawyers, and, perhaps most important, the local newspaper editor.

These years saw a massive effort to rationalize business management. Nowhere was this effort more apparent than in the search for solutions to the much discussed "human problem." Some such efforts, like graphology, physiognomy, and "character analysis," have been consigned to oblivion, but others have exercised a lasting impact. Among the latter we should briefly consider Taylorism, industrial psychology, welfare capitalism, and advertising, in addition to public relations itself.

The object of Taylorism was to order chaotic factory conditions by analyzing the tasks of each member of the work force and returning them to the worker in the most simplified, technically efficient form. Here was seen the spirit of the engineer, designed to eliminate human judgment from industrial tasks by reducing each one to a scientifically quantifiable scale.

Like scientific management, industrial psychology seemed to promise an end to guesswork in the plant by introducing scientific methodology. Practitioners claimed that through carefully fashioned tests they could determine the fittest candidates for jobs and promotions.[74] As with Taylorism, the enemy was perceived as "rule of thumb." Haphazard approaches may have obtained in small shops but in giant factories they were intolerable.

Welfare capitalism consisted of a set of programs aimed at maintaining the personal dimension in growing firms. Company-sponsored Sunday schools, churches, housing, recreation facilities and employee representation plans were supposed to show the worker that the manager cared for him as an individual as well as an employee. They would fend off unionism and also develop an improved worker: thrifty, clean, temperate, industrious and Americanized.[75]

Businessmen have always tried to govern the working habits of their employees, but the development of these three fields and the intense interest which the business community was devoting to them (trade journals were packed with articles extolling them) showed that twentieth-century industrialists were recognizing to a greater extent than ever before the necessity of understanding the "living world" contained by their factories.[76] Interestingly, these new endeavors could be seen as sometimes working at cross purposes. Scientific management and industrial psychology raised impersonality to an important objective while welfare capitalism plainly sought to counteract it.[77] Businessmen so needed the help of science that they were willing to discard, to a degree, the anti-intellectual bias of their predecessors and exploit the scholarly community for help in labor relations. And yet, through welfare capitalism, they hoped to preserve their self-image as benevolent paternalists. They were marching backward into the future.

Just as they realized they must understand the world their factories contained, businessmen were seeking a new relationship with the world that contained their factories. During this period, advertising was assuming its modern aspect. Once again, the bigness of business was a major factor. Companies were serving larger markets and were looking for a way to stimulate sales systematically through big-city newspapers with growing circulation and through the national magazines.

The turn of the century was a time of ferment in both the vocational and the technical sides of advertising. *Printers' Ink* was transforming itself from an organ devoted to the promotion of the interests of one important agent, George P. Rowell, to a journal servicing the whole trade. Advertising clubs, the first successful example of which was founded in 1894, were springing up all over the nation, to be united in 1905 in the Associated Advertising Clubs of America. Such pioneers as Albert D. Lasker were showing how sales could be increased by writing copy which featured an aggressively stated "reason why" the consumer should buy rather than announcement accompanied by claims to excellence which were merely ornamental.[78]

The development of public relations should be seen within this context. Businessmen well knew the power of public opinion. They respected its impact on the conduct of strikes, on legislation, on sales, and on their own morale. As their firms grew larger, they came to realize the importance of controlling the news which they could not avoid generating. Thus publicity departments appeared in corporate organizational charts.

Public relations did not develop only because articulate authors were attacking big business. Had Ida Tarbell written for a small, struggling newspaper with modest circulation about a local firm whose owner was a leading citizen of the town in which she lived, he probably would not have needed an Ivy Lee to help him institute "a policy of broad common sense" or to "humanize" him. Instead, she wrote in a popular magazine about a trust with nationwide and worldwide interests. Its owners and managers were merely names to its suppliers and customers. It seemed dangerous, unchecked, malevolent. In other words, this vocation developed from a matrix created by a whole constellation of circumstances. Business bigness, a search for order within corporations themselves encouraging an impersonal approach to management and at the same time suggesting the organization of the publicity which great corporations naturally attracted, high literacy rates, nationally available periodicals, and vigorous reform politicians all played a part in addition to the fact that the articles which appeared were often critical. The muckrakers were an important factor because they heated up the atmosphere. It is difficult to imagine hard-pressed executives devoting as much time and money to cope with a spate of complimentary articles.

Public relations was a product of the rationalization of corporate press relations which resulted both from a general movement to increase efficiency and from the specific desire to respond to journalistic criticism which was reaching a wider audience than ever before. In the 1920s attacks on business diminished in tone and number. Nevertheless, changing concepts of public opinion and of the role of the corporation in society in addition to startling developments in mass communication stimulated an increased interest in the function.

NOTES

1. Thomas C. Cochran, *Railroad Leaders* (Cambridge, Mass., 1953), p. 1.

2. Quoted in Matthew Josephson, *The Robber Barons* (New York, 1962), p. 34.

3. Quoted in James MacGregor Burns, *Roosevelt: The Lion and the Fox* (New York, 1956), pp. 332–333.

4. The descriptions in this paragraph appear on the following pages of *Robber Barons:* 14–15, 18, 81–82, 113, 117, 264, 291.

5. Ibid., pp. 276, 441, 187.

6. N. S. B. Gras, "Shifts in Public Relations," *Bulletin of the Business Historical Society*, 19 (October 1945), p. 104.

7. Cochran, *Leaders*, pp. 150, 123–125.

8. Alfred D. Chandler, Jr., "Henry Varnum Poor," in William Miller, ed., *Men In Business* (New York, 1962), pp. 276–280.

9. Edward C. Kirkland, *Industry Comes of Age* (Chicago, 1961), pp. 102–104, 116–120: Robert H. Elias, ed., *Chapters of Erie* (Ithaca, N.Y., 1966), p. 98.

10. Bernard Bailyn, *The New England Merchants in the Seventeenth Century* (New York, 1964), pp. 42, 44.

11. The phrase is that of Frederick B. Tolles, *Meeting House and Counting House* (New York, 1963), p. 46.

12. See the discussion of the death of Stephen Girard in Sigmund Diamond, *The Reputation of the American Businessman* (Cambridge, Mass., 1955), pp. 5–22.

13. Paul Goodman, "Ethics and Enterprise: The Values of the Boston Elite, 1800–1860," *American Quarterly* 18, No. 3 (Fall 1966), p. 441.

14. Tolles, *Meeting House*, p. 143.

15. Goodman, "Ethics," p. 440.

16. See Richard Hofstadter's discussion of business and intellect in *Anti-Intellectualism in American Life* (New York, 1963), pp. 233–252. The words quoted are those of Henry Huttleston Rogers. For a brief but colorful discussion of the tycoon, see Justin Kaplan, *Mr. Clemens and Mark Twain* (New York, 1969), pp. 378–380. For Rogers' skill at concealing his business dealings, see Daniel J. Boorstin, *The Americans: The Democratic Experience* (New York, 1974), pp. 417–418.

17. See Milton Friedman, *Capitalism and Freedom* (Chicago, 1962), pp. 133–136, and Earl F. Cheit, "The New Place of Business," in Cheit, ed., *The Business Establishment* (New York, 1964), pp. 163–164.

18. "The most strongly sanctioned justification for opinion or conduct was profit for the stockholders. To this end economy and efficiency should always be advocated and waste deplored." Cochran, *Leaders*, p. 78.

19. *New York Times*, October 13, 1882, p. 5. But instead of printing a retraction, the *Times* printed, directly under Vanderbilt's denial, a statement by the two reporters who wrote the story that Vanderbilt was unhappy not because their story was incorrect but rather too correct. Another version of the story was published by the Chicago *Tribune* and copied verbatim in the *Railroad Gazette*. This version was considerably tamer. The closest Vanderbilt came to "the public be damned" was:

Q: "Do your limited express trains pay or do you run them for the accommodation of the public?"

A: "Accommodation of the public! Nonsense, and they do not pay either." *Railroad Gazette* 14 (October 13, 1882), p. 627. The suggestion has been made that the *Tribune* changed the text of the interview to avoid offending Vanderbilt. Wayne Andrews, *The Vanderbilt Legend* (New York, 1941), p. 194. When the *Railroad Gazette* reported Vanderbilt's denial, it editorialized: "What Mr. Vanderbilt said, according to the *Tribune* report, . . . was not very wise, but by the Associated Press report it was simply brutal. . . . [W]hen Mr. Vanderbilt talks to a reporter he makes a speech to the entire nation, and a very large part of it is sure to take it seriously." Vol. 14, p. 629.

20. Lee Benson, *Merchants, Farmers and Railroads* (Cambridge, Mass., 1955), p. 183; Alvin F. Harlow, "William H. Vanderbilt," *Dictionary of American Biography*, Vol. 19 (New York, 1936), pp. 175–176; Josephson, *Robber Barons*, p. 187.

21. Edward C. Kirkland, *Dream and Thought in the Business Community* (Ithaca, 1956), p. 156.

22. Kirkland, *Industry*, p. 120.

23. Quoted in Ralph and Muriel Hidy, *Pioneering in Big Business* (New York, 1955), pp. 214–215.

24. The third volume of Daniel Boorstin's trilogy is replete with examples of entrepreneurial sensitivity to public opinion in the so-called public-be-damned era. This sensitivity manifested itself through the creation of attention getting events and efforts to "humanize" the corporation. Such activity greatly increased during the 1920s, but it did not originate in that decade. Boorstin, *Democratic Experience*, pp. 93, 103, 121–124, 180–183, 311–316, 332–335, 535–537.

25. See Adam Smith's discussion in *The Wealth of Nations*, Edwin Canaan, ed. (New York, 1937), pp. 58–61.

26. Daniel J. Boorstin, *The Americans: The National Experience* (New York, 1965), p. 127. He may exaggerate the uniqueness of the American booster. See Gottlieb Mittleberger's complaints about the Newlanders in *Journey to Pennsylvania* (Cambridge, Mass., 1960), pp. 26–32.

27. Neil Harris, *Humbug* (Boston, 1973), p. 4.

28. Gould "labored . . . to stir up the local population" to save his tannery (p. 40); Cooke used "ballyhoo" in his bond drives (p. 54), and corrupted the press "with edibles and bibibles" (p. 56). He also "unloosed" "a mighty propaganda" to

stimulate immigration and bond sales (p. 97). Anthony Drexel "owned" the head of the *Philadelphia Ledger* and used this connection to spread anti-Cooke rumors (p. 167). Gould's press organ "published news and opinions as he wished" (p. 208). Huntington bought newspapers "to 'control or burn' them" (p. 227). The examples could be extended.

29. Robert W. Fogel, *The Union Pacific Railroad* (Baltimore, 1960), pp. 75–81.

30. Henrietta M. Larson, *Jay Cooke* (New York, 1968), pp. 126–132, 169–172.

31. Leila A. Sussman, "The Public Relations Movement" (unpublished M.A. thesis, University of Chicago, 1947), p. 7; Elmer Davis asserted that the *Times* permanently discontinued this practice around 1900. *History of the New York Times* (New York, 1921), pp. 311–322.

32. Reproduced in Alfred McClung Lee, *The Daily Newspaper in America* (New York, 1937), p. 436.

33. Cochran, *Leaders*, p. 187.

34. Bernard A. Weisberger, *The American Newspaperman* (Chicago, 1961), pp. 97, 89.

35. Lee, *Newspaper*, p. 434.

36. Allan Nevins, *The Evening Post* (New York, 1922), p. 430.

37. Villard made vigorous use of publicity to entice settlers to the Northwest for the sake of his railroad interests. Indeed, publicity had been an important tool in peopling the sparse continent since the seventeenth century. James B. Hedges, "Promotion of Immigration to the Pacific Northwest by the Railroads," *Mississippi Valley Historical Review* 15, No. 2 (September 1928), pp. 183–203. There is an excellent collection of clippings in the Villard papers showing the extent of the promotional material which was inserted into news columns. Many of these articles show amusing and garish examples of the booster spirit at work. For example, the following headline from the November 7, 1881, edition of the San Francisco *Chronicle:* "MOSES MISTAKEN; The Land of Promise Found East of Portland." Henry Villard papers, Baker Library, Harvard Business School, Box 60. See also Box 96.

38. Weisberger, *Newspaperman*, p. 126; Julius Grodinsky, *Jay Gould* (Philadelphia, 1957), pp. 20, 281–282; Nevins, *Post,* p. 440.

39. Kirkland, *Industry*, p. 73.

40. Ray E. Hiebert, *Courtier to the Crowd* (Ames, I., 1966), p. 56.

41. Ibid., pp. 56–57; Eric F. Goldman, *Two-Way Street* (Boston, 1948), p. 8.

42. Hiebert, *Courier*, p. 83.

43. Ibid., p. 67.

44. Daniel A. Pope briefly discusses this idea in "The Development of National Advertising" (unpublished Ph.D. thesis, Columbia, 1973), p. 32. Some churches were extremely publicity-conscious during the Progressive era. See, for example, Christian F. Reisner, *Church Publicity: The Modern Way to Compel Them to Come In* (New York, 1913).

45. Anderson Pace, "Building a Line to the Public," *Railway Age Gazette* 61 (August 25, 1916), pp. 324–325.

46. See "Department of Public Policy and Relations," *Railway Age Gazette* 59 (August 27, 1915). pp. 376–377.

47. See Alan Raucher, *Public Relations and Business, 1900–1929* (Baltimore, 1968), pp. 47–63.

48. Thomas C. Cochran, *Basic History of American Business* (Princeton, N.J., 1968), p. 83; Charles W. Cheape, "The 1907 Contract, or How Philadelphia Learned to Live with the Traction Monopoly," unpublished paper delivered at Brandeis University colloquium on business history, April 30, 1974. The Philadelphia Traction Company responded quickly to complaints about passenger discomfort and poor service but failed to reap any credit for its efforts.

49. *Electric Railway Journal* 44 (October 3, 1914), pp. 651–752; (October 15, 1914), p. 862.

50. Norton E. Long, "The Public Relations of the Bell System," *Public Opinion Quarterly* 1 (October 1937), p. 10.

51. Albert Bigelow Paine quoted in ibid., pp. 11–12.

52. Scott M. Cutlip, "The Nation's First Public Relations Firm," *Journalism Quarterly* 43, No. 2 (Summer 1966), p. 275.

53. L. L. L. Golden, *Only by Public Consent* (New York, 1968), p. 27.

54. Raucher, *Public Relations*, pp. 49–53.

55. Albert Bigelow Paine, *In One Man's Life* (New York, 1921), p. 239.

56. Glenn Porter, "A Picture from Life's Other Side: Pocket Robber Baron," *Reviews in American History* 4, No. 3 (September 1976), p. 419.

57. Paine, *Life*, p. 24.

58. Hidy and Hidy, *Pioneering*, pp. 201–217, 698–699; Joseph I. C. Clarke, *My Life and Memories* (New York, 1925), pp. 343–352. Clarke was hired as a member of the legal department. He resigned in 1913. Jersey Standard was inconsistent in its public realtions policy. Raucher, *Public Relations*, pp. 22–24; George S. Gibb and Evelyn H. Knowlton, *The Resurgent Years* (New York, 1956), pp. 252–259.

59. John A. Garraty, "The United States Steel Corporation Versus Labor," *Labor History* 1 (Winter 1960), p. 1; Robert D. Hessen, "A Biography of Charles M. Schwab, Steel Industrialist" (unpublished Ph.D. thesis, Columbia, 1969), pp. 214–216; Robert H. Wiebe, *Businessmen and Reform* (Chicago, 1968), p. 187; Golden, *Consent*, pp. 247–254.

60. Raucher, *Public Relations*, pp. vi–ix.

61. Wiebe, *Businessmen*, pp. 17–18; Martin, *Enterprise*, pp. 80–84; Raucher, *Public Relations*, p. vii.

62. Ibid., pp. 52–53. For economic reasons, U.S. Steel should have been closely integrated, but such centralization might have been viewed askance by a public frightened by bigness. On the other hand, without centralization, the corporation risked bad publicity because of irresponsible activities of subsidiaries. Garraty, "U.S. Steel," p. 1. The Ford Motor Company did not have a department with the title "Public Relations" until April of 1944, but a student of the firm believes that it spent more money on public relations activities between 1903 and 1932 than any other company in the country. The automobile industry as a whole used publicity stunts such as races and long trips to try to convince a doubting public that the automobile was no passing fad but here to stay. David L. Lewis, "Henry Ford: A Study in Public Relations" (unpublished Ph.D. thesis, University of Michigan, 1959), pp. 519, ii–iii, 8.

63. *Business in American Life* (New York, 1972), p. 152.
64. David M. Chalmers, *The Social and Political Ideas of the Muckrakers* (New York, 1964), p. 15; Louis Filler, *Crusaders for American Liberalism* (Yellow Springs, Ohio, 1961), p. 10; Arthur and Lila Weinberg, eds., *The Muckrakers* (New York, 1961), pp. xiv, 187.
65. Chalmers, *Muckrakers*, p. 44.
66. Quoted in Weinberg, *Muckrakers*, pp. xx–xxi.
67. Filler, *Crusaders,* p. 365 and pp. 359–378 *passim;* but see also Hofstadter, *Reform*, p. 196.
68. Connie Jean Conway, "Theodore Vail's Public Relations Philosophy, Pt. II," *Bell Telephone Magazine* 37 (Winter 1958–1959), p. 51; Hiebert, *Courtier,* p. 41; Goldman, *Street,* p. 7.
69. Hofstadter, *Reform,* p. 187.
70. Louis Galambos, *The Public Image of Big Business in America, 1880–1940* (Baltimore, 1975), p. 254; Richard Hofstadter, "What Happened to the Antitrust Movement?" in *The Paranoid Style in American Politics and Other Essays* (New York, 1967), pp. 188 and 188–237 *passim.*
71. Almost three times as many Pulitzer prizes have been awarded for political reporting as for stories related to business since the citations were started in 1917. Edwary Jay Epstein, *Between Fact and Fiction* (New York, 1975), pp. 101–102. Chris Welles's "The Bleak Wasteland of Financial Journalism," *Columbia Journalism Review,* July–August 1973, is a good example of the many recent complaints of the low quality of current business reportage.
72. There were at least a dozen, and probably a good many more, universities sending out material to editors at the turn of the century. These included the University of Michigan, the University of Pennsylvania, and Harvard. Herbert Small to Charles W. Eliot, Folder 220, Box 115, Eliot papers, Pusey Library, Harvard.
73. Glenn Porter, *The Rise of Big Business, 1860–1910* (New York, 1973), p. 78.
74. Loren Baritz, *The Servants of Power* (Middletown, Conn., 1960), pp. 21–41. See also Richard S. Tedlow, "Henry Charles Link," *Dictionary of American Biography,* Supplement Five (New York, 1977), pp. 433–434.
75. Stuart D. Brandes, *American Welfare Capitalism* (Chicago, 1976), pp. 33 and *passim.* When the Bancroft family hired Miss Elizabeth Briscoe as the "welfare secretary" for their Wilmington, Delaware, textile mill she at first had no clear idea of what she was to do. But her employers soon defined her job as "interpreting the position of the employer toward the employees" and acting as "the representative of the employees, bringing before the firm any grievances that affect the employers individually or collectively." Daniel Nelson and Stuart Campbell, "Taylorism versus Welfare Work in American Industry: H. L. Gantt and the Bancrofts," *Business History Review* 46, No. 1 (Spring 1972), p. 8. The similarity between Miss Briscoe's experience and that of Ellsworth at AT&T (who did not know what his job was when he was hired) and of Lee's (who finally figured out that his job was to interpret the Pennsylvania to the public and *vice versa*) should be noted. Business auxiliaries were having similar troubles defining their roles and developing similar phrases for describing solutions to the "human question" in its many guises. Oddly enough, unlike the 1940s when public relations and

industrial relations specialists often worked hand-in-glove, collaboration such as that which took place between Lee and William Lyon MacKenzie King for Rockefeller after Ludlow seems to have been quite exceptional.

76. Baritz, *Power*, p. 15.

77. Taylor called welfare capitalism "a joke." Brandes, *Welfare*, p. 36.

78. Pope, "Advertising," pp. 282–289, 300; Richard S. Tedlow, "Albert Davis Lasker," *Dictionary of American Biography*, Supplement Five, pp. 410–412. As a percentage of the gross national product, advertising has never surpassed the 3.4 percent mark reached in 1904. Pope, "Advertising," p. 19.

Chapter II

Up From Press Agentry

The privilege of controlling the actions or of affecting the income and property of other persons is something that no one of us can profess to seek or admit to possessing.
John Kenneth Galbraith, 1952[1]

I

Historians have written of the 1920s as the businessman's decade in the United States. There is no need to recount the familiar evidence for this proposition; it suffices to say that such evidence does indeed abound. From all corners of the land came praise for the business system, and many counted it as among the highest of compliments to be referred to as a good businessman. An oft-cited example of the spirit of the age was the best-selling volume by Bruce Barton purporting to show that Jesus himself could best be appreciated as a dynamic go-getter. Tension between businessman and society had sufficiently abated by the middle of the decade that even the dyspeptic National Association of Manufacturers, spokesman for conservative small- and medium-sized enterprises, modulated the stringency of its anti-union platform.[2]

In the early years of U.S. Steel, a former Carnegie ironmaster was once moved to observe that "I have always had one rule. When a workman sticks up his head, hit it."[3] Yet by the 1920s this attitude seemed to have been largely abandoned. The same U. S. Steel, the largest firm in that most brutal of industries, reduced the workday at Gary from twelve to eight hours in 1923. Three years later, Ford instituted a five-day work week, while International Harvester granted its workers a two-week annual paid vacation.[4] Productivity and national income soared as America became the richest nation in the world.

Just as important, business seemed on its way to justifying its claim as benefactor of the human race, "the civilizer."[5] It seemed that William Gibbs McAdoo's motto of 1908, "the public be pleased," was being adopted by numerous tycoons of the New Era.[6] Many of the new industries establishing themselves, especially in the fields of entertainment, transportation, and products for the home, had a direct impact on the lives of consumers, promising an end to age-old drudgery and new frontiers of enjoyment.[7] Only a tiny portion of corporate effort by modern standards was devoted to weapons of war. With the stock market going ever upward, the business decade reached it apogee with the election of Herbert Hoover. The first successful businessman to become President since George Washington (and the last until Jimmy Carter), Hoover lived the rags-to-riches ideal and, with his unique background in humanitarianism and science, embodied hope for the future. Ex-muckraker Lincoln Steffens can be forgiven for gushing about "the distribution of wealth" looking as if it was "within sight in my amazing country."[8]

The 1920s were probably the most depressing decade in its history for the great enemy of the hegemony of big business, organized labor. During the Progressive era, union leaders had attained a modicum of respectability and at least the appearance of influence through such organizations as the National Civil Federation. With World War I, labor gained more than that; the nation needed union support and the price was greater recognition. But after the war, government-business-labor comity dissolved, and attempts to solidify earlier gains were crushed in 1919.[9]

Thomas Cochran has speculated that ascendancy in public relations was a significant factor in making business popular in the 1920s.[10] A look at the efforts of the unions in this realm shows that business did indeed far outstrip its competitor.

Despite the instinctive appreciation of some of its leaders of the importance of public relations, as indicated, for example, by the sensitivity of the UMW's Mitchell during the 1902 anthracite strike, the moribund labor movement was incapable of rising to the corporate challenge. Periods of prosperity, the conventional wisdom had it, were best suited to the growth of unions. During the '20s, however, membership plummeted. One reason was management's carrot-and-stick approach to the work force. Employers threatened workers with their "open shop" drives, seeking, with some success, to brand all union activity as radical and un-American. Concurrently, some of the largest firms stole labor's thunder. Welfare capitalism with its company unions offered such benefits as group life insurance, old-age pensions, and assistance with housing. Industrial relations experts "humanized" management by increasing communication with the men through new grievance procedures. The power of foremen was curbed in the drive to rationalize employment policy. In a few companies, as we have seen, wages and hours were favorably adjusted.[11]

Employee representation plans did not, of course, grant collective bargaining rights. Any improvements in the lot of the workers were paternalistic gifts, rather than concessions to power, and valuable benefits accrued to but a small percentage of the work force. Some employees recognized this and did not delude themselves about the motives of management. Many, however, especially among the semi- and unskilled, were won over by management's largesse.[12] Their actons may not have sprung from unadulterated altruism, but the progressive executives of the New Era seemed to be doing more for the laborer than the squabbling, visionless union leaders.

Effective public relations was throttled by the labor movement's aimlessness. "Should propaganda seek to bring about an immediate general overthrow of the existing order," asked an observer of the labor scene in 1928, "or should it lay stress on accomplishing reform bit by bit?" The former was clearly out of tune with the times and anathema to leading laborites. Unions had enough trouble with charges of un-Americanism without courting this kind of disaster. The latter, however, seemed to be progressing quite well without labor's involvement. Some leaders of the AFL, notably President William Green, eschewed conflict in favor of the corporate vision of a harmony of interests within the capitalistic system. Shortly before his death, Samuel Gompers even made peace with Taylorism in order to counter charges of impeding productivity. But these men were almost as out of place as accommodationists as they would have been as revolutionaries. Worst of all, their potential constituents were utterly bored with the twists and turns of their confusing philosophy and with their conventions, their legalisms, and their inaction. As Green himself ruefully admitted, the workers' attitude toward organized labor was one of "appalling indifference." Until workers understood that paternalism was a weak reed upon which to support their welfare and until labor leaders themselves learned what they were about, the unions would be unable to put together an effective public relations program.[13]

Despite a labor movement unable and a government unwilling to challenge corporate power, it would be erroneous to underestimate the deep currents of unease which persisted in the business community. Part of this was the result of a built-in inability to enjoy power in America because, as Hans Speier has pointed out, public opinion tends to suspect that its enjoyment indicates its abuse.[14] But there were other, quite tangible causes. One was the persistence of labor difficulties. A second were new and disquieting perceptions, growing out of the experience of World War I, about the nature of public opinion. And a third was the development of new communications technologies.

The postwar era commenced on a threatening note. The nation suffered economic dislocation and labor disputes shocking in their ferocity. In January, Seattle was hit by a general strike. In September it was the Boston policemen and the steelworkers, 350,000 strong. In November 425,000 coal miners walked out. These disruptions were punctuated by occasional violence and sundry bombings. Lenin was in power in Russia; anything seemed possible.

In the event, each one of these disputes was settled satisfactorily from the employers' point of view, thanks in no small part to the superiority of the corporations in selling the general public their point of view.[15] But the historian must keep in mind Frederick W. Maitland's famous dictum to the effect that things which are now in the past were once in the future. There was no way for the businessman to know that 1920 or 1921 would not see another union power grab as had 1919. Behind much of the seemingly disinterested benevolence of welfare capitalism was the very practical desire to prevent unionization.[16]

Furthermore, not all labor problems were directly related to unions, and those which were not persisted in the '20s. Employers were beginning to realize how the unorganized worker could slow production. Western Electric, for example, conducted the lengthy and costly Hawthorne experiments to learn how to deal with informal groups of workers who insisted on setting their own pace.[17]

Many corporations had thus been successful in winning public approval for their anti-union approach both during strikes and in times of labor peace. And yet the big businessman still had no established standards of practice for dealing with the press and with public opinion. In the 1920s, the necessity of establishing such standards acquired a new urgency because of new ideas about opinion formation and attitude change.

It had been a staple of democratic theory that the public was rational and, given the facts, could be trusted. The muckrakers, for example, did not see themselves primarily as "leaders, revivalists, agitators, or anything more than mere informers of the public."[18] ". . . [F]acts," Ray Stannard Baker later explained, "facts piled up to the point of dry certitude, was [sic] what the American people then needed and wanted."[19] By themselves, without persuasive interpretation, facts would lead to the right conclusions. Secrecy was a breeding ground for conspiracy against the commonweal. Muckrakers insisted that if business agreements were openly arrived at covenants, an informed public would excise evil-doing from the economic scene. Publicity was a keystone in the Progressive house of reform. By itself, it was a "potent force" which constituted a "continuous remedial measure" against chicanery in business and politics.[20] Ivy Lee attracted attention in the business community by arguing that the public could be trusted and that management would benefit by giving it the facts. His 1915 essay on "Publicity—A Cure for Railroad Evils" could have been published in *McClure's*.[21] An appropriate motto for the age would have been the slogan of the Scripps-Howard newspapers: "Give light and the people will find their own way."

But "[p]ublicity, the hope of the Progressive Era, became propaganda, the scourge of the twenties. . ." Shocked by the malleability of the masses before World War I propagandists, depressed by the renunciation of reform in favor of the Gamalielese mentality, and influenced by the emphasis of Freud and others on the role of the subconscious in decision making, many intellectuals abandoned their former faith in the public. The truth would not out through mere factual exposition. The public had to be persuaded, and this was a game at which more than one could play. For Walter Lippmann, the educated citizen of the Progressive era became the audience that arrived in the middle of a play's last act and left before the final curtain, having stayed just long enough to identify the hero and the villain but basing even this judgment upon inadequate information. Depth of understanding was beyond it; prejudice, stoked by random data, ruled it.[22]

In place of the Scripps-Howard motto, the '20s could have substituted another aphorism: "There are no facts, only interpretations." And of a sudden the woods were full of professional propagandists—press agents, publicity men, and public relations counselors—anxious to persuade the public to their clients' point of view by airing certain facts. "Factoids" might be a better word, for these paid advocates dealt only in usable truths. Persuasion for ulterior motives rather than disinterested enlightenment was the goal. "This is the underlying reason," wrote Walter Lippman in 1922, "for the existence of the press agent."

> The enormous discretion as to what facts and what impressions shall be reported is steadily convincing every organized group . . . that whether it wishes to secure publicity or avoid it, the exercise of discretion cannot be left to the reporter. . . . The development of the publicity man is a clear sign that the facts of modern life do not spontaneously take a shape in which they can be known. They must be given a shape by somebody, . . . and since there is little disinterested organization of intelligence, the need for some formulation is being met by the interested parties.[23]

These new attitudes toward persuasion were not confined to intellectuals; they were paralleled, in some cases preceded, by the writings of advertising agents, public relations men, and industrial psychologists. Merle Curti's analysis of articles in *Printers' Ink* has shown that from the founding of the publication in 1888 to about 1910, the view of man as a rational creature predominated. Men possessed plenty of common sense, and though perhaps liars themselves, hated lying and were shrewd enough to spot it. The customer was the sovereign of his own decision making and was liable to resent attempts at persuasion. The basic function of the advertising man, therefore, was to inform. A minority during this same period looked to emotions rather than reason and accepted the task of persuasion rather than mere announcement. They pointed to egocentricity, vanity, and prejudice as universal traits which the copywriter would do well to take advantage of.[24]

Shifts in the relative numbers holding these positions were evident around 1905, and from 1910 to 1930 the minority and majority had reversed themselves. The importance of nonrational impulses became generally recognized: "Thus advertising was to operate by suggestion, the use of forceful concrete details and pictures, by attention arresting stimuli, by playing on human sympathy, and by appeals to the senses." That this transformation was taking place not only in the pages of *Printers' Ink* was shown by Daniel A. Pope in his study of life insurance advertising, which "moved from a presentation of financial information (or misinformation) to persuasive appeals to pride and fear."[25]

The work of Walter Dill Scott was important in effectuating this change. In a 1901 speech to a Chicago advertising club, Scott spoke of the importance of appealing to the emotions as well as to the intellect, a thesis he elaborated on in *The Psychology of Advertising* which he published in 1905.[26] Most advertising men in the early years of this century were skeptical about the possible applications of academic psychology and sociology to their trade, but by the 1920s they were eager to put the social sciences to work to help them solve the problems of selling to an irrational public.

The important point is that the change in perception of public opinion from being essentially rational in the formation of its judgments to primarily emotional was as upsetting to businessmen as to intellectuals. The self-righteousness of their own pronouncements and the widespread faith in Lee, with his doctrine that the public could be trusted with the truth, showed that executives' belief in their own rectitude was genuine. But their beneficence might be obscured from a public which would not accept the facts (as executives saw them). The wiles of the rabble-rouser now loomed as as great a threat to acceptance of the business "truths" as did manipulations of corporate publicists to the "truths" of labor leaders and political and intellectual critics of the business system.

From the point of view of the struggling farmer, the unemployed coal miner, or the exploited textile hand, corporate executives may have seemed masters of the nation. From the entrepreneur's own eyes, however, one sees a chaotic array of difficulties and proposed solutions to the "human problem." The businessman confronted what appeared to be an ineluctable contradiction. On the one hand he needed a docile and "wantless" labor force. On the other, he needed consumers for his products and therefore placed advertising which promised youth, beauty, and security. This advertising was designed to arouse feelings of discontent and envy[27] and thus worked at cross purposes with labor policy. On top of these contradictory demands made for economic reasons, for, that is, frugal workers and extravagant consumers, he also had to cultivate a general ambience favorable to private property and free enterprise. He had to deal with the political threat of an irrational and potentially anti-corporate public opinion.

During the war, public opinion had shown its susceptibility to demagogic appeal. Matters were further complicated by the development of a new means of mass communication, the radio, with its momentous implications for influencing society. It could transform even Calvin Coolidge into a man of warmth. The executives who put together the Radio Corporation of America in 1919 were not sure how their new property would operate. Neither were business publicists. The technology of broadcasting had developed independently of corporate public relations and advertising. Suddenly, in the mid-1920s, businessmen were faced with a weapon of great potential for integrating or agitating an atomized society, but they did not know what to make of it. Local merchants, hotels, department stores, and newspapers did establish stations to attract publicity and win community good will, but a decade would pass before Ford and Du Pont pioneered in using radio nationally for artfully wrought institutional messages. Here was a case of the means of communication preceding its content.[28]

Generalizations concerning public opinion are hazardous, but Hans Speier's remark about the prohibition of enjoyment of power (and, he might have added, wealth) is applicable to the 1920s. Business journalist William Feather was right in observing that "the American businessman is the foremost hero of the American people today," but the fact that many executives harbored "an acute distrust of any power with a popular base" shows that this sentiment was not fully reciprocated.[29]

Dealing with public opinion was an interstice in corporate organization which had to be filled. During the course of this century the public relations counselor has assumed this duty. But his road to acceptance by businessmen has not been an easy one. Three men—Ivy L. Lee, Edward L. Bernays, and Arthur W. Page—were pivotal in developing that acceptance.

II

A businessman who wanted to influence public opinion could choose any of a number of methods. He could speak out personally. He could direct his advertising agency to manipulate contracts in order to sway editorial opinion. He could charge his legal staff to represent him in the "court of public opinion." Or he could hire a press agent or publicity bureau. All these approaches have been attempted during the course of the twentieth century, at times simultaneously within a single corporation. Each has presented its own particular drawbacks.

Andrew Carnegie showed that success as an entrepreneur did not preclude success as a publicist. For every Carnegie, however, there has been at least one George F. Baer. Often businessmen combined the qualities of both men. Henry Ford, once again, comes to mind as does Charles Schwab.[30]

Public relations counselors have encouraged business leaders to speak out. Ivy Lee, for example, said that "My theory of a publicity agent is that he should not act as an intermediary. . . . My idea is that the principal himself should be his own publicity agent . . ." As Lee realized, however, it was not practical for the "principal" of a firm with interests in every corner of the nation and perhaps the world to assume the task of publicity agent without help. "[T]he functions of a person like myself," he continued, "should be to advise with the man who is going to take the responsibility for the act itself as to what he should do and what he should say. . . ." In the modern era, the custodianship of the corporate image has proven too large a job to be handled without the aid of a specialist.[31]

The question of the integrity of the newspapers in the face of advertiser pressure was hotly debated in the early part of this century. Upton Sinclair dealt with this issue in *The Brass Check*. He found that "not merely is there a general control of the spirit and tone of the paper [by the major advertisers]; there is a control in minute details, sometimes grotesque." In the late nineteenth century, patent-medicine manufacturers inserted a "red clause" in their advertising contracts which declared the contract void "if any law is enacted by your State restricting or prohibiting the manufacture or sale of proprietary medicines." This all but eliminated criticism of such nostrums. Advertisers also exercised powerful influence over the foreign language press. In the age of big-business journalism ushered in by William Randolph Hearst in the early twentieth century, A. J. Liebling has charged, publishers naturally tend to use their properties "to form public opinion the N. A. M. approves." It was unnecessary to coerce what the publishers themselves wanted.[32]

The weight of the evidence dispassionately considered, however, suggests that advertising expenditures have not given corporations the control over journalism that some newspapermen and critics have imagined. Newspapers have been aware of who their large advertisers are and may remember them in editorials and puff them in news columns. But they also must report the news; they suppress it at their peril. In a study of the newspapers' usefulness for historical research. Lucy Maynard Salmon concluded that on the whole they were not reluctant to report even the elevator accident in the department store which purchased their advertising space.[33]

The corporation which did elect to influence editors through advertising could eliminate, or threaten to, its advertising in an offending publication, or dramatically increase its linage to win good will. The first avenue was largely ineffectual against established journals, and the second created the "Mouse that Roared" possibility of small newspapers blackmailing great corporations by threatening to publish unflattering stories unless paid off by advertising.[34] Although at times effective, this approach was basically negative, more likely to result in the suppression of bad news than the positive expression of a corporate viewpoint, and no doubt quite unsatisfying to the executive who felt his company had a good case that deserved a hearing. Manipulating advertising would have availed little to change the stand of a paper like the New York *Call,* for example. But when Ivy Lee published a book defending the railroads in 1915, he sent the *Call* a copy. Although the editorial staff was not converted (one editor claimed in mock alarm that when the package from Lee was received, fear swept the offices that it was a bomb), the paper did devote three articles to the book, and Lee reached a readership he otherwise would not have had.[35] He and those of like mind may have derived some pleasure from confronting the lion in his den.

If the corporation were in fact on trial before the public, it seemed a natural impulse to have it defended by those who appeared in its behalf before courts of law. Some corporation lawyers have succeeded in a public relations role, Judge Elbert Gary being the best example.[36] By and large, however, the corporation lawyer has not proven sufficiently skillful in speaking the people's language. The analogy between the courts of law and public opinion, so often drawn by public relations men, was far from exact.

Thus we come to our fourth possibility, the creation of a special corporate function for dealing with public opinion arising from the old press agent. This appeared to be a sensible solution, but the obstacles were nonetheless impressive.

The press agent had a bad reputation. He "ranked about with a tramp printer—a rootless quasi-vagrant, and all too often, an alcoholic incompetent." He was a "blustery individual with loud voice and loud pants, who sought to wheedle editors by flattery and poor cigars." "He whisked panthers in and out of hotels, conducted ballyhoos on Broadway, originated lacteal ablutions, and contrived fake suicides." He was "the only man in the world proud of being called a liar." He was "the direct descendant of P. T. Barnum, astute author of immortally funny hoaxes which were at the same time cruel and more than a little repulsive. It is difficult to conceive of such types in the board room with Alfred P. Sloan, Jr. or Pierre S. du Pont.[37]

George V. S. Michaelis's Publicity Bureau, the first agency of its kind, was a victim and a further cause of this bad repute. In September of 1900, the Bureau began working for Harvard at the fee of $200 per month. Approximately two years later, however, President Charles W. Eliot concluded that the prestige of having Harvard as a client was so valuable that the Bureau should furnish its services gratis, and, according to a member of the firm, ". . . we had to agree with him." In a classic muckraking article on railroad anti-Hepburn Act publicity, Ray Stannard Baker described the Bureau as having represented "high-class clients; notably Harvard University." He would have been less impressed had he known the conditions of its retention.[38]

Michaelis exacerbated the precarious status of his firm by a serious transgression against the Telephone Company and overzealousness in his railroad work.

It has always been difficult to judge the effectiveness of public relations work. Corporations have usually placed great store in the kinds of articles appearing about them, assuming these to be both indicative of and influential over public opinion. But how can they be sure that favorable publicity results from the work of their public relations men? Michaelis apparently tried to take advantage of this situation when employed by AT&T. Theodore Vail had hired another publicity man, George Harvey, unbeknownst to Michaelis, and when the Bureau tried to claim credit for Harvey's efforts, its untrustworthiness was revealed.[39]

The Bureau's most elaborate campaign was waged on behalf of the railroads in 1905 and 1906. It established offices in five eastern and midwestern cities and employed agents elsewhere. In Chicago, where its headquarters were most appropriately housed in the Orchestra Building, it employed forty-three people, mostly ex-newspapermen. They scanned all the publications within their district noting key information about them and assembling it in a card catalogue called the "Barometer."

> Possessed of this knowledge, how adroitly and perfectly the well-equipped publicity agents can play upon each town and influence each editor! Every card bears also, in columns, a list of numbers. Every number refers to an article sent out by the firm. Most of these articles are especially prepared by the staff writers for a certain town, or group of towns. There is no confused firing of wasteful volleys; each shot is carefully aimed.[40]

When confronted by a radical editor unmoved by this propaganda barrage, it was not unknown for the Bureau to send out an agent to the editor's town to stir up opinion against him. Did the system work? An employee told Ray Stannard Baker that in the week ending June 5, 1905, Nebraska newspapers carried 212 columns of antirailroad copy and only two favorable columns. Three months later, the box score was almost precisely reversed: 200 favorable columns to four unfavorable.[41]

Baker, while conceding the right of the roads to place their case before the public, was incensed that the Bureau's agents would not identify who was paying them for their work. Nor would they identify the sources of the press releases which would arrive on editors' desks "out of the blue heavens like a sort of manna." "If these agents had appeared frankly before the court of public opinion as railroad employees, no one could have quarreled with them; and they would have deceived no one. And why, if the railroad men have a really good argument, should they not make it openly and frankly?"[42]

The railroads may have been impressed with Baker's assessment. When they established the Bureau of Railway Economics in 1910, the purpose of which was to present their case to the public, it was stipulated that the organization avoid incurring "the stigma attaching to the so-called 'Publicity Bureaus' that have developed during recent years and have justly excited the antagonism of the newspapers."[43]

The founders of the Publicity Bureau differentiated their work from that of advertising agencies and press agents.[44] They were on the right track, providing employers with organized and effective service in a businesslike fashion quite unlike that of the circus publicity stunt man. During its brief existence, however, the Bureau frightened liberals, angered local editors, and in the end failed to impress the railroad men or Telephone Company. The Publicity Bureau was a false start.

Despite the Bureau's shortcomings, businessmen continued to explore solutions to their image problems. One man who did much in the early years to invest public relations with respectability and to show how the reporter's skills could be used to shore up rather than attack a business's reputation was Ivy L. Lee. Lee's career has been dealt with in detail elsewhere,[45] so our purpose will be merely to highlight his contribution to improving the public relations of public relations among executives.

Lee's first important clients were the anthracite coal mine operators. The anthracite industry had suffered a difficult strike in 1902, during which the handling of the press by the United Mine Workers and management showed a marked contrast. The union's John Mitchell was congeniality itself with newsmen, but the owners were clumsy and haughty, not a good combination. Their "arrogant stupidity," to use Theodore Roosevelt's phrase, won for them opprobrium and certainly did not help their cause.[46]

When another strike threatened in 1906, the operators put their image problems in the hands of Lee, from whom emanated forthwith an "authorized statement" announcing that the owners would supply as much information as they could to an interested public.[47] Like many another successful public relations man who was to run an independent agency after him, Lee was an astute self-publicizer. He took the occasion of this announcement to send to editors a Declaration of Principles, in which he attempted to answer some of the current objections to his craft:

> This is not a secret press bureau. All our work is done in the open. We aim to supply news. This is not an advertising agency; if you think any of our matter ought properly to go to your business office, do not use it. Our matter is accurate. . . . In brief, our plan is, frankly and openly, on behalf of the business concerns and public institutions, to supply to the press and public . . . prompt and accurate information concerning subjects which it is of value and interest to the public to know about. . . . I am always at your service for the purpose of enabling you to obtain more complete information concerning any of the subjects brought forward in my copy.[48]

Lee promised, in other words, to identify himself and his employer in the material he sent to editors. He promised not to use advertising revenues or other levers to force them to print it. Thus he acknowledged the justice of Ray Stannard Baker's two major objections to the Publicity Bureau's work and pledged to avoid them. Thirdly, Lee would tell the truth. There would be none of the prevarications of a Charles "Dollar-a-Line" Smith or a Harry Reichenbach in his releases.[49]

From the mine owners, Lee brought the sober press release to the Pennsylvania Railroad and, following the "Ludlow Massacre," to the Rockefeller interests. The core of his message was that corporate relations with labor, press, and public were by nature harmonious. Most criticism of management resulted from misunderstanding. Thus, if businessmen managed news carefully, they would be appreciated by a public which might otherwise be misled.

Many public relations counselors have aspired to the role of om- ←· budsman within the corporation. When their client's actions strayed from the public interest, they have claimed to try to change those actions by bringing forward the public's point of view. They possess, some have asserted, a broader perspective on business problems than their employer: the ability to see beyond the immediate tactics of labor or political conflict to a long-term strategy for security in the public eye. ← This aspiration was implicit in Lee's assertion that he not only interpreted his client to the public but the public to his client. In relatively minor matters, he did at times liberalize his employer's policy. But in times of turmoil, he showed himself to be a company man. So, indeed, have his successors. For the first requirement of an ombudsman is impartiality, and no matter how genuine the desire of some counselors to advance the public interest, they must always support their client, right or wrong, in the final analysis.

Thus during the Ludlow incident, Lee worked surreptitiously for Rockefeller for over six months prior to the announcement of his appointment, writing press releases for an organization calling itself the Coal Mine Operators Committee. He therefore violated one of his cardinal precepts: to work "in the open."[50] Even Lee's sympathetic biographer has admitted that most of his strike bulletins, while literally true, were basically misleading. He also publicized an outright untruth when he grossly exaggerated the salaries of the strike leaders. Lee had been misled by figures the company had supplied him and had been too busy to make an independent inquiry. He thus violated another clause of his Declaration of Principles: "to supply . . . prompt and accurate information," and he was excoriated for it. Carl Sandburg called him a "paid liar," and Upton Sinclair gave him the nickname "Poison Ivy." When Austin B. Garretson of the Commission on Industrial Relations asked Lee if his mission had not been "that of the average publicity agent, . . . to give the truth as the man you were serving for saw it?" the hearing room rang with derisive laughter. It was not the only laugh to be had at Lee's expense during the investigation.[51] Ludlow was an emergency, and Lee was in no position to urge basic policy changes on his employer.

Despite his clumsiness in this instance, Lee's reputation within the business community grew. Numerous letters from leading executives testified to their gratitude for his effectiveness. During the '20s, he stood at the summit of his vocation, working for some of the "big men" of the time and advising trade associations as well.[52]

He knew how to handle executives. He has been described as a "physician to corporate bodies," but a more accurate label would be a masseur for corporate egos. He understood that public criticism was not only a threat to the economic and political security of businesses but that it hurt executive feelings as well, and he counteracted it both through personal counseling and through influencing newsmen in his employers' behalf. As Lee W. Huebner has pointed out, "Lee's message to executives was not one of reform but of consolation."[53] While this function may have been far from that of the ombudsman, it was considerably more prestigious than that of the sideshow swindler that publicity advisers had formerly been considered.

Despite his image as an effective adviser to executives, Lee's attempts to solve another obstacle to professional recognition, the lack of a sensible definition for public relations, were not successful. His first serious attempt to describe what he did and to differentiate it from advertising and press agentry came in *Human Nature and the Railroads*,[54] ten speeches published in 1915. The portrait he painted was blurred by many inconsistencies. On the question of the public's opinion of the railroads, he found that ". . . somehow or other the public has come to have the idea that . . . essential evils are imbedded in the railroad business . . ." and that the public's "state of mind . . . is manifesting itself in harassing legislation, in burdensome taxation and in a general withdrawal of confidence." In complimenting the roads on their successful publicity program, however, he observed that "the people are with us" and now favor a rate hike. He synthesized these opposing views toward the end of the book: ". . . [A]t the present time the American people have no policy whatever toward railroad corporations."[55]

As were many other men of affairs of the Progressive era, Lee was convinced of the omnipotence of public opinion. "The people now rule. We have substituted for the divine right of kings, the divine right of the multitude. The crowd is enthroned,"[56] he lectured, and railroad men could ignore that fact only at their peril. How then was one to deal with the public? What was the basis of attitude formation and change? "The public is reasonable," we are assured in the introduction, but on page 14 we learn that "in the first place, crowds do not reason." Lee seemed to believe in the pre-eminence of reason, but, as these quotations indicate, he was inconsistent here as well. Ten years later he published *Publicity—Some Things It Is and Is Not*, which failed to reconcile these contradictions.[57]

Although his grasp of economics and social psychology was believed to be great, Lee rarely discussed the theses of the many books he referred to and found himself unable to remember correctly the titles and authors even of works which he considered particularly significant. His stumbling has led Alan Raucher to speculate that he did not read these books at all.[58] His confusion about the nature of his work led to embarrassment, as in this instance of his interrogation by Samuel Untermyer at the New York Transit Commission hearings in 1927:

Q: You are not exactly what you would call a publicity agent, are you?
A: No, sir, I don't think so.
Q: What is the difference between the vocation you follow and that of the publicity agent?
A: I don't know, sir.
Q: You cannot see any difference between the activities you follow . . . and the activities . . . of a publicity agent?
A: Well, I am quite prepared to say no.[59]

His employers shared Lee's inability to describe his function. After the Pennsylvania hired him, for example, he traveled the nation's railroads from 1906 to 1910 to study them. His passes described him variously as "Manager, Publicity Bureau," "Press Agent," "Advertising Agent," and "Publicity Agent," and he was referred to in letters of introduction as a man "with whom we have an advertising arrangement" and one who was handling matters of "publicity." When he left his partnership to devote himself exclusively to the Pennsylvania, he was given the title of "Director of Information," and when he returned after a two-year leave of absence he was dubbed "Executive Assistant." He was not at home with the title "public relations man" and after twenty-five years in the business, confessed that "I have never been able to find a satisfactory phrase to describe what I do."[60] The imprecision in his title reflected the confusion about his duties. When Untermyer demanded of the IRT's general counsel what Lee was being paid $12,000 a year for, the reply was "Brains." "Just for holding them in his head?" inquired Untermyer. For preparing news releases, the witness hesitantly answered.[61]

Although Lee was at the height of his fame in the 1920s, his innovations were already behind him. He should be viewed as the representative public relations man of the Progressive era, but that position was occupied by Edward L. Bernays in the postwar period. While Lee waffled back and forth between rational and emotional concepts of crowd psychology, Bernays accepted unflinchingly the contemporary emphasis on prejudice and the subconscious in attitude change. Lee was tongue-tied when asked to explain his job, but Bernays sallied forth in books, articles, and speeches not only to define public relations counseling (a term he coined in 1920) but to outline its methodology and suggest a code of ethics. While Lee thought of his trade as an art which would not outlive his career, Bernays conceived of public relations as the ongoing science of the "group mind" and "herd reaction." In tune with the rhetoric of the times, he insisted that he performed a valuable service which merited professional status.

But before launching into a description of Bernays's career, we must pause to note the impact on those who would mold opinion of the propaganda activities during World War I. The war saw the culmination of trends in journalism, advertising, and public relations of the preceding generation. Hundreds of journalists and publicists were drafted to deal with information—censoring it or spreading it—for government, the armed forces, or charities involved in war work.

American journalism has been taken to task for "discard[ing] the muckrake for the stars and stripes" during the war.[62] In a sense, however, the writers who worked for George Creel's Committee on Public Information (CPI) conducted a muckrake campaign of their own. None of the faults of the German political system or military machine were overlooked and some of the ugly rumors about the "Hun" were not authenticated before they were spread broadcast. Americans, who so recently had begged for the details of the corruption which surrounded them, could now rejoice in their nation's selfless devotion to freedom and democracy. Compared to the monstrous foe, the governments of St. Louis and Philadelphia approached the Platonic ideal while the frenzied finance of Wall Street was a mere peccadillo.

The staff of the CPI has been described as a "roll call of the muckrakers,"[63] but numerous advertising and publicity men also rushed to Washington to help "carr[y] the gospel of Americanism to every corner of the globe."[64] Side by side, former antagonists now labored for the same employer. Will Irwin, author of "The Press Agent: His Rise and Decline," and Carl Byoir, founder of one of the two largest public relations agencies in the country, both held high positions (though not simultaneously) with the CPI's foreign division. Among the coming leaders of public relations and related fields who saw wartime propaganda service were Byoir, Lee, Bernays, Frank Fayant, Arthur W. Page, Harry Reichenbach, William H. Baldwin III, Guy Emerson, and John Price Jones.

Belief in the power of propaganda grew throughout the interwar years, fueled by exposés of wartime activities and "confessions" of British and American propagandists. German right wingers further supported this thesis, claiming that they had been tricked into surrendering by Allied lies, among other things. Propaganda, though frightening many, seemed devastatingly effective, perhaps even more potent than bullets.[65]

Bernays was later to claim that the CPI actually developed theretofore unknown techniques of revolutionary effectiveness for manipulating public opinion. Using the kind of words he would later regret, he declared, "It was, of course, the astounding success of propaganda during the war that opened the eyes of the intelligent few in all departments of life to the possibilities of regimenting the public mind." In fact, the CPI techniques had been familiar before the war; what was new was the scale of operations.[66] Nevertheless, Bernays was right in emphasizing how the war experience heightened interest in professional opinion manipulation.

A nephew of Sigmund Freud and the scion of a distinguished central European Jewish family, Bernays surprised his family by choosing to become a Broadway press agent after graduating from Cornell. He joined the Committee on Public Information in 1917, and following the war he sought to broaden his work. He experimented with several names, including "press agent," "publicity manager," and "public information" (this last being an attempt to identify himself with the Creel Committee's reputation for effectiveness). He finally settled on "counsel on public relations," which he later defined as "giving professional advice to our clients on their public relationships, regardless of whether such advice resulted in publicity."[67] The term "counsel" was self-consciously borrowed from the legal profession. It is more than mere coincidence that advertising men, also seeking to establish their status as professionals, were regularly referring to themselves as attorneys rather than agents as early as 1892. The attempts of public relations men to force their field into a professional mold mirror similar attempts by advertising men but usually seem to occur about twenty to thirty years later. For example, on the eve of World War I, advertising agents were calling themselves engineers more often than attorneys, and in 1935 Bernays too switched metaphors, publishing an article entitled "The Engineering of Consent."[68]

Bernays complained that opinion leaders rejected this newly christened vocation. Newspapers feared declining revenues because of "space grabbers," advertising agents worried that their commissions would be lost, and the lingering ill-repute of the press agent caused potential employers to be hesitant. Bernays therefore decided to, in his words, "take on an uphill one-man campaign for public relations. [It] would become a continuing free client."[69] His success in this endeavor prompted another pioneer counselor, William Henry Baldwin, to remark in 1948 that "Bernays had more to do with developing acceptance for . . . public relations counsel than any half dozen other persons."[70]

Bernays began publishing a four-page newletter called *Contact* in the early twenties to expose "readers to the role public opinion played in their lives."

The typography, layout and paper were designed to give an impression of dignity and restrained distinction. . . . Doris [his partner and wife] selected short items she found in magazines and newspapers that had a bearing on our concept of public relations and in a deft paragraph or a telling head-line pointed up its public relations theme. The idea of viewing events from a public relations standpoint was new: *Contact* became an immediate suc-cess. I sent it to 15,000 editors, publishers, heads of organizations, profit and non-profit, and many leaders of groups.

Bernays was impressed by the interest shown by *Contact*'s readership and by the fact that it was commented upon in other publications.[71] He exaggerated, however, in saying that it established him; his own reputa-tion for effectiveness did that. And he was quite incorrect in claiming originality. As he was undoubtedly aware, Lee had begun publishing a similar newsletter intermittently two or three years previously. It was another way to attract attention which facilitated his search for clients.

In 1923, Bernays was engaged by New York University to teach what is usually regarded as the first course devoted specifically to public rela-tions ever offered by an American university,[72] and he also wrote *Crystal-lizing Public Opinion,* the first book devoted specifically to the "new pro-fession of public relations counsel."[73]

Bernays suggested to one of his clients, the publisher Horace Live-right, that the time had come for a book on public relations. The volume reaped the advantages of the kind of prepublication publicity which Bernays had developed for Liveright's other authors. Advertising circu-lars were mailed to book stores, and Liveright wrote important men in journalism to ask their opinions about the need for the proposed vol-ume.[74]

Despite all the publicity that public relations had received, few of those who responded to Liveright's mailing understood it. Paul U. Kellogg of the *Survey* wrote that "I guess there is a big need in my part of the world for a new book on public relations counsel, for—hell—I didn't know there was any such animal." Those who did understand didn't like it. Ben Mellon, for example, an associate editor of *Editor & Publisher,* de-clared:

> The only conceivable use to which I can see that such a book would be put, would be for the men and women who pose as counselors in public rela-tions to buy it up in large quantities and distribute it in their own defense among the men whose good graces they are trying to win. Even then, I doubt if the book would be read. . . . Some persons are wrongly under the impression that the ranks of public opinion lobbyists are made up of a high type of successful newspaper men. That is not true. In a large measure

they are the type of men who could not climb to any great heighths [*sic*] and have been able to use their acquaintance and knowledge of the newspaper business for their personal profit—which is perfectly all right.

Liveright agreed with this assessment but, perhaps encouraged by Mellon's admission that some people would indeed "buy it up in large quantities," he brought the book out.[75]

Crystallizing Public Opinion is a pastiche of sociological and psychological speculations and incidents from the author's young career. Unlike Lee, Bernays was a genuine student of his sources. He argued that public opinion, a "decisive factor" in modern life, is usually not the product of a careful weighing of issues. ". . . [P]ersons who have little knowledge of a subject almost invariably form definite and positive judgments upon the subject," and, having done so, "are often intolerant of a point of view that is contrary to their own."[76] Therefore, simply bludgeoning the public with claims and assertions, even true ones, may be counterproductive. An individual or group wishing to communicate with the public should instead consult the specialist, the public relations counselor, just as he would consult a legal counselor for a legal problem.

The public relations counsel is "first of all a student" whose "field of study is the public mind." "He brings the talent of his intuitive understanding to the aid of his practical and psychological tests and surveys."[77] He uses his tools to divide the public into various segments and then devises messages which subtly get a point across. The public is neither challenged nor argued with; it is coaxed and romanced.

The client's message reaches the public through the "created event." "The counsel on public relations not only know what news value is, but, knowing it, he is in a position to *make news happen.*"[78] He can stage events in such a way that the newspapers cannot ignore them. His client thus obtains attention in the media at a price much lower than the equivalent number of column inches at advertising rates. And, because he was an outsider, the counselor, Bernays claimed, could bring much-needed perspective to corporate dilemmas.

Bernays ventured a discussion of the theory of public opinion based upon Walter Lippmann's *Public Opinion,* published the previous year (1922), William Monroe Trotter's *Instincts of the Herd in Peace and War,* and Everett Dean Martin's *The Behavior of Crowds* and influenced by the theories of Freud. Each individual, he wrote, regardless of his intelligence, was subject to the prejudices of the groups with which he identified. The success of the public relations man at influencing public opinion depended upon his ability to play on these unconscious allegiances. Bernays's willingness to accept irrationality was as characteristic of the

'20s as was Lee's (albeit inconsistent) faith in reason and "facts" of Progressivism.

Bernays struggled to mitigate the antidemocratic aspect of opinion manipulation in two ways. First, unlike the lawyer who believed in everyone's right to a day in court, he held that the public relations counselor must refuse to represent before the "higher court of public opinion" clients who were "unsocial or otherwise harmful." Second, he must change his clients' policies to conform to the public interest if the two diverged: "He helps to mold the actions of his client as well as to mold public opinion."[79]

It was this second function which was supposed to differentiate the public relations counsel from the press agent and publicity man. Bernays made explicit what Lee had implied: the counsel must have a voice in policy. Was this transformation actually taking place in the 1920s, or was it merely representative of the attempts of many occupations to elevate themselves to professional status? The pre-eminent counselors were indeed assuming greater responsibilities than had their press agent predecessors, but not as great as their own promotional writings might lead one to believe.

Bernays's relation with Cheney Brothers serves to illustrate this point. Cheney, the nation's oldest and largest silk manufacturer, engaged him in 1923 in order, according to Bernays, to restore the style leadership which had been slipping away. His first move was to associate Cheney's clothing with the fountainhead of ladies' fashion, France. As he described his work, he inaugurated

> a free style service for fashion editors of the U. S., supplying them with news about silk usage and style in Paris. We sent French *croquis*, drawings of dresses (to be made of Cheney silk) to newspapers. We released photographs of models dressed in Cheney fabrics to 150 rotogravure sections of newspapers. We added a free mat service of Paris fashions for 300 small newspapers, and we corresponded with hundreds of newspaper editors about French fashions. . . . We even used French terminology to make our point, labeling our folder *"Chronique de la Mode"* above the imprint "Cheney Style Service."[80]

In the succeeding five years, according to his own account, Bernays had Cheney products displayed in the heart of the French textile district at Lyons and at a silk exhibition at the Louvre, and he managed to have Henry Creange, the firm's art director, appointed to the American commission to visit the International Exposition of Modern Decorative and Industrial Arts in Paris in 1925. He arranged to have the Architectural League of New York award Creange a medal for bringing art to industry, and he commissioned Georgia O'Keeffe to paint five pictures which were used to push Cheney colors. He also had the company present Mrs. Warren G. Harding with a dress length of Cheney silk.[81]

After a few months on the job, Bernays's work was "well known and very favorably commented upon in the trade." Cheney products began to appear prominently in important publications. Despite this evident success, Cheney Brothers terminated its relationship with Bernays on May 1, 1928. This action was taken with "reluctance" for two reasons: the company's own sales department had developed sufficiently, in part thanks to Bernays's help, to the point where it could handle much of his work, and because the company planned a reduction in some of the aspects of Bernays's program.[82]

Notwithstanding the doubts raised by his dismissal, Bernays did seem to attract publicity to the firm. If he was right in his evaluation of Cheney as a declining concern before his retention, and he is not consistently trustworthy as a historical witness,[83] he can be credited with making the company aware of important fashion trends and with modernizing the outlook of the executives. Creange once praised him "for bringing the viewpoint of the public to us and in a subtle way."[84] On the other hand, the problems he dealt with were almost completely those of moving merchandise through favorable publicity. He never had contact in this instance, and only rarely with his other clients in the early years, with such important political problems of the modern corporation as labor, community, and government relations. Much of what he wrote in *Crystallizing Public Opinion* was more reflective of his desires than the reality of his work at the time. And clearly his talk of invisible governments and mass mind control arose from a lack of perspective, an "upgrad[ing] of the frivolous to the portentous" which sometimes characterized him.[85] As Creange also wrote, "To me, Mr. Bernays is worth a dozen salesmen."[86]

Bernays, like Lee, had an impressive list of clients by the decade's end, but neither man had much policy input outside the realm of publicity. It is fair to assume that the multitude of other independent counselors had no more.

Arthur W. Page represented a different kind of public relations man. He was not an independent counselor but was permanently associated with one firm, AT&T. He did not have to keep his name before the business public in a constant search for clients and is therefore less well known to historians than the mysterious Lee and the flamboyant Bernays. Nevertheless, his work and that of other in-house counselors was probably more important than that of the independents in making public relations an integral factor in business decisions.

Page was born in Aberdeen, North Carolina, in 1883. His father was Walter Hines Page, editor of the *Atlantic Monthly* and *World's Work,* partner in the publishing house of Doubleday, Page, and Company, and later Wilson's wartime ambassador to Great Britain. He recalled approvingly that his father's philosophy of editing was to publicize the good that people did instead of exposing the evil, which is the essential function the public relations counselor performs as opposed to the muckraker.[87]

Page graduated from Lawrenceville and, in 1905, from Harvard where he edited a magazine and admired what he viewed as the cautious liberalism of Charles W. Eliot. He joined *World's Work* directly after his graduation at a time when the magazine's policy was changing from one of muckraking to conservatism. He traveled to London when his father became ambassador, and in the summer of 1918 wrote propaganda for the army. Unlike Bernays, Page did not find his wartime propagandizing impressive. At war's end, he entered the family publishing business, but increasing difficulties with the Doubledays convinced him to quit in 1927. He had no prospects, but, coincidentally the very day of his decision, he received a phone call from Walter Gifford who requested a meeting.[88]

Gifford, a Harvard classmate, had worked for AT&T or a subsidiary since graduation, and in 1925 he had become president. James D. Ellsworth was still running the information department, with the help of one assistant and one secretary. Ellsworth was ready to retire, and Gifford needed a replacement.[89] Quite without warning, Gifford offered Page the job of directing AT&T's communications. Page later said that

> What was in his [Gifford's] mind was that I'd been writing editorials about what was the duty of big business in a democracy and how should they get along, and giving them a lot of free advice. I told him I was interested. What he asked me to do was to come to AT&T and see what I could do.
>
> So I told them that if they were serious about it—that is, I didn't want to go there as a publicity man—but if they were serious about taking that point of view as the general policy, nothing would please me more than to try to do something instead of telling everybody else to do it. So that's the transition between editorial work and the telephone company, between writing and talking.[90]

Page believed that "all business in a democratic country begins with public permission and exists by public approval." He often spoke of the United States as if it were a direct democracy. As did other advocates of welfare capitalism in the 1920s, he favored managing the company with "the long run" in mind. The primary concern had to be the provision of efficient and polite service at reasonable rates. Employees had to be educated to a genuine esprit de corps, technological improvements fostered, prices kept low, and regulation welcomed. Under these circumstances, capital would eventually earn a "reasonable" return. "If it gets too much at one time, the public will insist on too little at another, so that in the end the stockholder will receive no more."[91]

The justification of profits has been one of the most persistent and difficult problems for corporate public relations departments in this century. Bell's approach was to subordinate them to political considerations in order to make the company politically secure and keep it in private hands. The Federal Communications Commission's investigation of AT&T in the 1930s uncovered evidence of awarding contracts for the printing of telephone directories to the highest bidder "due to local political reasons" and of maintaining a larger number of bank accounts than necessary in order to keep local financial leaders friendly. A critic has compared this practice to the "award of contracts by machine-controlled municipal administrations to political favorites. How different, in other words, are the 'business methods' of a private utility widely heralded as a very efficient example of private enterprise from those of the 'corrupt politicians' whose municipal government is widely proclaimed to be inefficient and wasteful?"[92]

It was the task of Page and his department not only to "sell" the company but also to take on the "perhaps more intangible and more important" job of apprising Bell of the facts the public wanted it to get.[93]

He supervised press releases, annual reports, advertising, pamphlets, public speaking, office tours, and motion pictures. This function cost the company what Page considered the paltry sum of less than one cent on every dollar earned. Page vigorously defended the company against charges of corrupting the press through advertising bribes. He insisted that advertising was placed without regard to editorial policy and that lapses from this standard were regrettable and exceptional. Like Professor Salmon, he believed that people thought that advertisers had a greater effect on editorial judgment than was the case. Although advertisers supported newspapers financially, a favorite method for raising circulation, upon which advertising charges were based, was attacking big business. He claimed to "take great pains" to notify the audience of the source of Bell publicity, a policy which the company had not scrupulously followed prior to his advent.[94]

Page was vehement on the subject of politics: "The Bell System has no political influence and wants none." This of course was an overstatement, but it did represent the company's policy of avoiding partisanship and eschewing participation in the great free enterprise campaigns conducted by manufacturers in the 1930s. Business was heterogeneous, and any attempt to promote the "American business system" led inevitably to disagreements and politics. It was the duty of each individual firm to tell its own story and no more. He actually went further, trying to differentiate Bell from the common representative of big business even before the Depression so that the company would not be washed away if there were an anti-big-business tide.[95] It is ironic that this, the most admired of public relations programs among other businesses, felt no sense of class solidarity.

Page did endeavor to bring the public's desires as he saw them to the attention of management. His close relationship to Gifford guaranteed that the chief executive would be informed of his assessments of public feeling. By 1941, Page was vice-president and one of the three operating officers sitting on the company's board of directors. His department was committed to the extensive use of opinion surveys which appear to have been important factors in the deliberations of the company's policy makers.[96] During Page's tenure, AT&T probably learned more about its customers' wishes concerning its service—down to such details as the introduction of dial phones and the placing of memo pads in public booths—than any other large company in the United States. And Bell acted on this information.

Under Page's leadership, the company's public relations department grew. It instituted public relations classes for employees and answered the many questions of management. By the time of his retirement in 1947, public relations was a recognized and respected staff function. It is for this achievement that some students have called Page the public relations counselor with the greatest influence upon the practice in the modern corporation.[97]

By the close of the 1920s, the list of executives who had praised public relations men and methods was long. Outside the business community, journalists, novelists, and intellectuals also spoke often of the "new profession," although usually with a good deal less affection. One of the main characters of John Dos Passos's trilogy, *U. S. A.,* the first volume of which *(The 42nd Parallel)* was published in 1930, was J. Ward Moorehouse, a public relations counselor. The ambitious Moorehouse, whose occupation, according to Maxwell Geismar, was supposed to represent the "embodiment of the highest form of success in the United States," was modeled loosely after Ivy Lee.[98] In 1932 John T. Flynn commented in the *Atlantic* that "By no system of honest elimination can Edward L. Bernays be excluded from a list of representative men in America. He has made an extraordinary success." Other observers were struck by the idea of the public relations man as the logical product of the American system. According to *The New Yorker,* he "may be viewed with fitting pride as a strictly local product. It is not conceivable that any other country could have produced him, any more than any other country could have produced P. T. Barnum."[99]

And these propagandists seemed ubiquitous. "We live," wrote John Dewey in 1929,

> exposed to the greatest flood of mass suggestion that any people has yet experienced. The need for united action, and the supposed need for integrated opinion and sentiment, are met by organized propaganda and advertising. The publicity agent is perhaps the most significant symbol of our present social life. There are individuals who resist; but, for a time at least, sentiment can be manufactured by mass methods for almost any person or any cause.[100]

By their exaggerated lamentations, these custodians of traditional forms of communication helped the counselor become more than a press agent in the eyes of management.

The public relations man, publicity man, press agent, or propagandist—whatever label the corporate public opinion manipulator adopted—*seemed* powerful; and, therefore, in a world in which nature so often imitates art, corporations were investing him with the power to mold thier images. Nevertheless, his influence in making policy, especially if he were an independent, was overestimated, as the Cheney Brothers example and many others illustrate. His ability to mold the "public mind" was doubtless overestimated as well. Clever public relations might increase sales or good will, but cause and effect were, and have continued to be, very difficult of measurement. How much did Bernays's work add to Cheney's sales? Would sales have increased less if old-fashioned advertising had been used? How many more people "liked" the National Electric Light Association after "Light's Golden Jubillee,"[101] a famous "created event" of 1929 supposedly designed to commemorate the invention of the electric light, than had liked it before? Was this increased affection worth the trouble? What benefits would accrue because of it? Businessmen had not invented a balance sheet upon which such results were tallied. When public relations activities backfired, good will was sacrificed. When a company got caught in a widely publicized lie, as did the mine operators at Ludlow, its opponents had a powerful weapon to use against it. The "boomerang" effect was real and dangerous. On the other hand, the steel companies' success in hanging the radical label on the unions in 1919 did indeed help their cause. In this confusing situation, many businessmen would no doubt have sympathized with John Wanamaker's remark about his advertising budget: He knew half of it was money thrown away but he did not know which half.

One thing can be concluded. Though overestimated at the time by counselors and critics, the influence of public relations in the managements of corporations and trade associations was increasing during the 1920s. Belief in the importance of public opinion and the hazards of neglecting it was widespread among businessmen. They needed assistance in reconciling to the public and the labor force the contradictory demands they made upon society.

Ivy L. Lee convinced many of the value of publicity as a political tool and of the importance of an expert's help in being attentive to public opinion. Edward L. Bernays showed how unorthodox publicity could serve firms in highly competitive markets, and he gave his vocation a rationale. Arthur W. Page showed how to integrate the function into the management of a major corporation. Thanks to their work and similar efforts by lesser lights who entered the field after the war, public relations assumed a prestige which had never been accorded press agentry. Businessmen would be able to call upon and further refine it when the stock market crash transformed the dimly perceived fears of the 1920s into the reality of the 1930s.

NOTES

1. *American Capitalism: The Concept of Countervailing Power* (Boston, 1952), p. 28.

2. Allen M. Wakstein, "The National Association of Manufacturers and Labor Relations in the 1920's," *Labor History* 10, No. 2 (Spring 1969), pp. 171–173.

3 Ida M. Tarbell, *The Life of Elbert H. Gary* (New York, 1925), p. 156.

4. William E. Leuchtenberg, *The Perils of Prosperity* (Chicago, 1958), pp. 178–179.

5. Ernest Elmo Calkins, *Business the Civilizer* (Boston, 1928), pp. 118–119, 294–295.

6. This phrase was developed in conscious contrast to Vanderbilt's supposed dictum. This proved to be a remarkably skillful appeal. William Gibbs McAdoo, *Crowded Years* (Boston, 1931), pp. 101–105; John J. Broesamle, *William Gibbs McAdoo* (Port Washington, N.Y., 1973), pp. 25–41.

7. Advertising men seemed particularly aware of the "amelioration of the housewife's lot." Bruce Barton wrote the following slogan for a General Electric campaign of the '20s: "Any woman who does anything which a little electric motor can do is working for 3¢ an hour!" Calkins, *Civilizer*, pp. 12–19; Otis Pease, "Bruce Barton," in John A. Garraty and Jerome Sternstein, eds., *Encyclopedia of American Biography* (New York, 1974), pp. 62–63.

8. *The Autobiography of Lincoln Steffens* (New York, 1931), p. 855.

9. Melvyn Dubovsky, *Industrialism and the American Worker, 1865–1920* (New York, 1975), pp. 109–134.

10. Thomas Cochran, *Business in American Life*, p. 152.

11. Irving Bernstein, *The Lean Years* (Baltimore, 1960), pp. 144–189; Joseph G. Rayback, *A History of American Labor* (New York, 1966), pp. 290–291. Management-sponsored employee opinion polls were begun in the early 1920s. King MacRury, "Employee Morale: Analyses of Absence Records and Opinion Polls," *Industrial and Labor Relations Review* 2, No. 2 (January 1949), pp. 240–241.

12. Bernstein, *Lean Years*, 182–186; David Brody, "Labor and the Great Depression: The Interpretive Prospects," *Labor History* 13, No. 2 (Spring 1972), p. 242; Brandes, *Welfare*, pp. 135–148.

13. Willard E. Atkins, "Aspects of Labor Propaganda," in J. B. S. Hardman, ed., *American Labor Dynamics* (New York, 1968, first published 1928), p. 366; Bernstein, *Lean Years*, pp. 83–143; Brody, "Prospects," p. 242.

14. Speier, "Public Opinion," p. 110.

15. The steel strike, David Brody has written, "was fought out on two fronts—in the steel towns and before the public." For a time, the unions succeeded in slowing production, but management outflanked and routed them before the court of public opinion. United behind the suave and experienced Judge Gary, the steelmen branded the strikers radicals and claimed not to be opposed to organized labor but merely in favor of the open shop. Divided among themselves and inept at press relations, union leaders failed to convince the public of the justice of their cause. *Steelworkers in America* (New York, 1960), p. 243; Philip C. Ensley, "The Interchurch World Movement and the Steel Strike of 1919," *Labor History* 13, No. 2 (Spring 1972), pp. 217–230.

16. This is an important theme in Brandes, *Welfare*. See, for example, pp. 48–51.

17. Baritz, *Power*, pp. 77–95.

18. Lee W. Huebner, "The Discovery of Propaganda" (unpublished Ph.D. thesis, Harvard, 1968), p. 106.

19. *American Chronicle* (New York, 1945), p. 183.

20. Louis D. Brandeis, *Other People's Money* (New York, 1967), pp. 62–63.

21. See *Human Nature and Railroads* (Philadelphia, 1915), pp. 79–84.

22. Huebner, "Discovery," pp. 200, 274; Walter Lippmann, *The Phantom Public* (New York, 1925), p. 65. A striking example of the effect of this change on a man of action is the career of Robert Moses. In the Progressive era, he had faith in the public's willingness to weigh the facts and arrive at the rational conclusions. He had been disillusioned by the mid-1920s, and he degenerated into a skillful and brutal manipulator of opinion—a master of public relations in the worst sense. Robert A. Caro, *The Power Broker* (New York, 1975), pp. 85, 218, 241, and 1-282 *passim*.

23. *Public Opinion* (New York, 1965), pp. 217–218.

24. Merle Curti, "The Changing Concept of 'Human Nature' in the Literature of American Advertising," *Business History Review*, 41, No. 4 (Winter 1967), pp. 338–342.

25 Ibid., p. 374; Pope, "Advertising," p. 171.

26. Edmund C. Lynch, "Walter Dill Scott," *Business History Review* 52, No. 2 (Summer 1968), pp. 151–154.

27. Stuart B. Ewen, *Captains of Consciousness* (New York, 1976), *passim*.

28. Erik Barnouw, *A Tower in Babel* (New York, 1966), pp. 54, 58–74, 99, 105; Raymond Williams, *Television: Technology and Cultural Form* (New York, 1975), p. 25.

29. James W. Prothro, *Dollar Decade* (Baton Rouge, 1954), pp. 44, 175.

30. For Schwab's problems with image making, see Hessen, "Schwab," pp. 215–217.

31. U.S. Senate. Industrial Relations: *Final Report and Testimony* Submitted to Congress by the Commission on Industrial Relations created by the Act of August 13, 1912. Document No. 415, 64th Cong., 1st Sess. (1916) (hereinafter, CIR), Vol. 8, p. 7911.

32. Upton Sinclair, *The Brass Check* (Pasadena, 1931), p. 282; Ewen, *Consciousness*, pp. 62–65; James Harvey Young, *The Medical Messiahs* (Princeton, N.J., 1967), p. 29; A. J. Liebling, *The Press* (New York, 1975), p. 17. NAM executives would certainly have disagreed with Liebling's remark.

33. Lucy Maynard Salmon, *The Newspaper and the Historian* (New York, 1923), pp. 434–435. Albert Lasker, a man in a position to know, stated that at the turn of the century, ". . . The separation of the business office and the editorial office was absolutely complete. . . . An advertiser made no difference. If an elevator fell, the story got all over the front page. If the advertiser didn't like it, that was just too bad." Lasker memoir, Columbia Oral History Collection (hereinafter, COHC), pp. 10–11. Lasker also remarked, rather too unspecifically, that the change from this policy was one reason for the decline in the influence of newspapers. When, one wonders, did this policy change and who were the people most responsible? Harry Reichenbach had a predictably less respectful view of the integrity of the newspapers. "Don't they have sacred cows?" he once asked Edward L. Bernays in defense of his hoaxing. "Do they print stories about shoplifting in department stores?" Edward L. Bernays, *Biography of an Idea* (New York, 1965), p. 203.

34. Instances of this phenomenon are not, however, unknown. In 1923, for example, AT&T bought space in a rural Mississippi journal which had been unfriendly. The paper changed its attitude as a result. N. R. Danielian, *AT&T* (New York, 1939), pp. 315–317.

35. Peter Schlausen, "Our Own Bomb Outrage," New York *Call,* July 20, 1915; "The Rockefeller Institute for the provision of munitions for the class war has just issued a neat little asphyxiating bomb entitled *Human Nature and Railroads,*" New York *Call,* July 22, 1915; Chester M. Wright, "Unto the World Has Been Given a Book by Ivy Lee." Wright cited research by Scott Nearing to refute Lee's assertions. New York *Call,* July 25, 1915, Box 18, Lee papers, Princeton University.

36. Brody, *Steelworkers,* pp. 156–167.

37. Bruce Bliven to Edward L. Bernays, October 28, 1961, Bernays papers, his possession, Cambridge, Mass.; Cleveland *Plain Dealer,* November 11, 1934, Box 47, Lee Papers; *Printers' Ink,* July 21, 1927, p. 179; Will Irwin, "The Press Agent: His Rise and Decline," Collier's, December 2, 1911, p. 24.

38. Cutlip, "First Firm,' p. 269–274; Ray Stannard Baker, "Railroads on Trial," *McClure's,* March 1906, p. 537.

39. Cutlip. "First Firm." pp. 275–276.

40. Ibid., pp. 277–278; Baker, "Trial," p. 537.

41. Ibid., pp. 537–538.

42. Ibid., p. 538.

43. Quoted in Martin, *Enterprise Denied*, p. 257.

44. Cutlip, "First Firm," p. 280; Herbert Small to Charles W. Eliot, May 4, 1901, Folder 220, Box 115, Eliot papers.

45. See Hiebert, *Courtier;* Raucher, *Public Relations;* and Huebner, "Discovery."

46. George E. Mowry, *The Era of Theodore Roosevelt* (New York, 1962), pp. 134–140.

47. In its obituary for Lee, the *New York Times* observed that he "probably did as much as any man to turn the gathering of news into a matter of collecting prepared statements from news sources." "Ivy Lee Dies at 57 of Brain Ailment," *New York Times,* November 10, 1934, p. 15.

48. Hiebert, *Courtier,* p. 48.

49. For the activities of "Dollar-a-Line" Smith during the Hughes investigation of the life insurance industry, see Pope, "Advertising," pp. 161–162. For Reichenbach, see Harry Reichenbach and Donald Freedman, *Phantom Fame* (New York, 1931).

50. Graham Adams, Jr., *Age of Industrial Violence* (New York, 1966), p. 167; Raucher, *Public Relations*, p. 26.

51. Hiebert, *Courtier*, pp. 101, 298; CIR, Vol. 8, p. 7910. In a brochure called "Publicity" which Lee published in the ealy 1900s. Lee claimed that "my strength is being uniformly careful to send to the press only such information as I can make myself responsible for personally." Box 6, Lee papers.

52. A survey conducted by the University of Michigan in 1970 found Lee to be the outstanding figure of modern public relations. David L. Lewis, "The Outstanding PR Professionals," *Public Relations Journal* 26, No. 10 (October 1970), p. 78.

53. Huebner, "Discovery," p. 18.

54. *Human Nature and the Railroads,* (Philadelphia, 1915.)

55. Pp. 9, 28, 59, 108.

56. Ibid., p. 8

57. (New York, 1925.)

58. *Public Relations,* pp. 125–126.

59. "Duties of an Advisor in Public Relations," *Printers' Ink,* July 7, 1927, pp. 73–74.

60. Boxes 8 and 18, Lee papers; Raucher, *Public Relations,* p. 21; Hiebert, *Courtier,* p. 62; "Duties of an Advisor in Public Relations," *Printers' Ink,* p. 73.

61. "The Difference between 'Public Relations Advisor' and 'Press Agent,'" *Printers' Ink,* June 19, 1927, p. 10; but for a different interpretation of the same interview, see Hiebert, *Courtier,* p. 234.

62. Sydney Stahl Weinberg, "Wartime Propaganda in a Democracy" (unpublished Ph.D. thesis, Columbia, 1969), p. 35.

63. Louis Filler, *Crusaders,* p. 375.

64. The phrase is part of the subtitle of George Creel's *How We Advertised America* (New York, 1920).

65. Weinberg, "Wartime Propaganda," pp. 93–97.

66. Edward L. Bernays, *Propaganda* (New York, 1928), pp. 27–28; Raucher, *Public Relations*, p. 69.

67. Bernays, *Idea*, p. 288.

68. Pope, "Advertising," pp. 314–316. The metaphors of law and engineering have predominated in the attempts of public relations counselors to explain their vocation to the layman. Comparisons to medicine have also been made. Thus a 1934 article on Ivy Lee described him as a "Family Physician to Big Business." Lee's friend John Mumford called him a "physician to corporate bodies," a description Lee liked. And Bernays once explained that the public relations man was primarily concerned with producing "social metabolism." Wayne W. Parrish, "Ivy Lee, Family Physician to Big Business," *Literary Digest,* June 9, 1934, pp. 30ff.

69. Bernays, *Idea*, pp. 288–289.

70. Eric F. Goldman, *Two-Way Street* (Boston, 1948), p. 21.

71. Bernays, *Idea*, pp. 289–290.

72. Bernays taught at a university which at the time offered more courses in advertising than any other in the nation. His students were few and his pay a mere $200, but, as Eric F. Goldman has observed, ". . . Neither the size of the class nor the amount of the salary was the point." The "point" was that the prestige of both public relations and Bernays were enhanced by associating them with a prestigious American institution—the university. The final examination showed that the course followed his book closely. Raucher, *Public Relations,* p. 138; Goldman, *Two-Way Street*, p. 16. The title of Bernays's course was "Business Relations." Here is the text of the final exam:

1. What is public opinion? How is it formed?

2. How can it be molded and modified?

3. In what fields does the public relations counsel function?

4. What is meant by "group and herd"?

5. What characteristics of the group and herd make it possible for the public relations counsel to function?

6. What is group leadership?

7. Name the universal desires and instincts upon which human motivation is based.

8. Work out a plan a counsel on public relations might offer to the Music Chamber of Commerce to help effect a more favorable public opinion toward music.

9. Work out a plan a counsel on public relations might offer to the New York University to build up among the people of the nation a proper conception of its scope and functions.

10. Work out a plan a counsel for public relations might offer
   a. The Rolls-Royce automobile.
   b. The Ford automobile.

Quite a lot of ground to cover in two or three hours. A copy of this test is in the Bernays papers.

73. (New York, 1923), p. v.

74. Bernays, *Idea*, pp. 291, 277–286; Raucher, *Public Relations*, p. 130.

75. Paul U. Kellogg to Horace Liveright, August 10, 1922; Ben Mellon to Horace Liveright, August 2, 1922, Bernays papers. Liveright's agreement with Mellon is indicated by a marginal note on this letter.

76. Bernays, *Crystallizing*, pp. 63–65.

77. Ibid., pp. 52–53.

78. Ibid., p. 197.

79. Ibid., pp. 56–57, 87, 122, 216.

80. Bernays, *Idea*, pp. 301–302.

81. Ibid., pp. 299–312.

82. H. W. Smith of the *American Silk Journal* to Boni and Liveright, March 12, 1924; Frank W. Cheney to Edward L. Bernays, February 12, 1925; J. C. Heckman to Edward L. Bernays, January 23, 1928, Bernays papers.

83. Bernays has written an 816-page autobiography and given interviews to numerous scholars. He has also deposited 92 boxes of his papers at the Library of Congress and a lengthy memoir with the Columbia Oral History Collection, both of which sources will be made available after the deaths of him and his wife. His views are, therefore, receiving and will continue to receive wide publicity.

His recollections must be used with care, however. When his autobiography was published in 1965, Simon and Schuster was "bombarded" with letters written to correct various alleged mistakes Bernays had made. Philip N. Schuyler, "Bernays' Big Memoirs Hugely Entertaining," *Editor & Publisher*, November 20, 1965, p. 54. And some people charged "that there are gross inaccuracies that cannot be attributed to a normal distortion of memory." *Public Relations Quarterly*, Winter 1966, p. 97.

The fallibility of his memory is most interestingly illustrated by the manner in which he handled his encounter in 1923 with Henry R. Luce and Britton Hadden in his autobiography. A mutual acquaintance "begged me," he wrote, to meet the two men. At the Yale Club of New York, Luce and Hadden outlined their ideas for *Time*, but Bernays was unimpressed. He turned down their request that he invest in it and "I declined their offer of $125 a week for public relations counsel because I thought their evaluation of the market was incorrect and I didn't want to take their money for a project I felt would not succeed. Besides, our fees were higher than they could afford to pay."

Later, Bernays invested in *Time*. He never bothered to calculate how much money he would have saved had he taken advantage of this golden chance, because "life always has new opportunities. The pragmatic test is to take advantage of more opportunities than one misses." *Idea*, pp. 363–364.

Thus Bernays gave us to believe that he was much sought after and as early as 1923 could afford to turn down a $125 weekly retainer. W. A. Swanberg accepted this story, describing Bernays as a "kindly but expensive public relations counsel [who] thrust away a fortune, which he would amass anyway by his own efforts." *Luce* (New York, 1973), p. 86.

Letters in Bernays's papers give a dramatically different impression of the episode. On April 9, 1923, Bernays wrote Luce a three-and-one-half-page letter proposing a six-pronged public relations campaign which Bernays was willing to direct for only $100 a week. He seemed, in this letter, to be quite anxious to land the account. More than two weeks elapsed before Luce got around to replying.

"... [W]e are not yet ready," he explained, "to undertake any considerable obligations for public counsel relations [*sic!*]." Bernays quickly wrote back, expressing a most clear and forceful belief in the magazine. Bernays to Luce, April 9, 1923; Luce to Bernays, April 27, 1923; Bernays to Luce, April 30, 1923, Bernays papers.

84. Henry Creange to Charles Cheney, February 25, 1923, Bernays papers.

85. The phrase is Marvin Barrett's, "Cart before the Horse," *Reporter*, December 30, 1965. p. 44.

86. Henry Creange to Charles Cheney, February 25, 1923, Bernays papers.

87. Arthur W. Page memoir, COHC, pp. 1, 21–22.

88. Ibid., pp. 9, 43–47; William Kettle, "The Making of Public Opinion," *Arena*, July, 1909, p. 448.

89. Golden, *Consent*, p. 42.

90. Page memoir, pp. 71–72.

91. Arthur W. Page, *The Bell Telephone System* (New York, 1941), pp. 154, 3, 16. This de-emphasis on profits has reached many corporations today. In the midst of the energy crisis of 1973–1974, the chairman of the board of Exxon sent a letter to stockholders in which he essentially apologized for all the money he was making for them, an attitude which would have left William H. Vanderbilt quite puzzled.

92. Danielian, *AT&T*, pp. 287–290.

93. Briarcliff Publicity Conference, April 28, 1927, "What Publicity and Advertising Can Do To Help Organization," Vol. 5, Arthur W. Page papers, State Historical Society of Wisconsin, Madison.

94. Page, *Telephone*, pp. 154–163. Before Page, the telephone company financed three books without acknowledging its connection with them. They were Herbert N. Casson, *The History of the Telephone* (Chicago, 1910); James Mavor, *Government Telephones* (New York, 1916); and Arthur Pound, *The Telephone Idea* (New York, 1926). See Danielian, *AT&T*, pp. 292–296.

95. Ibid., p. 170; "Public Relations," General Operating Conference, May 1930, Page papers, Vol. 5, p. 1. Roger Barton, "What Should a Business Do About Public Relations?" *Advertising and Selling*, October 1946, pp. 41ff.

96. Joseph M. Shaw to Paul N. Olive, September 15, 1943, Box 1, Joseph M. Shaw papers, State Historical Society of Wisconsin, Madison.

97. Cutlip and Center, *Effective Public Relations*, p. 90; Golden, *Consent*, p. 47.

98. Lee's biographer has justly complained that this treatment was "blatantly false to the supposed model." Nevertheless, he noted, "the characterization became widely accepted as a portrait of the public relations counsel." Dos Passos had Moorehouse opening up an office on 100 Fifth Avenue and calling himself a "public relations counsel" in 1914. The term was not actually coined until after World War I. Moorehouse may have been unlike Lee in his freewheeling private life, but Dos Passos did give him the correct script:

> American industry, like a steamengine, like a high-power locomotive on a great express train charging through the night of old individualistic methods.... What does a steamengine require? Co-operation, coordination of the inventor's brain, the promoter's brain that made the development of these high-power products possible.... Co-operation of

capital, the storedup energy of the race in the form of credit intelligently directed . . . labor, the prosperous contented American working man to whom the unprecedented possibilities of capital collected in great corporations had given the full dinnerpail, cheap motor transport, insurance, short working hours . . . a measure of comfort and prosperity unequaled before or since in the tragic possessions of recorded history or in the known regions of the habitable globe.

The 42nd Parallel (New York, 1952), pp. ix, 304; Hiebert, *Courtier,* p. 299.

99. "Edward L. Bernays, The Science of Ballyhoo," *The Atlantic,* May, 1932, p. 563; "A Reporter at Large: Merchants of Glory," *The New Yorker,* clipping in Bernays papers.

100. *Individualism Old and New* (New York, 1930), pp. 42–43.

101. The National Electric Light Association used this occasion to combat advocates of public power. Bernays, *Idea,* pp. 344–345, 444–460; Leonard W. Doob, *Propaganda* (New York, 1935), p. 195. Light's Golden Jubilee is yet another example of the controversy which has arisen over Bernays's career. Fred L. Black, a publicity aide to Henry Ford for over 25 years, was present in Dearborn in 1929. According to his recollection, Bernays played a distinctly minor role but did anger Ford by his persistent attempts to have himself photographed with the distinguished guests. At length, Ford supposedly took Black aside and told him to "get Bernays the hell out of here or I'll have Harry Bennett's men throw him over the fence," a warning which Bernays heeded. So incensed was Bernays when this account was published by Alan Raucher that he investigated the possiblities of suing him for libel and wrote a scathing review of his book. In his defense, Bernays points proudly to a letter from Edsel Ford: "It was a great pleasure to work with you in connection with the plans for Light's Golden Jubilee at Dearborn, and I can assure you that without the assistance of you and the General Electric group the affair could not have been worked out as well as it was." Edsel Ford to Bernays, November 6, 1929; Thomas Edison to Bernays, October 22, 1929; Napoleon Boynton to Bernays, October 25, 1929; Bernays papers; Lewis, "Henry Ford," pp. 453–454; Raucher, *Public Relations,* p. 106; *Annals* of the American Academy of Political and Social Science, 383 (May 1969), pp. 214–215.

Chapter III

The National Association of Manufacturers and Public Relations during the New Deal

The question is, who is going to have the most influence with the 130,000,000 owners of America?

Bruce Barton, 1936[1]

The focus of public relations in the early years was on political struggles with regulatory agencies, politicians, and leaders of organized labor. This focus shifted during the 1920s because the needs of potential employers changed. The primary problem was increasing consumption, so counselors marketed themselves as masters of psycho-social secrets which made them equal to "a dozen salesmen." During the Depression, stimulating consumption was, obviously, still of enormous importance, but an even greater need, some executives felt, was protecting the power position of business in the face of the New Deal and an awakening labor movement. The response to the decline in prestige resulting from economic collapse was, to use an infelicitous phrase soon to gain currency, to try to "sell the American way of life to the American people." It was to this call, similar to that of the Progressive era but on a broader scale, that a growing public relations establishment rallied.

Fittingly, the leading exponent of public relations as an engine of anti-union and anti-government propaganda among not only large but medium-sized and small businesses as well was a trade association, an organization of businessmen which produced nothing tangible to sell that might distract it from the "selling" of its philosophy. The National Association of Manufacturers' (NAM) public relations campaigns of the Depression were prefigured by decades of effort to "control national

59

questions of importance to manufacturers."[2] The most important of these questions, following a change in leadership in 1902, was the status of organized labor.[3] The Association's officers during the Progressive era expressed a single-minded determination to stamp out unionism. Since they recognized the power of public opinion, this goal could best be achieved by conducting a mighty propaganda designed to bring the public back to the proper American and Christian viewpoint. By 1918, the Association was publicizing its opinions through a news-plate service and an extensive speakers' bureau, whose lecturers were attracting a gratifyingly large amount of publicity. It produced and distributed three series of posters, a newsletter, *American Industries* (the official magazine of the Association), and even a motion picture.

The NAM also recognized the strategic role of the press in influencing public opinion, and its leadership was not bound by respect for the integrity of the Fourth Estate. One of its presidents encouraged members to patronize with their advertising only those publications which were "bold and fearless" on the labor issue and withdraw all support from the "cowardly" ones "whose columns and pages are filled with cheap sensational trash tending to breed discontent, chaos, and anarchy."[4]

Under the presidency from 1921 to 1931 of John W. Edgerton, a relatively benign and paternalistic textile manufacturer from Tennessee, the Association continued to concentrate on the labor issue. It lent its support to the Open Shop movement which was springing up around the country at war's end and also endeavored to attract publicity for its conventions and other activities.

The Depression had a devastating effect upon the organization. To cut expenses, firms terminated their affiliation or went into arrears on their dues. By 1933, membership dropped from a high of 5,350 in 1922 to under 1,500, and resignations were averaging 65 a month. Publication of *American Industries* ceased in 1930, and various other economies were instituted. By the end of 1931, the Association had clearly reached a crisis,[5] and it must have been apparent even to Edgerton himself that his regime was incapable of coping with it. He wanted to resign his post at the end of 1931, after eleven years of service. The board of directors, however, agreed that his retirement might further injure Association morale, so he was promoted to the newly created position of chairman of the board despite stringent cost cutting elsewhere.[6]

Robert L. Lund was nominated to take the office which Edgerton thus vacated on December 18, 1931. He had no illusions about the difficulties he faced. As conditions of acceptance, in justice, as he put it, to the Association and to himself, Lund insisted that each member of the Board contribute $250 for an emergency fund and that each secure twenty-five new members. Five directors resigned forthwith, but the remainder persevered, and the modern history of the National Association of Manufacturers began.[7]

Lund was a member of the "Brass Hats," a group of industrialists who were not content to see "radicals" and "demagogues" supplant them and their colleagues as the leaders of the nation. The group's origins are obscure, but it seems to have been informally organized as a dinner club in 1931 or 1932, meeting first in Detroit and later in New York City.[8] Its prominent members included Tom Girdler, president of Republic Steel and leader of the employers in the "Little Steel" strikes; Robert B. Henderson, president of Pacific Portland Cement; Charles R. Hook, president of American Rolling Mill and a future president of the NAM; Ernest T. Weir, chairman of National Steel; and finally Lund, president of Lambert Pharmaceutical and a former vice-president of the Association.[9] That three of these men hailed from an industry with a traditionally hard line toward organized labor indicated the conservative persuasion of the group as a whole.

The evidence suggests that neither Lund nor the other Brass Hats had any preconceived notions about a public relations program for the defense of business before they assumed control of the NAM. Even after a year in the presidency Lund did not mention public relations, publicity, or propaganda as the rationale for the organization's survival. Its principal purpose, he felt, was to provide leadership for other business organizations.[10]

On September 7, 1933, however, Lund issued a memorandum which indicated that he had discovered the purpose for which the NAM had been groping. He observed that the National Industrial Recovery Act had "brought revolutionary changes in the industrial picture," the most significant of which were in the realm of labor relations. The act had unleashed an intense organizing activity on the part of unions, including not only the AFL but also "the communistic groups whose activities, as time passes, may bring highly serious consequences."

Lund added:

All of these organizations, having lost in the Act their long-time conventional appeals to workers, have resorted to untruthful or misleading statements about the law, particularly that it requires workers to join unions; that the worker cannot secure the benefits contemplated by the law unless he joins such unions; that employers' organizations of workers are prohibited by the law; and other statements.

It is reasonable to expect that a campaign based upon such false statements will ultimately defeat itself as the facts come to light. The outcome, however, will depend upon the activity of employers in combatting these misstatements. . . . The dire need of the strongest possible employer opposition is obvious.

Four major tasks, therefore, now faced the NAM, he said. It must develop a legislative program to deal with problems arising from the NIRA. It must step up its efforts at consolidating manufacturers' organizations. It must become the authority on business statistics. And finally:

> The problem of public relations must have an active consideration that the Association has never been able to give it. The public does not understand industry, largely because industry itself has made no real effort to tell its story; to show the people of this country that our high living standards have risen almost altogether from the civilization which industrial activity has set up. On the other hand, selfish groups, including labor, the socialistic-minded and the radical, have constantly and continuously misrepresented industry to the people, with the result that there is a general misinformation of our industrial economy, which is highly destructive in its effect.
>
> The Association must have a more effective publicity staff than at present. The task of public relations, however, involves more than telling the public of the activities of the Association. Discretion and careful planning must be used in carrying it out and all channels through which the public may be reached must be used. The job, it will be recognized, is similar to that which has been done for individuals and large corporations by men such as Lee, Bernys [sic], Bruce Barton, and others.[11]

Lund's memorandum contained the kernel of the NAM's message during the thirties. Industry's problems, he believed, were caused chiefly by public misunderstanding of its great services. This misunderstanding had resulted from industry's failure to "tell its story." Businessmen should launch "an active campaign of education."[12] The memorandum also showed that Lund and like-minded businessmen had no intention of relinquishing their claim to national leadership. Arthur M. Schlesinger, Jr. has written that by the time of Roosevelt's inauguration, any such claim "had long since collapsed" not only because of the hardships caused by the Depression but also the gross misconduct revealed in the Senate Banking and Currency Committee investigations in 1932, the suicide of Ivar Krueger, and the disintegration of the Insull empire. Not only had the nation lost confidence in business, but business, it seemed, "was losing confidence in itself."[13] The very existence of the Brass Hats, their decision to rejuvenate the NAM, and their determination as early as September of 1933 to launch the kind of public relations program described by Lund proved that at least some big businessmen even in the Depression's darkest days had not lost faith in a business-dominated social and economic order.[14]

The thrust of Lund's critique was that labor was his primary opponent in the battle for men's minds. He was willing to assume that the government would act in the interests of business. However, by his proposal for the preparation of a legislative program, he gave notice that he was not going to leave this good will to chance.

Lund's vigor contrasts with the Association's tardiness in jumping on the "Open Shop" bandwagon following World War I. Anti-union activity at that time developed spontaneously in dozens of cities across the country in response to tensions generated by union organizing activity, the failure of the President's First Industrial Conference, the great steel strike, and the other labor disruptions mentioned in Chapter II. The NAM hesitated for almost a year before assuming national leadership of the movement. By contrast, the Association seized the direction of anti-union efforts during the Depression without waiting for widespread local agitation against the labor provisions of the NIRA. Its propagandistic activities in these two cases were similar, but it is a testimony to the increased prestige of public relations that that label was not used following World War I but was during the Depression. As a result of a decade of the "two-way street" gospel of public relations and the paternalistic attitude of welfare capitalism, a new dimension was added to the NAM approach. The aim in 1920 was solely propaganda, but during the New Deal, as we shall see, the Association also sought in a modest way to reform and educate employers.[15]

To run the public relations program, Lund picked the combative Walter W. Weisenberger, an ex-newspaperman and a former executive of the chamber of commerce of Lund's native city of St. Louis, who became executive vice-president of the Association. Weisenberger's chief aide was another former journalist, James Selvage, who was given the title of public relations director.[16] Two committees were formed to oversee the campaign. The Public Relations Committee, with a membership of from forty to fifty businessmen, was founded in 1934 to evaluate the plans of Weisenberger and his staff. The National Industrial Information Committee was founded in 1935 to raise money specifically for the NAM's public relations crusade.[17]

Although Association propaganda of the 1930s resembled in some ways that of the Progressive era, it also differed in important respects. Chief among these was an increased sensitivity to the opinions of others rather than the mere expression of the NAM viewpoint. For example, one of Weisenberger's first moves was to commission Cherington and Roper to conduct a nationwide poll of over 6,000 employees of large and small manufacturers. Probably no such effort had been made by the Association up to this time. The new NAM sought to sell free enterprise the way Procter & Gamble sold soap. Weisenberger, therefore, ordered a market survey to discover the opinions of and the best appeals to reach the potential consumers.[18]

Another departure from the old ways was the attitude toward the press. The new public relations program made extensive use of paid advertising, thus encouraging the allegiance of advertising men and newspapers alike. Perhaps because it was run by former newspapermen, the program did not try to lecture or threaten journalists but sought to work with and through them.

As had their predecessors, the public relations directors tried to make use of every medium of communication to put their message across, including radio programs, motion pictures, film strips, paid advertisements in newspapers and magazines, outdoor billboard advertisements, direct mail, displays for schools and plants, clipsheets for plant publications, a speakers' bureau, and more. The financial support behind this effort grew geometrically.[19] There were numerous propaganda campaigns directed against the New Deal organized by individual businesses and other business associations, but Lund claimed that the NAM's generated a greater "volume of publicity . . . than all other programs combined."[20]

The public relations department had three basic guidelines for the preparation of copy: avoid involved explanations using complicated statistics; emphasize the self-interest of those at whom the message is directed; and be positive and assertive rather than negative. These rules, only inconsistently followed at best, resembled the teachings of Ivy Lee. The staff was too pugnacious, however, to accept some of the subtler precepts of Edward L. Bernays, who tried to avoid direct replies to critics of his clients. Such replies, he argued, onlys served to polarize the public, which had no way of discovering the truth in such a dialogue. The NAM, on the other hand, issued immediate replies to attacks.[21]

The central theme of NAM public relations material was that industry's managers were the true leaders of the nation. The public interest, and especially the workingman's interest, was safe in their hands. Business was on trial. (Although the staff was constantly warning itself that its propaganda should not be defensive, a recurring theme of its material was a courtroom scene at which industry stood accused by radical agitators or social planners while the judge was the American public.) False leaders were attempting to usurp its rightful place. Should they succeed, the great blessings of the American system would be forfeit.

"A man is worth the wages he can earn," pronounced a business journalist of the 1920s,[22] and so was an economic system, according to the NAM. The public relations staff sought to show that despite temporary difficulties, the American worker could afford more food, clothing, and luxuries than the worker of any other nation. This great achievement was the result of American business genius. The benefits of the system, however, were not described solely in material terms. The civil liberties everyone so cherished would be endangered should the social planners gain control. Freedom was indivisible; it could not be subtracted from enterprise without also taking it from speech, press, and religion.[23]

Although some students have argued that 1936–1937 was a turning point in business-sponsored anti-New Deal propaganda, the basic message of the NAM did not vary through the decade.[24] There did seem to be a softening of the tone of its annual Congress of American Industry,[25] but when looking for moderation or stridency of expression, the dividing lines are more likely to conform to the nature of the medium of communication and the audience than to chronology.

The speakers' bureau lecturers, for example, spoke to small groups whose composition they knew. When one Dr. Allen R. Stockdale addressed the Kiwanis convention in Poland Springs, Maine, on September 22, 1939, he declared that "crackpots and demagogues have been trying to indict business before the bar of public opinion, but American business is getting out of the dog-house."[26] These were not calm or moderate words, and they were eschewed in the mass media program.

In the case of radio, with an indeterminate audience, the message was appropriately muted. The most effective broadcasting effort was a serial called "The American Family Robinson." According to an advertising brochure for the program, it provided "industrial information which becomes entertainment—it stresses the value of the very business principles now most under fire by those advocating reform before recovery." Included in its cast of characters was Luke Robinson, "the sanely philosophical editor of the Centerville *Herald,* [who] espouses a fair deal for business and industry" and Professor Broadbelt, "prototype of the panacea peddler, organizer of Arcadia, Inc."[27]

In one series of episodes, an accident at a local plant leads to rioting by citizens who charge the owner with pocketing his profits instead of replacing unsafe machinery. At a "trial," Luke Robinson shows that the plant had actually been operating at a loss, and the owner dramatically returns from another town to announce that he has just sold some property to meet the payroll. He thus wins the support of the community, and the trial concludes with Robinson explaining that reform is necessary but only when brought about "within the rules of the game."[28] Industry is acquitted; its managers are shown to be sensitive and decent men. Rabble-rousing is discredited. Because the business leader is trustworthy, the success of his enterprise will foster an harmonious polity.

The harmony of all classes was a pillar of Association public relations. The clearest statement of this belief can be found in a series of twelve newspaper advertisements which the Association bought and distributed in 1936 and 1937. They were originally composed by Charles A. Mac-Donald of the "small but enterprising" South Bend, Indiana, advertising agency of MacDonald-Cook. They were published at the expense of a citizens' committee or employers' association in the local papers of such hotbeds of labor unrest as Canton, Ohio, and Johnstown, Pennsylvania. The NAM public relations staff was so impressed with the copy that it bought the rights to it and, after revising it, sent it out to 367 newspapers across the country. All or part of this package appeared in over 200 newspapers.[29]

A typical advertisement featured a construction worker high on a steel girder looking down and waving at a man in a chauffeured limousine. The headline reads: "I knew him when he pushed a wheelbarrow," and the text purports to show that in America, every man and his offspring have an equal chance of success. ". . . [U]nder no other flag and under no other social plan" has such a high degree of economic mobility been achieved. There is opportunity for all primarily because of "the spirit of good will among all groups." At the bottom of the page is the motto of the campaign: "Prosperity dwells where harmony reigns."[30]

Here was a remarkably mild, insubstantial message for these climactic years of labor-management conflict. Employers preached harmony while the LaFollette Committee on Violations of Free Speech and the Rights of Labor "found war."[31] What did those who distributed these advertisements hope to accomplish? According to MacDonald, they were designed

> to promote industrial harmony and a clear understanding between the workers and management, to help avoid misunderstandings which were costing thousands and thousands of dollars in communities, loss of employment, loss of incomes that were taking care of families, homes, women and children and general business in the community.[32]

This explanation can be quickly dismissed. They did not dispel misunderstanding, and it is hard to believe MacDonald himself really thought they did. Were they aimed at labor? Were they supposed, for example, to convince the demonstrators at Republic Steel's South Chicago plant that they should go back to work peacefully because their children might someday be like Tom Girdler? Though the worker seemed to be the principal target, the advertisements showed little comprehension of his point of view or goals. Were they, as has often been charged of public relations propaganda, merely examples of management talking to itself? Over 40 businessmen belonged to the Public Relations Committee of the NAM and more than 3,000 businesses paid for the advertisements through their dues and contributions. From firms of different sizes in all regions of the country and from competing industries, perhaps these businessmen could agree upon having themselves portrayed as self-made men and social benefactors but upon little else.

There is some merit in both these speculations. It may seem naive that employers thought they could overcome union sympathies through public relations, but some of the most outspoken advocates of public relations in the NAM, like Ernest T. Weir and Fred Crawford of Thompson Products, were also among the most paternalistic. They sincerely believed that if management would simply talk to workers, "outside agitators" would never gain a foothold.

It is probable that organizational dynamics also had a hand in shaping the harmony campaign. The NAM has long worked for "unit thinking and unit action" among the membership in order to increase the strength of its positions,[33] but it has not always been able to contain conflict. Holcombe Parkes, the energetic director of the Association's postwar public relations, correctly assessed the particular difficulties of his position. It simply was

> not possible for us to function as an advertiser should function. . . . [W]e are wrapped with endless red tape in an association of this kind, hence, our advertising must always be partly unrealistic and admittedly naive in that it represents the common denominator of the vigorous views of fifty or more people.[34]

The principal force behind the design of this and other NAM campaigns may have been other than a desire to reach the workers, flatter employers, or meet organizational exigencies. One scholar has suggested that the true goal was to influence the middle classes, small businessmen, farmers, skilled craftsmen, professionals, and white-collar workers. By the 1930s, much American advertising directed its appeal to this broad middle stratum rather than to the industrial worker. The belief was then current that "the market is a diamond" rather than a pyramid. That is to say that regardless of numerical composition, the middle classes have the most purchasing power and are therefore the most important consumers.[35] The idea may have been that the "sale of ideas" should follow the lead of the sale of products, since the middle classes had the most political power as well.

The idea of harmony was not original with the public relations staff of the NAM nor was the Association's the only version of it. American businessmen have traditionally expounded a belief in a fluid society in which there was an harmonious relationship between employer and employee. The linchpin of this system in the nineteenth century was the protective tariff, which enabled industry to grow and maintain acceptable profit margins and thus facilitated high wages for labor.[36] The executive's primary duty in corporations like large railroads where ownership and management were separate was narrowly interpreted as maximizing profit for the stockholders.[37] To better achieve this goal, he had to steel himself against excessive sentimentality and cultivate the "gumption" necessary to make the hard decisions.[38] The ultimate outcome of this apparent selfishness was general prosperity, thanks to the guidance of "the invisible hand." Frederick W. Taylor's scientific management also claimed to accommodate the interests of everyone. The differential piece rate would keep total labor costs low, thus making possible a higher wage for workers who remained on the job and lower prices for the public.[39] Production would be supervised by experts, insuring fairness and efficiency.

In the 1920s, increasingly professionally trained "managerial" leaders came to look upon themselves not merely as extensions of the stockholders' will but as trustees, mediating the claims of employees, consumers, and the public as well as the owners. The managerial executive was not bound to abstain from involving his firm in public causes. He could foster social harmony by contributing profits to worthy charities and claimed to take the public impact of his firm's activities into consideration.[40] Thus an officer of a large New York bank explained in 1927 that most of "the best upper class men in business . . . would not consider a policy which enriched them or their company and was at the same time against the public interest."[41] In the nineteenth-century world of classical economics, such a policy would have been impossible by definition.

The NAM has usually been looked upon as one of the foremost exponents of the conservative, classical model of harmony, and not without reason. The keystone of its beliefs was business leadership. In the newspaper campaign referred to above and even more explicitly in such public relations material as "Uncle Abner Says," a series of cartoons designed to be inserted in plant publications, the politician was often denigrated and the role of the government minimized.[42] Thus in the 1940s, its public relations staff fought postwar price controls, the Full Employment Bill, and Keynesian finance while the more managerially oriented Committee for Economic Development gave qualified support to all three. Nevertheless, elements of the managerial approach were in evidence. The public relations staff portrayed the businessman as actively working for the best interests of the community as a whole. He was more than a mere automaton with the gumption to pursue exclusively the interests of the stockholders.[43]

What effect did the public relations program have upon the attitudes of Americans toward business? It is impossible to render more than a tentative answer. The wide exposure and constant repetition of the Association's message probably changed some minds, but on the other hand, as was the case with the Liberty League, its extremism provided a convenient foil against which defenders of the New Deal could crystallize sentiment. For although in the conservative context of the business community it served, the NAM's campaign could be a moderating force, to a Depression-racked nation its Horatio Alger homilies appeared ingenuous at best.

Its sponsor certainly thought it in large measure succeeded. "I shudder to think," ran a set speakers' bureau speech, "of the fix we would be in today if we had not developed industrial consciousness." Robert Lund, sensing that public opinion was at last turning to the right after the 1938 elections, declined to credit all the change to public relations, but he did believe that the "new era and new formula of public contact by industry" had played its part. An analysis of the Association's crusade prepared after the 1940 elections pointed out that, although business had recently been "about as popular as a skunk at a lawn party," Wendell Willkie had just polled more votes than any Republican predecessor, "and his open and avowed platform was industrial—those lost-sight-of fundamentals that NAM began preaching seven years ago." Even though many seemed unaware of the "imminent danger" private enterprise was in, at least now "they favor the system, all right. That phase of our job has been well done."[44]

But what of the businessmen of the NAM? Public relations counselors have often asserted that the social utility of their vocation rests on two-way communication, with business changing as well as the public. Did increased communication facilitated by public relations lead executives to adopt different policies toward employees, plant communities, the government, etc.?

Walter Weisenberger took his responsibility seriously in this regard. He was particularly proud of a nation-wide survey of employee relations policies which his department assembled and distributed. For this project, the department retained a physician

> to advise us in the assembling of material as to what constitutes good hygiene, good sanitation, good lighting, good health. There again the object is to set forth to the average-sized manufacturer who cannot employ experts, that here are the things that are done by others and how they can adopt them economically and the good business side of putting those practices in. All of this is self-analysis which I believe no other national group has made as much progress [in] as we have. . . .[45]

The results of this study, which were even mailed to some nonmembers, excited considerable interest and went through at least two printings. From meetings and correspondence, Weisenberger concluded that the information was being put to good use.

There is, however, another side to this story. The NAM's corporate executives may have had a different idea from that of the public relations staff of the true aim of the program. In replying to a question about the financing of the harmony campaign, the then president of the Association Colby M. Chester wrote that "the main purpose of the NAM public information program is to stimulate increased publicity and advertising that truthfully tell industry's story." Nowhere in his letter did he mention the two-way street idea.[46] When pressed before the LaFollette Committee about the meaning of a letter soliciting funds for public relations, Ernest T. Weir, an original Brass Hat and the first president of the National Industrial Information Committee, characterized the embarrassing passages as "the elaborations of a salesman," an answer that must have made Weisenberger acutely uncomfortable. Backed into yet another corner, Weir claimed to "know very little about advertising and publicity. . . ." If this were true of a man so closely connected to the public relations program, one must wonder how much other businessmen knew of it.[47]

Another incident shows the limits of the application of the two-way street concept. When Remington Rand's Ilion, New York, plant was hit by a strike in June of 1936, James H. Rand, Jr. broke the union by what came to be called the Mohawk Valley Formula. This consisted of the use of strikebreakers, espionage, and pervasive propaganda in an aggressive fashion later denounced by the National Labor Relations Board. Weisenberger and an aide felt that all industry should be apprised of the Mohawk Valley Formula, so they prepared an article about it for the NAM Law Bulletin. In gathering information about the strike, Weisenberger spent a few hours, and his aide two days, interviewing the company's publicity man and the head of the company-supported citizens' committee. The result was an unqualified endorsement of the company and the citizens' committee for their contributions to "law and order" and "civic dignity." At no time did Weisenberger or his staff give a fair hearing—or any hearing—to the other side. No attempt was made to play the role of ombudsman. Remington-Rand was a prominent member of the NAM, and James Rand sat on the board of the National Industrial Information Committee. He was proud of his conquest of the union and would not have approved of mediation from the public relations staff even had it been offered.[48]

Weisenberger, like some other public relations counselors, did make honest attempts to reform his employers. But these attempts were only possible when they did not seem forced, when, that is, they could be interpreted as resulting from the businessman's paternal regard for employee or customer and not from the push or threat of a countervailing power like organized labor or government. In the latter situations, the corporate public relations man is forced to close ranks with the beleaguered businessman.[49]

The LaFollette Committee, which investigated NAM public relations in the late 1930s, ridiculed the Association's talk of educating the public. Its campaign "cannot be said by any stretch of argument to contribute to a better understanding of our 'Industrial Economic Society,' or to an easier adjustment of prospective recruits from schools and colleges for industrial employment." It was a propaganda barrage, pure and simple.

> Unnerved by the impact of the depression, apprehensive of the growing strength of labor, enraged at critics of the failures of business and rejecting almost in toto the devices of the new administration in Washington to find solutions to the problems it inherited in 1933, the leaders of the association resorted to "education," just as they had done in 1903–08, and 1919–21 under the guise of the "industrial conservation movement." They asked not what the weaknesses and abuses of the economic structure had been, and how they could be corrected, but instead paid millions to tell the public that nothing was wrong and that grave dangers lurked in the proposed remedies. In addition to this broad political objective, the association considered its propaganda material an effective weapon in its fight against labor unions.[50]

This criticism was not without justification. The corporate public relations apparatus had indeed sought to quell labor unionism, and it had been used in tandem with the most vicious of anti-union tactics in order to protect the public opinion flank of the conservative corporation. Thus we see the NAM supporting the Mohawk Valley Formula of Remington Rand, or the public relations firm of Hill and Knowlton looking after the reputation of Republic Steel's Tom Girdler while he was equipping a private army, employing an extensive espionage network, and locking workers out of plants.[51] And public relations had aided in the formation of citizens' committees, which acted as a vehicle of employer intimidation of workers after direct communication for this purpose was prohibited by the Wagner Act. There was, however, another side to the role of public relations in labor-management conflict, one which the LaFollette Committee, with its prolabor bias, failed to recognize.

Symbolic of this other side was a March 1937 *Printers' Ink* article, which the NAM's public relations staff felt was sufficiently important to circulate a summary of it to Association members. The article held that though many manufacturers seemed to think that advertising was of no account as an antistrike weapon, if they would invest just

> one-tenth of the money in advertising preparation that they are apparently quite willing to invest in labor spies, tear gas, and other methods, which have proved worse than useless, they will stand a far better chance of winning public support than is possible under present circumstances.[52]

The LaFollette Committee condemned the ulterior motives for corporate communication revealed by this article and endorsed by the NAM. Victory over the unions, rather than rational dialogue, was the goal. The Committee did not see that the article's point of view could lead to more peaceful labor relations. Some public relations and advertising men of the thirties were telling employers that their profession offered a better way to deal with unions and strikers than the brutal methods of the old-time industrialists.[53] The National Labor Relations Board disagreed with this assessment, as did LaFollette himself.[54] But over the past thirty years, most major employers have abandoned strong-arm tactics while increasing their investment in public relations.

It is not intended here to assert that public relations counseling caused the demise of espionage, the yellow-dog contract, private corporate armies, and violence, or even that it was the major factor in setting such practices on the road to ultimate extinction. Scholars have given the lion's share of credit for the civilizing of industrial relations in America to the Wagner Act and its liberal interpretation by the National Labor Relations Board.[55] Nevertheless, public relations did play its part. For although its methods and messages may not have satisfied the liberal politician or union leader, it did provide the employer with a nonviolent means of expressing himself. And its basic tenet since the earliest days of Ivy Lee had always been that an underlying harmony of interests existed which needed only proper communication to be generally recognized.

Talk, after all, rather than violence, was what public relations was all about, and as Professor Marvin Meyers has observed, "With talk begins responsibility." Perhaps the employer came to believe some of the rhetoric of industrial harmony and "adjustment" which his own public relations men were composing for the consumption of others.[56]

Confusion about the opposition to public relations did not disappear immediately with the NAM's adoption of it. Businessmen did recognize the need to make the "fundamental institutional sale" of private enterprise to the American public, but uncertainty persisted as to how.[57] As one public relations counselor wrote in 1936, "The American businessman may not know what public relations work is, but he pretty generally thinks it is a good thing."[58] Opponents to public relations work were still plentiful in law, journalism, and advertising. And there remained opponents to the Association approach among businessmen themselves. Texas manufacturer Milo Perkins might have had the NAM in mind when he remarked in 1934 that "the capitalist system can be destroyed more effectively by having men of means defend it than by importing a million Reds from Moscow to attack it."[59]

By the end of the decade, however, both confusion and opposition had begun to dissipate. Whether they agreed with the Association message or not, businessmen were according public relations recognition as a staff function whose responsibilities included organizing the news that a corporation generated with an eye to maintaining a good reputation for it and keeping the executives up-to-date about trends in public opinion. Political duties overshadowed economic ones, thanks in no small degree to the NAM's emphasis.

Thus the National Association of Manufacturers was influential in establishing public relations as a permanent fixture in the American corporation and trade association. The NAM had embraced public relations in the depths of the Great Depression and, more than any other organization, promoted its use. Its campaigns, supported by 3,000 businesses in the mid-1930s and by almost four times that many a decade later, and its intense discussions at the annual Congresses of American Industry introduced the function to a wide audience of businessmen, small as well as large, and further increased its stature.

Among practitioners its influence has also been great. Almost every major independent and many in-house counselors were to attend at least one Association-sponsored public relations conclave. Although agreement with the content of its program was not unanimous, they were all exposed to it, and some probably had their search for clients facilitated by it. The NAM remained an indefatigable booster of their trade and a home base to which they kept returning.

The Roosevelt Administration was not mute in the face of corporate propaganda. In addition to detailing the activities of some leading independent counseling firms during the 1930s, we must also discuss the arsenal of the enemy.

NOTES

1. "Winning Public Approval," *Advertising and Selling*, May 21, 1936, p. 29.
2. Albert K. Stiegerwalt, *The National Association of Manufacturers, 1895–1914* (Grand Rapids, 1964), p. 42; Circular of Information No. 23, February 10, 1898, pp. 1–2, papers of the National Association of Manufacturers, Eleutherian Mills Historical Library, Greenville, Wilmington, Del. (cited hereinafter as NAM papers).

3. It should be noted that even before this change in leadership, the Association recognized "the value of printers' ink" and conducted a "general propaganda." It is not correct to call the early NAM, as Robert H. Wiebe did, a "relatively quiet organization." *Businessmen and Reform* (Chicago, 1962), p. 25.

4. *Proceedings* of the 19th annual convention of the NAM, 1914, pp. 167–168; *Proceedings* of the 16th NAM, 1911, p. 87; Clarence Bonnett, *Employers Associations in the United States* (New York, 1922), pp. 340–342. In addition to the helpful discussions of early Association propaganda by Wiebe, Stiegerwalt, and Bonnett, see Albion G. Taylor, *Labor Policies of the National Association of Manufacturers* (Urbana, 1928), and Allen M. Wakstein, "The National Association of Manufacturers and Labor Relations in the 1920's," *Labor History* 10, No. 2 (Spring 1969), pp. 163–176. Considering the amount of research on NAM publicity from 1895 to 1930, it is surprising that so little has appeared about it during the New Deal.

5. *The NAM and Its Leaders* (privately printed, 1947), p. 7, Drawer No. 11, File Cabinet No. 6. NAM papers: "Renovation in NAM: Industry's Intransigent Spokesman Now Says 'Yes' as well as 'No,'" *Fortune* (July 1948), p. 75.

6. Letter from Board of Directors to NAM membership, Dec. 18, 1931; Executive Committee Meeting of Board of Directors, Vol. 19, pp. 83–85, Minute Books of the Board of Directors of the NAM, office of the NAM, New York City (cited hereinafter as BOD). Edgerton, however, was to enjoy his new position for a mere six months. Minutes of Executive Committee Meeting of BOD, June 23, 1932, Vol. 19, p. 159. These minute books were made available to me with the help of Dr. Richmond D. Williams of the Eleutherian Mills Historical Library and through the kindness of Mr. John R. McGraw of the NAM.

7. Minutes of BOD meeting, Dec. 18, 1931, Vol. 19, pp. 73–75.

8. The report of the LaFollette Civil Liberties Committee stated that the Brass Hats organized themselves after the 1932 election. They then chose the NAM as the proper vehicle for "business salvation" and restructured it in 1933, making Lund president. Actually, Lund became president at the end of 1931, and the restructuring took place soon thereafter. The logic of events and my reading of the minutes of the meetings of the Board of Directors from 1931 to 1934 suggest to me that the Brass Hats were born in 1931 and became involved with the NAM not to "save" business but rather to fill the leadership void in the collapsing organization. Not till September, 1933 did they recognize the necessity of having a public relations spokesman for industry or the potential of the NAM for that role. See U.S. Senate, Committee on Education and Labor, *Labor Policies of Employers Associations*, Report No. 6, Part 7, 76th Cong., 1st Sess., 1939, p. 211 (cited hereinafter as *Labor Policies*).

9. Ibid., pp. 211–212; John N. Stalker, "The National Association of Manufacturers" (unpublished Ph.D. thesis, University of Wisconsin, 1950), p. 3.

10. BOD minutes, Nov. 15, 1932. The question of a "program of industrial education" was given lengthy consideration at the February 12, 1932, meeting when a staff member submitted a five-page memorandum inspired by the "dissemination of economic errors."

11. "CONFIDENTIAL. A Consideration of the Policies and Programs of the National Association of Manufacturers by Robert L. Lund, President, Sept. 7, 1933." BOD, Vol. 20, p. 119.

12. This refrain has been sung throughout this century. As early as 1916, an official of the NAM called a "campaign of education" a "hackneyed phrase," yet in 1974, M. A. Wright, chairman of the board of Exxon, rued the fact that "business has failed to do an effective job in communicating its point of view to the general public." This explanation of business unpopularity has the advantage of not requiring businessmen to change their actions. It assumes that there exists a harmony of interests in an economy characterized by free enterprise and that the only cause for dissatisfaction is an inability to see this harmony, or as some of the more direct public relations men put it, "economic illiteracy." *Proceedings* of 21st NAM, 1916, p. 1960; Wright is quoted in J. K. Gallbraith's review of *The Assault on Free Enterprise, The New York Times Book Review,* Sept. 15, 1974, p. 7; John W. Hill, *The Making of a Public Relations Man* (New York, 1963). pp. 169–170, 174–178, 220–222.

13. Arthur M. Schlesinger, Jr., *The Coming of the New Deal* (Boston, 1958). pp. 423–425; Linda Keller Brown, "Challenge and Response" (unpublished Ph.D. thesis, University of Pennsylvania, 1972), pp. 174–179.

14. An NAM in-house historian gave great emphasis to the immediacy of the Association's opposition to F.D.R.: "At 1:08 p.m. on March 4, 1933 the New Deal began. Business overnight came under attack, and, as president of the NAM, Robert L. Lund became one of the leaders of the defense." *The NAM and Its Leaders,* p. 8. The activities of the Brass Hats suggest to me that the New Deal "honeymoon" was not quite as ardent an affair as some have supposed.

15. Allen M. Wakstein, "The Origins of the Open Shop Movement, 1919–1920," *Journal of American History* 51, No. 3 (December 1964), pp. 460–475.

16. When Selvage was first hired, the titles "Publicity Director" and "Director of Public Relations" were apparently used interchangeably. "Report of the Secretary," Dec. 7, 1933, BOD, Vol. 20, p. 139.

17. *Labor Policies,* Report No. 6, Pt. 5, pp. 154–155.

18. *Proceedings* of 39th NAM, 1934, pp. 359–360, 370–372.

19. NAM Expenditures on Public Information (Public Relations):

Year	$ for Info. Program	Total Income	Public Info. as % of Total Income
1933	—	$ 240,900	—
1934	$ 36,500	480,317	7.2
1935	112,659	617,143	18.2
1936	467,759	1,171,390	33.9
1937	793,043	1,439,548	55.1

Source: Labor Policies, Report No. 6, Pt. 5, p. 168.

Figures for the succeeding years are not completely reliable, but the budget for public relations did continue to increase. Nor do these expenditures tell the whole story. The NAM was receiving space in publications, outdoor billboards, and radio time at either greatly reduced rates or free. It was given over $1,250,000 worth of outdoor advertising space, $1,000,000 in newspaper space, and over $1,000,000 in radio time free in 1937. U.S. Senate, Subcommittee of the Committee on Education and Labor. *Hearings* Pursuant to S. Res. 266,

Violations of Free Speech and Rights of Labor, 74th–76th Congs., 1936–1940, Pt. 17, pp. 7761–7762 (cited hereinafter as LaFollette Committee *Hearings*).

20. *Proceedings* of 43rd NAM, 1938, p. 10.

21. Bernays, *Biography of an Idea*, p. 241; "Brief Outline of Purpose and Operation of the Industrial Mobilization," February 1940, Drawer No. 1110, NAM papers.

22. Prothro, *Dollar Decade*, p. 34.

23. In 1940, the NAM launched the "Tripod of Freedom" public relations symbol designed to illustrate graphically that "individual freedom in this country rests on a tripartite foundation. . . . One leg of that tripod is representative democracy, the second is civil and religious liberty, and the third is free private enterprise." Remove one leg and the whole structure collapses. *NAM and Leaders*, p. 26.

24. Students of business opposition to the New Deal have made various attempts to periodize it. Two contemporary journalists, Strother H. Walker and Paul Sklar, saw the election of 1936 as a turning point. Businessmen had "relied too heavily on . . . persuasive material" prior to the election, but Roosevelt's overwhelming electoral endorsement made them turn inward. Public relations, they now decided, must begin with the corporation itself. The product, in other words, must be improved and emphasis placed not on slick advertisements but on down-to-earth community relations. *Business Finds Its Voice* (New York, 1938), pp. 59–63.

Two historians have also seen 1936–1937 as a turning point, but in different ways. Thomas C. Longin believed business propaganda was more emotional and extreme before the election that it was afterwards. Lloyd M. Wells has asserted that big business based its self-defense on constitutional law during F.D.R.'s first term and turned to public relations during his second. "The Search for Security" (unpublished Ph.D. thesis, University of Nebraska, 1970), pp. 17–18. Longin contradicted himself on this point on pp. 299–300; "The Defense of Big Business" (unpublished Ph.D. thesis, Princeton, N.J., 1955), p. 48.

25. *Business Week* headlined an article on the 1935 NAM convention "The NAM Declares War" (Dec. 14, 1935), pp. 9–10. The headline for the 1938 convention read, "We're Ready to Talk It Over" (Dec. 17, 1938), p. 20. Frances Perkins is said to have "rubbed her eyes with astonishment" at the liberality of the 1939 resolutions. Lee R. Tillman, "The American Business Community and the Death of the New Deal" (unpublished Ph.D. thesis, University of Arizona, 1966), pp. 28–29.

26. Press release, Sept. 23, 1939, p. 1, Drawer No. 1110, NAM papers.

27. "Industry's Own Radio Program," Drawer No. 1110, NAM papers.

28. "Synopsis of Succeeding Broadcasts of 'The American Family Robinson,'" Drawer No. 1110, NAM papers.

29. Walker and Sklar, *Voice*, pp. 18–19; LaFollette Committee *Hearings*, Pt. 18, pp. 7766–7778.

30. Drawer No. 1110, NAM papers.

31. Jerold S. Auerbach, *Labor and Liberty* (Indianapolis, 1966), p. 143.

32. LaFollette Committee *Hearings* Pt. 18, p. 7766.

33. Alfred S. Cleveland, "NAM: Spokesman for Industry?" *Harvard Business Review* 26 (May 1948), p. 360.

34. Memo, Parkes to R. S. Smethurst, Feb. 12, 1946, Drawer No. 1134, NAM papers. Smethurst, an NAM lawyer, scribbled "My deepest sympathy!" on the memo.

35. Robert A. Brady, *Business as a System of Power* (New York, 1943), pp. 274–276.

36. Henry C. Carey, the foremost American economist of the Middle Period, was a leading exponent of the tariff as an agent of harmony. After a brief flirtation with an advocacy of an ill-defined free trade, Carey came to believe that the tariff would do more than just advance the interests of entrepreneur and laborer alike. According to his biographer, he believed it would "find husbands for old maids and free the entire sex from an age-old bondage. . . , make Southern planters rich but . . . also ultimately free the slave. . . . [and] lower the bastardy rate, improve morals, eliminate crime and war." Arnold W. Green, *Henry Charles Carey* (Philadelphia, 1951), pp. 134–143; Joseph Dorfman, *The Economic Mind in American Civilization*, II (New York, 1946), pp. 789–805. See also an appropriately entitled book that Carey published shortly before the Civil War: *The Harmony of Interests, Agricultural, Manufacturing, and Commercial* (New York, 1856).

Businessmen preached harmony to the laborer but often justified their power to the community on the grounds that they had proven their fitness by rising to the top of the competitive cauldron. Competition among businessmen led to general prosperity. Businessmen and their propagandists have never entertained the possibility that competition between workers and management for profits might serve either the workers or the public better than harmony. William Graham Sumner, on the other hand, did acknowledge that employees "must be expected to develop their interests fully in the competition and struggle of life. It is for the health of the industrial organization that they should do so." Maurice R. Davie, *Sumner Today* (New Haven, 1940), p. 63.

37. Cochran, *Railroad Leaders*, p. 78.

38. Kirkland, *Dream*, p. 71.

39. Samuel Haber, *Efficiency and Uplift* (Chicago, 1964), p. 27.

40. Morrell Heald, "Management's Responsibility to Society: The Growth of an Idea," *Business History Review* 31, No. 4 (Winter 1957), pp. 375–384.

41. Quoted in Morrell Heald, "Business Thought in the Twenties: Social Responsibility," *American Quarterly* 13, No. 2, Pt. 1 (Summer 1961), p. 127.

42. There is a good collection of the NAM's "Service for Plant Publications" from July 1935 to December 1940 in Drawer No. 1111, NAM papers.

43. The "managerial" influence in the NAM was evidenced by the remark of its president, Colby M. Chester, following the 1936 election, that "industry must accept its responsibility for the national welfare as being an even higher duty than the successful operation of private business." Quoted in Heald, *Social Responsibilities of Business* (Cleveland, 1970), p. 194.

44. "Your City's Stake in Industry," Drawer No. 1111, NAM papers; *Proceedings* of 43rd NAM, 1938, pp. 8–10; "Certain Recommendations in Connection

with NAM's Public Information Program for 1941," pp. 1–2, Drawer No. 1111, NAM papers.

Further indication of the NAM's confidence in the future of public relations was its sponsorship of over a dozen national and regional public relations forums in the 1940s, where independent counselors, corporate public relations officers, and other executives could discuss and refine the function. These meetings were the most important of their kind up to that time, marking, it has been claimed, the "coming of age" of the vocation. The Association also continued its own public relations program, which gained the support of an increasing number of businesses. See "Industry's Public Relations" (New York, 1942) forward, Drawer No. 1110, NAM papers.

45. Wells, "Security," pp. 71–72; LaFollette Committee *Hearings*, Pt. 18, p. 7824; LaFollette Committee *Hearings*, Pt. 17, p. 7411.

46. Ibid., pp. 7761–7762.

47. It is also possible, of course, that Weir gave this answer in order to avoid responding to a difficult line of questioning. Ibid., pp. 7468, 7478.

48. LaFollette Committee *Hearings*, Pt. 18, pp. 7779–7800.

49. Those few historians who have given careful consideration to public relations have been skeptical about the extent to which the activities of public relations men have liberalized corporations or made them more responsive to society's needs. Alan Raucher acknowledged that some public relations counselors, such as Lee, Page, and Page's predecessor at AT&T, James D. Ellsworth, did attain high staff positions, but that did not necessarily mean they were influential in policy formation. Even if they did have some say, he doubted that their voices were significant. If they had little or no influence over policy, they obviously could not act as ombudsmen. "One of the basic flaws in the exaggerated claims of social significance," he concluded, "was simply that practitioners were not able to carry out those functions." The exaggeration of the power of public relations men was an important theme in Raucher's book. He felt their abilities to persuade the public had also been greatly overestimated. He discounted Lee's claims to knowledge of social psychology and labeled Bernays's description of his methodology "jabberwocky." *Public Relations*, pp. 148, 101, 154, 125–126, 134.

Thomas Cochran agreed with Raucher that pre-Depression public relations was primarily a matter of corporate persuasion of the public with very little feedback involved. He disagreed, however, with Raucher's belief in the ineffectiveness of this persuasion, giving it part of the credit for the increase in good will toward business in the twenties. ". . . [T]his older style of public relations was in the realm of words and pious exhortation" and utterly inadequate to meet the problems of the thirties. Only in the late thirties did the genuine two-way street approach begin to appear. *The American Business System* (New York, 1962), pp. 154–157; *Business in American Life*, pp. 152, 254.

In Morrell Heald's view, attempts to use publicity to broaden social approval during the New Era "were undoubtedly directed more toward public persuasion than toward self-examination. Nevertheless, a new sensitivity to community opinion had begun to take form." Heald saw the thirties as a retreat from even this modest beginning. Overall, he was extremely circumspect about the reforming impulse of public relations. Counsellors have so often flagrantly exploited the tools of mass persuasion that questions have been and continue to be raised "regarding the morality and the social utility of the public relations function." "Management's Responsibility to Society," p. 378; *Social Responsibilities of Business*, p. 86.

50. *Labor Policies*, pp. 175, 178.

51. Irving Bernstein, *Turbulent Years* (Boston, 1969), pp. 482–483.

52. *Labor Policies*, p. 178.

53. The element of self-interest was not absent in this advice, but public relations is no less noteworthy as a reforming influence as a result. Here was an example of counselors promoting the public interest (by advocating the renunciation of violence) while promoting their own.

54. In the Freuhauf case of 1935, the NLRB held that nothing "is more calculated to interfere with, restrain, and coerce employees in the right to self organization" than espionage—an impressive testimony to its effectiveness. The Board thus rated it more potent than advertising or public relations. On March 28, 1939, LaFollette introduced a bill designed to prohibit espionage, strikebreaking, use of gas and automatic weapons, and use of armed guards beyond an employer's premises. He contemplated no regulation or prohibition of public relations or advertising. Auerbach, *Labor*, pp. 57, 198.

55. Harry A. Millis and Emily Clark Brown, *From the Wagner Act to Taft-Hartley* (Chicago, 1950) pp. 252–268; Joseph G. Rayback, *A History of American Labor* (New York, 1968), pp. 341–436; R. W. Fleming, "The Significance of the Wagner Act," in Milton Derber and Edwin Young, eds., *Labor and the New Deal* (Madison, 1957), p. 151. See also the interesting discussion by H. M. Gittleman, "Perspectives on American Industrial Violence," *Business History Review* 47, No. 1 (Spring 1973), pp. 1–23.

56. *The Jacksonian Persuasion* (Stanford, Calif., 1960), p. ix. "Quite simply," according to Robert Heilbroner, "business has sold itself the bill of goods it originally intended to sell the public." "Public Relations—The Invisible Sell," *Harper's*, June 1957, p. 31.

57. *Economic Forum*, Winter 1936, insert following p. 324.

58. Bernard Lichtenburg to Bruce Barton, Feb. 13, 1936, Vol. 14, Bernard Lichtenburg papers, State Historical Society of Wisconsin, Madison.

59. Milo Perkins, "Grab the Torch, Men of Means, Grab the Torch!" *Nation* 139 (Nov. 28, 1934), p. 619. Donaldson Brown, vice chairman of the board of General Motors was disturbed about the stridency of the NAM and worked within the Association to moderate it. Heald, *Social Responsibility of Business*, pp. 196–197.

Chapter IV

The Fight for Public Opinion

Industry and Politics . . . are competitors for the confidence of the same patron, the public. Politics knows it; industry, for three years, has acted as if it did not.
Bruce Barton, 1936[1]

If you do not appreciate the full value of public relations, just check back in your thinking to the magic accomplished by the best public relations man *the world has ever known . . . the President of the United States.*
James W. Irwin, conservative public relations counselor, 1943[2]

"Business or Politics: Which Will Lead?" asked *Forbes* magazine in mid-1932,[3] and this question became more pressing with the advent of Roosevelt. Despite recent attempts by some historians to minimize it,[4] business conflict with the New Deal is a central theme of the '30s. As the Depression wore on, anti-Roosevelt sentiment became so widespread that individual firms and trade associations tied their particular quarrels to it. Without an appreciation of its intensity, the activities of the three public relations firms with which this chapter will deal—Ivy Lee and T. J. Ross, Carl Byoir and Associates, and Hill and Knowlton—are inexplicable.

The government was far from helpless in this fight for public opinion. Executive agencies had steadily been developing their publicity apparatuses during the '20s and these establishments enjoyed a sharp increase in number of employees, budget, and expertise during the '30s. They became effective defenders of agency activities through their press contacts. Political publicity was also making strides, and the paramount position of the President in the fight for public opinion was evidenced by Roosevelt's successes. As head of the party, government, and state, the President had at his disposal means which, though not a part of professional public relations, could mold opinion along desired lines. The best example, as will be seen shortly, were the administration-supported congressional investigating committees.

Some understanding of the history and character of administrative and political publicity is important for two reasons. First, public relations–conscious executives in the '30s, and to an extent since then,[5] have often viewed their activities as a response to government aggression, both verbal and substantive. A discussion limited to their sometimes extreme reactions makes them seem more unreasonable than they were. Second, government, especially on the federal level, has succeeded in arrogating to itself the paternalistic role which industrialists had so cherished prior to the stock market crash. Therefore its activities have been part of the businessman's reassessment of his image.[6]

Businessmen have seen themselves fight for the approval of the factor which sanctifies power in America—public opinion. Government has been one principal opponent. The other has been organized labor, and a special discussion of union public relations appears in Chapter V.

I

Federal public relations activity might be divided into two categories which are neither clearly defined nor mutually exclusive: administrative and political. One of the causes for the Republican party's defeat in the 1936 elections, according to the chairman of its National Committee, was the propaganda issued by federal agencies during the preceding three years.[7] Whatever the accuracy of this observation, press releases of an ostensibly nonpartisan caste emanating from a federal agency can indeed benefit politicians in power.[8] On the other hand, a distinction should be drawn between an information officer dispensing data on crops for the Department of Agriculture and the propagandizing of Charles Michelson, Louis McHenry Howe, Stephen Early, and Marvin McIntyre.

Agency publicity on the federal level dates back at least to 1839 when Congress appropriated $1,000 for the dissemination of agricultural information from the patent office. Other agencies receiving funds to publicize their work before the turn of the century include the Department of Agriculture, the U.S. Office of Education, the Public Health Service, and the Departments of Labor and Commerce.[9]

During Theodore Roosevelt's second term, the Forest Service conducted a vigorous educational campaign which, charged enemies of Roosevelt and Gifford Pinchot, was aimed more at persuading than informing. A provision of the Agricultural Appropriation Bill of 1908 enjoined the Forest Service from paying for the preparation of newspaper and magazine articles. Congressional objections to increasing executive branch publicity activities finally led to the passage of an amendment to a 1913 bill which prohibited the use of funds "for the compensation of any publicity expert unless specifically appropriated for that purpose."[10] This statute has never been repealed, but instead of limiting agency publicity, it has merely forced the camouflaging of government practitioners with phony titles (and, incidentally, made it difficult to obtain reliable information on the subject).

By the mid-'20s, *Printers' Ink* was complaining that since the war the government had been issuing hundreds of press releases monthly dealing with the business situation and had thus made itself part of an industrial drive for free publicity. The magazine's Washington bureau asked the director of economic information of the Bureau of Agricultural Economics why his agency did not dispense information through paid advertising rather than through releases. The director replied that his job was to disseminate information, not to sell anything, and that every paid advertisement caused demands from politicians that the money be spent on their favorite publications. "Hence, it is probable," moaned *PI,* "that political influence is an insurmountable obstacle to general government advertising."[11]

During the New Deal, administrative publicity by executive agencies blossomed. Even a relatively objective observer like Harvard's E. Pendleton Herring observed in mid-1935 that "never before has the Federal Government undertaken on so vast a scale and with such deliberate intent, the task of building a favorable public opinion toward its policies." Although acknowledging that ". . . the skillful and effective use of publicity is one of the essential devices of successful administration," he feared that the "two hundred-odd" public relations officers in the executive branch were beginning to compromise the independence of journalists. The only solution was countervailing propaganda, from the minority party and Congress. Like other critics, he viewed the confusion in the executive branch as the best safeguard against an irresistible campaign of persuasion.[12] This belief led to stout opposition to administration attempts to create a central information agency.

Such an attempt was the National Emergency Council. Bruce Barton charged that the NEC was "only a front for a bunch of 290 press agents" and introduced a bill calling for its dissolution in 1939. Roosevelt bowed to the outcry and abolished the agency, but it reappeared immediately "almost intact" in the guise of the Office of Government Reports. It is ironic that conservatives like Barton, who, as *Time* tartly noted, "knows a press agent when he sees one," fought the rationalization of government public relations, since one of their prime indictments of the New Deal was for its administrative inefficiency.[13]

It is impossible to say precisely how many public relations people the federal government employed because of the need to camouflage the function. Estimates range from about 250 in the mid-thirties to over 310 by the end of the decade. James McCamy, author of a 1939 study, found that their morale was steadily improving because of high pay, job security, and the interesting nature of the work. However, they still found themselves on the defensive due to the suspicion that publicity was a way of persuading people to do things they did not want to do. He concluded that

> the conditions of economic security and interesting work which favor good morale are outweighed by the hostility to publicity, by the lack of clear articulation and understanding between publicity agents and other officials within the agency, by the personal situation of the publicity agent which denies him public acclaim and removes him from his past loyalties of working for media instead of for news sources.[14]

Some of these public relations men did operate on the staff level, advising management of the effects of policy upon public opinion.

In the early twenties, Bernays had stressed the importance of psychological tests and surveys in determining the state of the public mind, thus inaugurating a debate which lingers to this day over whether public relations is an art or a science. McCamy discovered that scientific methodology had not yet made significant progress in the government's attempts to influence opinion. Rather, attitude measurement was based primarily upon informal samplings of letters and clippings.[15]

Not all media were effectively used and the creation of the appeal depended upon the intuition and experience of the individual counselor rather than upon careful study. Newspapers were favored and radio was largely ignored. McCamy provided an excellent summary of the methods:

> [Most believe] that an emotional appeal is better than a rational; that personal address is a more commanding medium than the printed page or the radio; that the prestige of the exhorter is very important; that the person whose initial attitude is more or less neutral shows the greatest change after bombardment by propaganda; that the federal government, at least in terms of prestige of employment, enjoys greater prestige than state and local governments; that the best efforts, in summary, will be obtained if the propaganda method involves vivid, novel, realistic, and emotionally charged experiences, if the propaganda has a clear field devoid of the

counter-influences or the opportunities to hear the complexities of and the objections to the point of view being advocated, and if the method uses individuals, institutions, groups, or their symbols, which have an established prestige value in their audience.[16]

Just as presidents of large corporations were often assigned propaganda tasks, so the President of the United States had a public relations mission to perform during the Depression. When Franklin Roosevelt made his famed pronouncement that "the only thing we have to fear is fear itself," he was essentially enunciating a public relations analysis of the economic collapse. If people would only change their outlook from fear to confidence, the substantive problems would solve themselves.

The appeal to public opinion through the cultivation of the press has been a part of the American Presidency since the days of the Founding Fathers. Not only aspirants who proclaimed the virtues of democracy and the common man but even their more conservative opponents developed networks of editors loyal to their respective views and leaders.

Perhaps no President before him, however, arrested public attention to the degree that Theodore Roosevelt did. He showed how a shrewd and striking political personality could dominate the headlines. An article in *Harper's* during his Presidency was entitled "Theodore Roosevelt: Press Agent."[17] His ability to "puff" himself was comparable to Henry Ford's. Mr. Dooley was quite taken in:

Whin Tiddy was blowed up in th' harbor iv Havana he instantly con-cluded they must be war. He debated th' question long an' earnestly an' fin'lly passed a jint resolution declarin' war. So far so good. But there was no wan to carry it on. What shud he do?

Mr. Dooley then quoted the Rough Rider on the question of who was the first to the top of San Juan Hill: "'. . . I will say f'r th' binifit iv Posterity that I was th' only man I see. An' I had a tillyscope.'" Mr. Dooley concluded that Roosevelt should have entitled *The War With Spain*, "Alone in Cuba."[18] Sinclair Lewis listed Roosevelt among the four "acknowledged masters" of publicity.[19]

Less recognized for his persuasiveness because of the pall that the Depression has cast over his reputation but nonetheless an innovator in political public relations was Herbert Hoover. Hoover's ambition and his sense of duty impelled him to seek political influence and office. He was handicapped, however, by what one student has labeled "his outstanding personality trait, his tendency to shrink before the public eye." In order to reconcile the conflicting demands posed by his "drive and diffidence," he spoke through journalists and editors. Assisted by public relations aides, he cultivated writers who he thought influenced public opinion. In their turn, journalists were drawn to him because of the selfless humanitarianism he exhibited as director of World War I relief.

> By 1917, Hoover had created a far-flung public relations apparatus. Through newspaper and magazine publicity, the instigation of specialized sub-campaigns at the community and state level, and the association of important public figures and renowned institutions with his work, he had been successful in securing the material and moral support necessary to bring Belgium safely through her period of national travail.[20]

Hoover brought his wartime expertise to the Commerce Department, which he headed from 1921 to 1928. He was convinced of the value of public relations as a device for educating the masses and for disseminating his political and economic philosophy. So far-reaching were his efforts that he has been judged "instrumental in bringing the techniques of administrative publicity to maturity in American government." This activity helped make Hoover "the most heralded public official in the country" by 1928 and aided his presidential bid. During the Depression, he continued his time-tested stratagems. Now, however, his actions, which had previously spoken at least as loudly as his words, failed to mitigate the disaster. Unemployment made a mockery of his public statements, and his reputation never fully recovered.[21]

Another reason for the eclipse of Hoover's reputation as a public relations specialist was the remarkable proficiency of his successor in the same realm.

In his first campaign, for the New York State Senate in 1910, Franklin D. Roosevelt showed that he had all of Hoover's drive but none of his diffidence. He was a natural glad-hander, bounding up to the average citizen declaring, "Call me Franklin—I'm going to call you Tom."[22] He got a taste of the problems of the politicians' quest for public approval when the Republicans tried to engineer a press boycott of his activities, forcing him to purchase $400 of advertising space in the journals of his native county.[23] In the midst of his campaign for re-election two years later, he was striken with typhoid and forced to rely heavily on an upstate newspaperman for help. Thus began an association which was to last a quarter century.

A cynical, shrewd, and suspicious *Niebelung* of a man, Louis McHenry Howe personified many traits which have drawn criticism to the corporate public relations adviser. Even his sympathetic biographer noted his "immense confidence in his ability to trick the ordinary man." "If you say a thing is so often enough," Howe advised, "it stands a good chance to become a fact."[24] An important part of his job was to cultivate the press, especially in rural areas, and this he did through various manipulations and by encouraging his boss to correspond with rural editors. His ploys educated his patron to the nether side of opinion-molding. Roosevelt made equally effective choices for Howe's colleagues and successors.

Following his tenure as Assistant Secretary of the Navy, where he sharpened his skills at dealing with people from a different social world,[25] Roosevelt suffered reverses in both politics and health which threatened to retire him from public life. But, displaying the self-possession which was one of his hallmarks, he did not abandon his ambitions. He remained high in Democratic councils and developed an extensive correspondence within the party. Always he urged his colleagues to unite, think out a sensible platform, and construct a publicity machine. He secured plenty of personal publicity as well, despite the sad state of his party and his physical handicap. After becoming governor of New York, he organized a press bureau to supply information to partisan journals, and Howe revamped his personal clipping service which now provided a nation-wide summary of editorial opinion.

Some people who knew Roosevelt as President were so amazed by his knowledge of public opinion that they thought he had a "sixth sense" which enabled him to divine it. Actually, as James MacGregor Burns has said, his mastery came not from the occult but from hard work: a careful examination of the daily press, a widespread network of correspondents,[26] a sensitive sounding out of those with whom he spoke about general conditions as well as specific requests, and a shrewd appraisal of the reactions of the crowds he addressed. Perhaps his most important tool was the public opinion poll. From his first term, when the science, or perhaps art, of polling was still in its infancy, he commissioned his own surveys and received information on others. In the midst of World War II, he even asked Hadley Cantril, a pioneer in the field, to conduct a poll in Vichy-controlled North Africa to determine whether the Americans or British would meet with greater opposition from the populace in an invasion.

Roosevelt was the first President to appoint an official press secretary. He had a talented staff of speech writers who were able to tailor messages gracefully to fit his style. He had a warm handshake and an engaging smile, and he was an accomplished public speaker. But most impressive was his mastery of that instrument which had rather puzzled business publicists in the 1920s—the radio. "Perhaps never before had there been so happy a coincidence of personal talent with technological opportunity" as in the marriage of Roosevelt and radio. He managed to project himself as friend and father to more Americans than could ever have heard a President before the electronic age.[27]

This, then, was what the business community and the party of Martin,

Barton, and Fish were to learn. In a contest of epithets they never had a chance, and the epithets were not long in coming.

With the signing of the Securities Exchange Act of 1934, the so-called New Deal honeymoon came to an end. As recriminations flew back and forth between the administration and leading businessmen, Chester, Sloan, Du Ponts, Hook and Girdler proved to be no match in prestige, popularity, or skillfulness as phrasemakers to the President. In a radio address in September of 1934, Roosevelt declared himself unalterably opposed to "a return to that definition of Liberty under which for many years a free people were being gradually regimented into the service of the privileged few" (a remark which calls to mind Bernays's earlier boasts about the possibilities of regimenting the public mind). In 1935, he observed, "I can realize that gentlemen in well-warmed and well-stocked clubs will discourse on the expenses of government and the suffering they are going through because the government is spending money on work relief." In 1936, he spoke of "privileged princes" and "economic royalists" and denounced "entrenched greed" and those "unscrupulous money changers" who were stealing the "livery of great constitutional ideals to serve discredited special interests."[28]

These cracks hurt.[29] Assailed by a President idolized by the masses, by the Congress which often had the President's blessing, and by the regulatory agencies, businessmen tried through public relations to prevent public opinion from being added to their host of adversaries and even hoped to use it to gain the offensive.

II

The 1930s saw three organizations firmly establish themselves as public relations counselors to large corporate clients. They were Ivy Lee and T. J. Ross, Carl Byoir and Associates, and Hill and Knowlton. The first of these, which was headed exclusively by Ross after Lee's death in 1934, reaped the prestige surrounding the name of public relations' founding father. The latter two have grown into what today are among the largest firms in the business. Both have acted as schools for individual counselors who went on to set up their own "shops" or who became directors of the in-house public relations apparatuses of big business and other bureaucracies. The late John W. Hill especially appears to have played a role in public relations similar to that of Albert D. Lasker and the Lord and Thomas Agency in advertising. All three have exercised great influence on the development of public relations nationwide and worldwide. An investigation of their techniques and "philosophies" is therefore essential.

These three firms were retained by varied clients during the '30s. But one characteristic unites their most important campaigns—conflict between business and government. In the case of Lee and Ross, the conflict was directly with one of Roosevelt's cherished projects. With Byoir, it was with a state-by-state regulatory movement which obtained powerful spokesmen in the House of Representatives. And in the third instance, conflict centered around labor policies which ran contrary to those endorsed by powerful senators. All three instances illustrate the defensiveness of big business which was rendered all the more exploitable because of the decline of business repute due to the Depression.

A good example of direct conflict between corporate public relations and the President, abetted by senatorial supporters, was the propaganda battle over the "Death Sentence" provision of the Public Utilities Holding Company Bill of 1935, also known as the Wheeler-Rayburn Bill.

That a battle should occur over utilities was no accident. Because they have historically occupied an insecure position in the enterprise ideology, utilities pioneered in the development of public relations. During the twenties, their spokesmen scrutinized school textbooks for objectionable passages and staged widely noted "created events."

Their opponents in the 1930s were not new to the power debate either. From early in his governorship, Franklin Roosevelt was concerned about power policy. He grasped what James M. Burns has called the "central issue": "How much should be done by the state in both developing and distributing electricity from the people's water power, and how much by private enterprise?"[30] He failed in his bid as governor to use the state to harness the power of the St. Lawrence. He had been opposed by the Republican legislature, the "power barons," and railroad interests and had been hindered by international ramifications. The defeat only served to heighten his resolve as President to deal with this problem.

The most threatening element of the Wheeler-Rayburn Bill to holding company executives was Section 10 of Title 1. This clause empowered the Securities and Exchange Commission to compel dissolution of holding companies which could not justify their existence on the grounds of geography or economics. The administration had opted for destruction of the holding companies rather than regulation, and utility executives, recognizing the danger, were determined to edit the death sentence out of the legislation.[31]

The Edison Electric Institute, a trade organization, decided through its Committee of Public Utility Executives to hire the firm of Ivy Lee and T. J. Ross to help arouse public opinion against the bill. Lee had died the previous year, under yet another cloud of suspicion caused by his work for I. G. Farben after Hitler's accession to power, but Ross intended, in the best tradition of his former partner and mentor, "to develop facts and the best method of presenting them to various groups of people in an effort to enlist their active support in the defeat of the present bill, or enactment of a bill to fairly regulate the industry." According to Philip J. Funigiello, Ross

> attempted to create among . . . various groups what might be described as a "conspiracy" neurosis. Non-utility corporations would be persuaded that the New Deal was conspiring to destroy business and the free enterprise system. Insurance companies, for example, were to be told that their assets would be seized and used to fund the debt; banks would be included in the definition of a holding company in order to subject them to the law's "destructive measures. . . ." In sum, Ross's plan was a blueprint for a comprehensive attack on all New Deal policies, one that would appeal to such zealous defenders of "the American Way" as the Committee for the Nation and the American Liberty League.[32]

Initial results were gratifying. A survey of one thousand newspaper editorials between February 10 and April 15 revealed over three-fifths opposed to some aspect of the bill, with the percentage climbing steadily in Ross's favor. But the bill cleared the Senate Commerce Committee intact in May, and with the blessing of the Committee of Public Utility Executives, Ross collaborated with N. W. Ayer & Son to appeal more directly to the populace. The new plan, budgeted for almost $300,000, included a series of fifteen-minute radio talks, extensive newspaper advertising, a write-in campaign, and a whispering campaign designed to call into question Roosevelt's health, mental as well as physical.[33]

Indications of public displeasure at the death sentence flooded Washington and, added to frantic lobbying, took their toll. In a test vote of July 1, the House rejected Section 10 of Title 1, to the great glee of the directors of the utility effort. Roosevelt had placed all his seemingly invincible prestige behind the measure. Now, for the first time since taking office, he seemed to have been soundly whipped. But he had one more card up his sleeve, and it proved to be the trump.[34]

Soon after the House vote, both the House and Senate empowered special committees to examine all the lobbying conducted for and against the bill. The House inquiry sputtered, but the Senate's, directed by Hugo Black, paved the way for final passage.

The primary purpose of the congressional inquiry prior to the New Deal had been to gather information to assist in the drawing up of legislation or to supervise the executive branch. "But during the thirties," Jerold S. Auerbach has written, "congressional committees assumed still another role: influencing public opinion to mobilize support for administration programs."[35] Since these programs often narrowed the sphere of decision making by the executives of private corporations, the investigations which supported them tried to win public support by portraying management as irresponsible. This was Black's assignment.

When Burnham Carter, one of Ross's assistants, informed the committee that he was a public relations counsel, Black asked, "You mean you are attorneys?" Despite his professed inexperience in such matters, Black played an important part in undermining Ross's objectives. After the House-Senate conference deadlocked over the death sentence issue, the administration unleashed Black, who went after the utilities like a prosecuting attorney. He laid bare the lengths to which they had gone to influence opinion: the bogus telegrams signed with names picked randomly from city directories; the shipping into Washington of influential persons; the (suspected) attempts at bribery; and, perhaps most damaging, the hundreds of thousands of dollars invested in the project, which monies were furnished by operating companies.[36]

Late in August of 1935, Roosevelt signed the Public Utilities Holding Companies Act, including the death sentence, into law. His triumph was facilitated by Black's exposé. "There is little doubt," concluded Funigiello, "that the sensational revelations of the lobby investigation, coinciding as they did with the congressional debates and the conference committee meetings, helped to swing public opinion against the industry. The administration encouraged Black in his investigation because it was confident that, in the long run, opinion would turn in its favor."[37] All the maneuvers of the chosen successor of the famed master of opinion molding, backed by all the utility money, were rendered nugatory through the simple expedient of publicizing them. This lesson was not lost on critics. From Ray Stannard Baker on, many have argued that publicity about public relations would destroy its power. This has not, however, invariably proven to be the case.

Unlike the Wheeler-Rayburn measure, chain-store taxation proposals did not arrest the President's personal attention. Nonetheless, such proposals were enacted by state legislatures and championed by some congressmen during the Depression. In order to fight them, the Great Atlantic and Pacific Tea Company resorted to public relations, rather than to more traditional lobbying techniques. The idea was to influence the legislation not through cloakroom whispers but by demonstrating a public sentiment favorable to the chains which it would cost politicians votes to violate. The firm awarded A&P's prestigious account was Carl Byoir & Associates. Its campaign deserves detailed examination for it illustrates some interesting implications of the way big-budget opinion creation tried to influence legislation.

Carl Byoir was a name prominently associated with Ivy Lee in 1933 and 1934. The firms of both men were investigated by the House Un-American Activities Committee because of their connections with German propaganda in the United States. In the case of Carl Byoir & Associates, the account in question was that of the German Tourist Information Office, which was solicited by an executive, Carl Dickey, apparently without Byoir's knowledge in October of 1933. The account was terminated about a year later, following appearances of Byoir, Dickey, and the German propagandist George Sylvester Viereck, who was on the Byoir payroll, before HUAC. Dickey actually did circulate Nazi propaganda, but not pursuant to any contract of the Byoir organization. Although Byoir himself was exonerated by Morris Dickstein in 1935, critics through the years have noted "a certain piquancy" in the fact that Byoir, a Jew, should have been employed by the Nazis and connected with Viereck.[38]

Carl Byoir (pronounced "buyer") was born in Des Moines in 1888. At the age of seventeen, he was city editor of the Waterloo, Iowa, *Times Tribune*. In 1906, he entered the University of Iowa with only $30 in his pocket and graduated four years later worth $6,500. Six years after graduation, he received a law degree from Columbia and went to work for the Hearst magazines. He was an important member of the Committee on Public Information, and following the war he became involved in international propaganda. He acted as a liaison between Czechoslovak Americans and their relatives in Europe and formed the Lithuanian National Council, the aim of which was to secure American recognition of the Baltic state. He also speculated in commodity shipments to the two countries, making money until the collapse of the foreign exchange markets drove him deeply into debt.[39]

Byoir avoided bankruptcy by promoting Nuxated Iron, "a high-priced iron tonic of low cost and little value"; Seedol, a bowel tonic; Kepmalt, a weight builder; Viaderma, a rub-on reducing compound; and finally Blondex, a hair dye. Having paid his debts, he moved to Havana in 1928, where he edited two English-language newspapers. Two years later, he persuaded the Cuban dictator, Gerardo Machado, to give him a $60,000-a-year contract to increase American tourism to the island. He opened an office in New York and assembled a staff which showed steadfast loyalty over the years. He met important industrialists during his Havana work, but his primary business until 1936 was as a promoter of tourism around the world.[40]

Byoir praised Ivy Lee's methods and regarded him as the greatest practitioner of his craft, but he believed that Lee did not go far enough.

Mr. Lee never at any time in his life made any effort to set up an affirmative organization, I think I would call it, to create or disseminate news to reach 140,000,000 people because his clients were of the type, the great railroads, Standard Oil, Mr. Rockefeller personally, that anything they said became news. It was not necessary to create a machinery for the transmission of that news because the great press associations, the great newspapers were only too anxious to get it.

So our concept was that you must set up a great affirmative organization, that you must have specialists in every field, that you must approach the newspapers not just with newspapermen but with sports writers as good as their own, with financial writers as good as their own, with fashion writers as good as their own and with men who would give the material in the proper spacing, not over-emphasizing it and trying to get a column when it deserved only an inch. It would be given to the different editors not as a mimeographed statement but in reply to a concept of that particular editor's concept of what news and news value were.[41]

In 1932, Byoir drew up a set of general rules to govern the way he wanted his firm to conduct its business. Of these, two are of particular interest: the firm would give special attention to news-creating events and would use what was sometimes referred to as the third-person approach. ("It is not," explained Byoir, "what a client says about himself that scores, but what another person, whom the public regards as an outstanding authority, says about him, that carries weight.") In 1937, Byoir initiated his campaign for A&P in which he would vigorously apply his aphorisms; controversy over his role would linger to 1954.[42]

Early in the '30s, the brothers Hartford (John was president of A&P and George, chairman of the board) let it be known that if the American people did not appreciate their services and wanted to tax them out of existence, they would not lift a finger to protest. The company illustrated the sincerity of its take-it-or-leave-it attitude in its response to labor difficulties. When the Teamsters struck its Cleveland stores, it simply closed up shop, announcing dourly through the local press that conditions no longer favored its presence.[43]

As the anti-chain-store movement gained momentum, however, the Hartfords began to see things differently. When they made their original declaration of unwillingness to fight discriminatory laws, only two states had such legislation on the books. By the fall of 1938, that number had increased to twenty-two, and the federal government, in the person of Representative Wright Patman, was readying itself for further assaults.

The previous year, the Hartfords had hired Byoir to fight legislation proposed in New York State which would have cost the chain $2 million.[44] Byoir made "no appeal for the chain stores as such." Instead, his firm explained to various groups and organizations what they would be losing if the state raised chain-store taxes and why they should protest to the legislature. "We went out to farmer organizations, cooperatives, and labor organizations, and civic groups, women's clubs, consumer organization . . . and preached the distributive method of the chain store. . . ." Traditional methods of influencing legislation were eschewed. "We never approached any member of the legislature," explained Byoir, "nor employed anyone to lobby nor any high-paid lawyers." Andrew Hacker has speculated that public relations, based on the theory that lawmakers respond to public opinion with at least as much sensitivity as they do to personally applied pressure, has become an important supplement to lobbying. "The intimate contacts of the capital cloakroom are bolstered by the practiced techniques of Madison Avenue." In this instance, the Byoir plan was so effective that its author has been credited with the bill's death in committee.[45]

Pleased with Byoir's activities in New York, the Hartfords loosed him upon the nation. "On the A&P account," recalled a Byoir executive,

> we had bills pending in 44 legislatures [in 1938] . . . to tax the chain stores. We went out and made common cause with those population groups that had a stake in the A&P's low cost operation: the potato growers, the peach growers, the shippers, the real estate men, the customers, the banks, labor unions, women's groups, every one that we could identify.

When Byoir researched the problems he confronted through nation-wide public opinion polls, he uncovered a paradox. Most people liked to shop the chains because of their low prices and yet favored anti-chain legislation and taxation. The American shopper wanted to get the best value for the money, but he or she was still nostalgic for the friendly neighborhood grocer. Byoir attacked this problem by publicizing the re-sults of discrimination against chains.[46]

His campaign cleverly combined openness with behind-the-scenes maneuvers. It commenced with a "Statement of Public Policy" which Byoir wrote for A&P and which was aimed specifically at Patman. The lengthy, double-column message was signed by George and John Hartford, and although the text was naturally biased in favor of their case, it was soberly presented and argued. It was not for themselves, explained the Hartfords, that the company had determined to fight the Patman measure, for they had more money than they knew what to do with and most of their income went to the government anyway. It was rather for the employee, who had given so many years of faithful ser-vice; for the consumer, whose standard of living was enhanced by A&P's low prices; and for the farmer, who benefited from the chain's low-cost distribution of his products.

> As we have said [ran the advertisement's noteworthy conclusion], Mr. Pat-man is an able politician, an able lobbyist and an able propagandist. In that field he is an expert. We are experts only in the grocery business. We believe the chain stores have a right to present their case to the American people. We will not go into politics, nor will we establish a lobby in Washington for the purpose of attempting to influence the vote of any

member of Congress. . . . Since the task we have set before us is one involving the widest dissemination of complete information to all of the American people, and since this is a profession in which we are not expert, we have engaged Carl Byoir & Associates, public relations counsel, to do this work. We realize that our views are seldom news. We know, therefore, that we must be prepared to spend a substantial sum of money in telling our story to all of the American people. We declare now that this money will be spent in the dissemination of information through paid advertising and every medium available to us, and in cooperating in the work or formation of study groups among consumers, farmers and workers, which provide open forums for a discussion of all measures affecting the cost of living.[47]

This statement won approval because at last counselor and client were willing to acknowledge their relationship. It was run in 2,000 newspapers across the country at a cost of $280,000 and was purposely held to a fifteen-inch, five-column space so as not to appear flamboyant.[48]

Byoir's strategy was to dramatize the already high level of chain-store taxation through third-party organizations and created events. These were not directly linked to him or A&P and, seemingly independent, could avoid being tarred with the brush of special pleading. Here was a classic public relations maneuver. A wider aim with which no one would argue—lowering taxes—was advocated by ostensibly independent groups who linked this aim to the preservation of the chain-store industry, against whose efficient operations costly taxes were being proposed.

The Byoir firm set up a subsidiary, Business Organization, Inc., which, with funding from A&P, created or supported third-party organizations all over the country. In New Jersey, it was the Emergency Consumers Tax Committee, which had representatives in over a hundred communities and helped defeat a proposed tax on supermarkets. In New York, the Consumers Tax Committee, labeled by its leader the "Minute Women of the Recession," collected and publicized information on hidden taxes. The Empire State was also the site of one of the cleverest stunts of the campaign. The president of the student union of Rensselaer Polytechnic Institute in Troy announced the formation of "Tax-CENTinels" in the spring of 1938 to fight taxes. Inspired by a Byoir aide, students managed to collect 800,000 pennies, one-half the city's normal supply, in eight hours and proceeded to pay one-quarter of the cost of each purchase they made with pennies to dramatize their complaint that nearly that percentage of the price of every article went to hidden taxes.[49]

The House of Representatives held hearings on the Patman legislation in April and May of 1940. One hundred eighty-nine witnesses, naturally predisposed against the legislation but also mightily encouraged by Byoir and with their travel expenses funded by A&P to the amount of

$51,505.68, journeyed to the capital to testify.[50] Few testified in favor, and Patman's plans died in committee. A&P, under Byoir's direction, had defeated the threat for a price of about $500,000.

But the government was not finished with the chain. On November 25, 1942, a federal grand jury in Dallas returned an indictment against A&P of New York, twelve subsidiaries, Carl Byoir & Associates, and Business Organization, Inc., for violations of the antitrust laws. After the indictment was quashed by a Dallas district court judge who called it "inflammatory," the government succeeded in having the charges tried before District Judge Lindley in Danville, Illinois. The defendants were found guilty. A&P was fined $175,000 and Byoir $5,000, and both immediately appealed to the seventh circuit.[51]

Their conviction was upheld, and the court's opinion, written by Judge Sherman Minton (later appointed to the Supreme Court by President Truman), was a revealing documentation of the relationship between Byoir and the company. As he followed the "devious manipulations" of the chain, Judge Minton concluded that it was not through economies of scale that A&P undersold the competition but rather through such abuses as blacklists, boycotts, and threats. A case in point was the Altantic Commission Company (ACCO), a wholly owned subsidiary which bought fruits, vegetables, and produce. ACCO bludgeoned supplier and competitor alike to build a two-price system, through which the chain obtained the highest-quality merchandise at the lowest prices, with the remainder being passed off to the independent grocer at higher prices.[52]

Through all this, Byoir was put in the embarrassing position of having to dissociate himself from his client. Even if A&P had comspired to violate the law, a contention he did not grant, Byoir claimed that he was unaware of it. Public relations men usually try to take all the credit they can get for their client's policy decisions, but here the reverse was the case.[53] Judge Minton's decision may have cost Byoir some money, but it stood as impressive testimony to the influence of this midwestern Jew in the deliberations of a corporation managed and almost completely owned by an eastern Roman Catholic family.

The evidence shows that Byoir was thoroughly familiar with the policies of A&P. Byoir is no babe in the woods, likely not to understand, but under the contract of his corporate puppet with A&P it was his duty to counsel, guide, and direct the policy making officers of his client. This obligation he faithfully performed even to the extent of initiating policy and personally participating in its adoption and implementation.

An illustration was Byoir's assistance in setting up a short-lived super co-op, which had as its aim a more complete control of the shippers by ACCO. He helped create this new structure despite the doubts of John Hartford. On the basis of this incident and others, Minton concluded that Byoir "could not have been ignorant of the thread of this conspiracy, which runs through the whole fabric of A&P's dealings. . ."[54]

A&P's problems were far from over. Seven and one-half months after the Minton decision, the federal government launched a civil suit to break up the chain. Byoir once again turned to newspaper advertisements. He placed a series of four full-page notices in 2,000 papers, at a cost estimated to have been $5 million. The government dropped the suit in 1954, without ever going to trial. Byoir's massive good-will campaign probably did have some effect; according to a Gallup poll, the public favored A&P's side of the case three to one.[55]

Carl Byoir & Associates represented one extreme among independent public relations firms. Though conservative of demeanor and habit, Byoir developed many gambits to capture attention and influence opinion. As his list of clients shows, he could attach himself to a variety of causes, publicizing dictator-run Cuba and Nazi Germany and also, with President Roosevelt's blessing, the Warm Springs Foundation.[56] The feature of his relationship to A&P which journalists, judges, and scholars found most distasteful was the false front or third-party technique, disguising the sources of support for organizations expressing his client's views. This approach was familiar from the time of Edward L. Bernays's Broadway press-agentry days before World War I, and it has become a permanent public relations weapon. Byoir used it effectively in later accounts. On the other hand, he was also willing to announce to the world in newspaper advertisements his connection with A&P. This shows how publicity can be used in tandem with secrecy. The original "Statement of Public Policy" scored debating points by implying that persuasion would be forthright. Byoir touted his relationship with A&P; he did not wait for some congressional committee to discover it. What he did not put in the advertisement was his method of persuasion. This consisted of creating the impression of spontaneous grass-roots sentiment where none existed until his third-party groups "crystallized" it.

Unlike Byoir, the founder of the other leading agency of the 1930s was an ideologue whose clients were usually major industrial firms or trade associations. Less daring than Byoir, John W. Hill established a reputation for right-thinking, integrity, and effectiveness which has nurtured his firm through the years. Beginning in 1909, following some college education, he meandered in and out of journalistic jobs in three midwestern states. He spent more than ten years working for a steel trade paper and learned enough economics to publish a syndicated column and supervise a newsletter on business conditions. In all, he gained sixteen years' experience as a newspaper reporter, business editor, and publisher. During this apprenticeship, especially in connection with his work for the steel trade paper, one of Hill's "jobs was to handle news about industrial companies, most of whose officials had no use for newspaper reporters and no desire to give out any news. Those who had news to report did it with incredible ineptitude." His interest was stimulated by Ivy Lee's *Publicity*. He was impressed by the concept that news management should not be merely press agentry but should actually be intimately interwoven with the policy making of a corporation, the idea that "[p]ublic relationships . . . involved not simply 'saying' but '*doing*'—not just talk, but action." In April of 1927, he decided to pursue "my real ambition to publicize industry." Through connections he had made as a journalist and with the help of a stroke of good luck, he secured two clients in the Cleveland area: a bank, which retained him at $500 a month, and a steel company. "I was in business and it was the greatest thrill of my life. I rented a small office and had some cards printed that said I was in the business of 'corporate publicity.'"[57]

For six and one-half years, Hill worked in Cleveland for industrial and financial clients. Despite the Depression, his business flourished until the bank failures of early 1933. When the Union Trust Company, Cleveland's largest bank, closed its doors that year, Hill went into partnership with Don Knowlton, one of the bank's advertising officers. In mid-November, Tom Girdler put Hill in touch with Walter Tower of the American Iron and Steel Institute in New York City. Hill was eager to establish himself in Gotham because, even in the depth of the Depression, he believed that public relations had an "obvious future" which would unfold primarily in New York, the nation's corporate headquarters. The Institute retained Hill's firm; the two have been associated ever since, and this connection has proved to be his "springboard" from provincial public relations to grandeur.[58]

Hill is the leading representative of a school of counselors committed to economic conservatism and business leadership. Unlike Bernays, who could work for a union with the same aplomb with which he would work for a corporation, or Byoir, who seemed to be willing to work for anyone, Hill was a genuine ideologue of the right. It is difficult indeed to imagine him advising a union or the Democratic party.

> The story [of American industry] is so big [he once wrote], so amazing, and so stirring, and is possessed of so many ramifications that it can never be

fully told nor can it ever grow boring. It must deal with facts only and with truth only.

Because industry must be truthful, it does not follow that it must be dull. There are rich mines of drama, of color, of personality and of human interest in every industry. They need only to be explored to yield shining nuggets.

Basically, the job is to let the public know as much about industry's achievements as it now knows about its faults and defects. The job is to tell the story of its services to mankind, of its ideas, of its aims, purposes, and activities. Under an enlightened public relations policy, nothing that is of interest to the public is hidden from the public.[59]

For a price, less ideological public relations men could crank out similar paragraphs. But Hill's client list and political activities showed how sincerely he held these views.

Hill's link to the Steel Institute and the industry was Republic's president and chairman of the board, Thomas Mercer Girdler. Girdler was cut from the mold of the old-time steel masters who held sway in the industry before the rise of the financiers and the managerial capitalism of Judge Gary. His labor relations policy was uncompromising. Girdler worked for Jones & Laughlin from 1920 to 1928, during which time he rose from manager of the Aliquippa works to president. Aliquippa, under his suzerainty, had "the most notorious anti-union reputation of any town in America." The company dominated every aspect of the residents' lives; Girdler himself called it "a benevolent dictatorship." John L. Lewis described him as "a heavily armed monomaniac, with murderous tendencies, who has gone berserk," and Irving Bernstein concluded that his "personality, if unlovable, was at least definite."[60]

Girdler and other leaders of the Institute turned to public relations following their efforts to draw up an NRA code in the summer of 1933. They had experienced difficulties "fending off the press" that hectic season and were ready to rationalize their press relations. Hill was the natural choice for the job. A Republican of the Robert A. Taft persuasion, he greatly admired steel's "rugged individualists" and fervently believed that America's salvation lay in keeping key economic decisions in their hands rather than having them transferred to politicians. The fact that he was retained by both Republic (until 1948 when the company set up its own department) and the Institute at a fee of $22,500 a year was testimony to the steelmen's concern about their difficulty in presenting their views to the public.[61]

Hill felt that "if I were to be of any value to the steel industry, it was important that I have the confidence of the policy makers." As a result, he attended every meeting of the board of the AISI for twenty years following 1933 and did make policy suggestions. On the other hand, he has observed that "some may have an exaggerated idea of the influence that counselors have in shaping corporate policy" because although they are often consulted and inform executives of popular sentiment, it is the client himself who makes the final decisions.[62]

As early as the end of 1933, Hill made a suggestion concerning labor relations which, while not adopted, was seriously discussed. He believed that unionization was inevitable unless employers attempted a dramatic move. They had, by their acceptance of employee representation plans, accepted the concept of collective bargaining. Therefore, an employer-sponsored confederation of company unions might answer the threat of the militants. "At least the officers of such a confederation would have been authentic steelworkers steeped in the steel tradition. This might be preferable," Hill recalled arguing, "to a union created by outside professional agitators and organizers."[63]

In order to make clear its opposition to the CIO, the Institute, in consultation with Hill and others, published a full-page advertisement in 375 newspapers around the country at a cost of $114,365 on July 1, 1936. Addressed to "the public and the employees in the steel industry," the advertisement complained that "persons and organizations not connected with the industry have taken charge of the campaign [of unionization]." "The true objective of the drive was the closed shop." The industry believed in collective bargaining and already had plans under which it functioned successfully. The union drive would undermine these arrangements and "with its accompanying agitation for industrial strife" would threaten the recovery of the industry from the Depression. "The Steel Industry," the advertisement concluded, "will use its resources to the best of its ability to protect its employees and their families from intimidation, coercion, and violence and to aid them in maintaining collective bargaining free from interference from any source."[64]

One of these resources was the anti-union propaganda which Hill and Knowlton developed and distributed, especially in the heavily industrialized and strike-torn Great Lakes states. In a letter to the secretary of the Greater Akron Association, Hill explained that there were five ways to disseminate information: speeches, news stories and editorials, paid advertising, radio, and booklets and circulars. Hill thought all should be used. The most important tool was "newspaper publicity—that is, news stories and editorials in the newspapers. To do this [*sic*] we should enlist the active support and cooperation of the editors and we would also have to produce events or circumstances which would give rise to news." Talks and speeches were also "particularly valuable" because of their dramatic nature and because they made news. Like the government publicity men, Hill was not impressed with the propaganda possibilities of radio. It was too easy to use it "so extensively as to destroy its own effectiveness."[65]

This aversion to radio was not shared by some in-house counselors. In 1935, Ford launched the "Ford Sunday Evening Hour," during which William J. Cameron delivered homilies approved by the elder Ford, and Du Pont began its sponsorship of "Cavalcade of America" in order to convince the American intelligentsia that it deserved better than the "Merchants of Death" stigma of the Nye Committee hearings.[66] Nor was it shared by Roosevelt or foreign propagandists. It was extraordinarily short-sighted for Hill and other independent counselors to surrender voluntarily such a potent weapon. The reason may lie in the one great advantage of newsprint to the airwaves: newspapers turn out a tangible record, while the spoken word is ephemeral. (Note that Hill liked speeches not because they convinced the immediate audience, but because they were reported as news.) In a field whose effectiveness must always be in doubt, a stack of clippings reassured a client that his money was not being wasted in a way that the report of a couple of words on the radio could not. The two companies which pioneered in image making through radio had long-range goals. The need for tangible proof of immediate impact was therefore diminished.

Hill claimed great skill in getting newspaper publicity, and it was his firm's activities in this regard which brought it to the attention of the LaFollette Civil Liberties Committee. In the Wheeler-Rayburn and Chain Store cases, business publicists initiated the fight for public opinion and then had to cope with the counterattack from President, Congress, and/or the courts. In this instance, a congressional committee struck first, reacting to propaganda which had been aimed not at influencing legislation or administration policy but at undercutting the CIO. As often happens, the methods of persuasion became a bigger issue than the substance of the message. Senator LaFollette pointedly asked Hill on July 21, 1938, in reference to the AISI advertisement of two years before, whether it was not "your experience that the wide distribution of advertising helps to improve the relations of a particular industry . . . with the press?" Hill rejected the suggestion that the advertisement had been placed to curry favor rather than simply to express a point of view. Continuous advertising over a lengthy period of time might have an advantageous effect in the editorial columns, "but," Hill told LaFollette, "I certainly don't think that, as the term is, a 'one shot' insertion would have any effect of that kind."[67] But on this point the Committee was not finished.

A few days before he was called to testify, Hill encountered one of

LaFollette's staff in a Washington restaurant, who told him that the Committee had found a "bombshell" in his files which would soon be detonated. After exploring some questionable aspects of the firm's relationship with conservative publicist George Sokolsky and the National Association of Manufacturers, the Committee called Edgar S. Browerfind, who had worked on the Republic account in Birmingham. Browerfind had written a memorandum concerning newspaper treatment of Republic in mid-1937 in which he suggested that "some pressure might also be exerted through the advertisers in Birmingham." It could not have shocked the cognoscenti of 1938 to learn that a public relations agency would employ pressure tactics to influence a newspaper. However, suspicion of such activity is one thing and exposure quite another. To Hill, who had long emphasized the importance of high standards of integrity in order to establish credibility with the media, the publication of the memorandum must have been especially disconcerting. His resentment of the LaFollette Committee never abated. In his autobiography, published in 1963, he called it "totally unfair" and observed that it handled its hearing "much like a Soviet purge trial, with no attempt at fairness or even decency." Referring to the Browerfind note, he complained that LaFollette pounced on this "juicy morsel and . . . proceeded to make the most of it. He read the brief document into the record just before adjournment of the afternoon session and handed out mimeograph copies to the press."[68] Perhaps Hill felt some professional jealousy at being beaten at his own game. LaFollette proved to be as skillful at publicizing his point of view as Senator Black had been.

Hill also objected that "we were given no chance at all to clarify the memorandum or refute his interpretation of it." Browerfind was, in fact, given a chance to explain it and also to explain why leading advertisers did pay a call on an Alabama publisher. He claimed that the advertisers were not acting at his suggestion nor was their visit to the publisher, Victor Hanson, an attempt at intimidation. Browerfind's "clarifications" were as follows:

> LaFollette: Suppose you were the editor or the publisher of a newspaper, and a group of men representing the economic power and the advertising accounts of the class and kind and weight of the committee that called on Mr. Hanson, came into your office, would the fact that they were men representing a lot of economic power and potential advertising come into your mind while they were interviewing you or not?
>
> Browerfind: I would say that I hope that I would have the strength of character enough to do what every newspaper editor that I know has done. [Laughter.]
>
> LaFollette: Order, please.

BROWERFIND: And that is to disregard entirely their position in the community. He is there to give the news as he sees it. . . . Why it [Browerfind's suggestion to apply advertiser pressure] was made, I do not know at this time, because it is entirely in conflict with any policy of Republic Steel Corporation or of Hill and Knowlton. We have never found that it is a wise thing to do or ethical thing to do.

LAFOLLETTE: Can you explain why you suggested it in this particular case?

BROWERFIND: I wish I could give a reasonable explanation beyond the fact that it was a sort of mental aberration.

Hill too declared that the memo was contrary to company policy, yet his biographer found no evidence that Browerfind was ever punished for it.[69] The last laugh, however, was Hill's. The LaFollette revelation failed to put him out of business, as some Civil Liberties staff members predicted it would. Instead, Hill and Knowlton flourished. In 1960, two polls conducted by *Printers' Ink*, one among newspaper editors and the other among public relations agencies, both ranked Hill and Knowlton the number one organization in the field. A Gallagher report survey of 344 public relations directors in 1963 also ranked Hill and Knowlton first with 23 percent of the votes, more than twice as many as the firm placing second. In 1966, Hill and Knowlton employed 250 men and women in fourteen offices worldwide and serviced clients whose annual gross sales were estimated to be $1 billion.[70]

III

In the 1930s public relations agencies often found themselves battling the government in order to prevent erosion of private management's prerogatives. In pursuing this goal, they used all media, sometimes making forthright declarations through advertising and sometimes concealing their activities behind false fronts. The firms played rough, coercing newspapers into adopting views favorable to their clients and spreading false and damaging rumors about opponents. They saw the importance of understanding public opinion and thus commissioned polls. Their employees were almost always ex-journalists, but their executives did display some awareness of academic sociology and psychology. They believed that changing public opinion was difficult but not impossible if group leaders could be reached and persuaded. Top counselors did have policy influence, but they sometimes became as committed to their client's original point of view as the client himself, thus making change difficult. Interestingly, being caught red-handed in activities which they themselves condemned, such as browbeating editors, spreading false rumors, or encouraging activities which violated the antitrust laws, did not seem to damage them professionally. Edward L. Bernays once noted that censure by journalists actually attracted clients, who reasoned that any such dangerous menace must at least be effective.[71]

We also see that one of the best sales jobs the public relations firms did was on their clients. They scored only sporadic successes, and in these instances it was difficult to determine if victory was won through an actual change in public opinion, through persuading vote-conscious politicians that public opinion favored their client, through good fortune in court, or through strategic lobbying. Business fell into ill repute in the thirties not because of corporate bad manners or insensitivity to public opinion, though both exacerbated the situation, but rather because of economic catastrophe. Anti-union industries succumbed to the CIO in spite of the promises of public relations men that such unpleasantness could be avoided through the well-funded manipulation of public opinion. And business regained some of its lost luster during World War II not because of public relations but because of the necessities of wartime unity and the proven accomplishments of the arsenal of democracy.

On the other hand, it is worth speculating about what might have happened without public relations. As the NAM speaker asked, what would have happened without the development of "industrial consciousness"? We will never know. It is at least arguable that management's prerogatives would have been yet further eroded.

Not all counselors engaged in imbroglios over public policy. Some, like Bernays and Harry A. Bruno, continued to use public relations primarily as an alternative to advertising to increase sales rather than sell a philosophy.[72] Others, struggling to survive, presented themselves as all things to all potential clients.[73] And slowly, the number of corporations increased which were changing the name of their publicity department to public relations and upgrading the prestige and salary of the in-house counselor.

Fighting the government and the unions was, however, the most important task during the Depression. Bruce Barton's complaint that industry was unaware that government was contesting it for public support was, in the light of the Liberty League and the NAM, unwarranted when he made it in 1936. It would have been even less justified four years later, for by then three firms—Lee and Ross, Byoir, and Hill and Knowlton—had been blooded in the battle for public opinion. Unlike the many ephemeral PR "shops" which died with their founders, these became established institutions. Together with trade associations and in-house counselors, they provided management with a formidable phalanx of professional opinion molders, albeit not usually as effective as they promised. Government was not silent in this battle. Though legally proscribed, public relations in administrative agencies burgeoned, and the opinion leadership of the President and congressional investigating committees proved a match for business. Firms developed specifically to serve politicians,[74] and corporate counselors (and advertising agents) sometimes worked for politicians when called upon at election time. Unions had press liaisons as well, but no firms with the facilities and experience of these three developed to serve them. And organized labor's need for opinion management was growing, especially after the seizure of private property during the sit-down strikes caused middle-class opinion to recoil at union power.

NOTES

1. *Economic Forum*, Winter 1936, insert following p. 324.

2. "Plain Talk to Business Men About Their Press and Radio Contacts," *Sales Management*, July 15, 1943, p. 46.

3. Brown, "Challenge," p. 169.

4. Barton J. Bernstein, "The New Deal," in Bernstein, ed., *Towards a New Past* (New York, 1969), p. 264.

5. Recent books by corporate public relations advisers have emphasized the role of government. See Golden, *Consent,* and Harold Brayman, *Corporate Management in a World of Politics* (New York, 1967).

6. The decline of welfare capitalism was probably in part a result of this reassessment. For other reasons for the demise of welfarism, see Brandes, *Welfare,* pp. 135–148.

7. James L. McCamy, *Government Publicity* (Chicago, 1939), p. 15.

8. At times, agency publicity intended to be strictly educational and unbiased could be quite antibusiness, as was sometimes the case with the Food and Drug Administration. Egbert S. Wengert, "The Public Relations of Selected Federal Administrative Agencies" (unpublished Ph.D. thesis, University of Wisconsin, 1939), pp. 95–96. For a stimulating discussion of the problems caused for public communication by the dual nature of government "as the community's business and . . . as the persons in power," see Zechariah Chaffee, Jr., *Government and Mass Communications*, Vol. II (Chicago, 1947), pp. 723–793.

9. T. Swann Harding, "Genesis of One 'Government Propaganda Mill,'" *Public Opinion Quarterly* 11, No. 2 (Summer 1947), pp. 227–235; Harwood Childs, *Public Opinion: Nature, Formation, and Role* (Princeton, N.J., 1965), p. 295.

10. Felice M. Goodman, "Origins of a Continuing Conflict" (unpublished M.A. thesis, University of Wisconsin, 1967), pp. 81–107, 134.

11. Harry Donald Knight, "Press Criticism of the Public Relations Function in Government" (unpublished master's thesis, University of Wisconsin, 1953), pp. 8–9, 56–57; "Is Uncle Sam Our Biggest Press Agent?" *Printers' Ink*, February 24, 1927, pp. 165–168.

12. "Official Publicity under the New Deal," *Annals* of the American Academy of Political and Social Science, Vol. 179 (May 1935), pp. 167–175; Elisha Hanson, "Official Propaganda and the New Deal," *Annals* of the American Academy of Political and Social Science, Vol. 179 (May 1935), pp. 176–186.

13. Knight, "Press Criticism," pp. 132–135; Weinberg, "Wartime Propaganda," pp. 122–137. For evaluations of Roosevelt as an administrator, see Schlesinger, *New Deal*, pp. 533–552.

14. Weinberg, "Wartime Propaganda," pp. 122, 134; McCamy, *Government Publicity*, pp. 5, 211.

15. Ibid., pp. 173, 161, 147, 149–150; Weinberg, "Wartime Propaganda," p. 125.

16. McCamy, *Government Publicity*, pp. 159, 148–149.

17. J. J. Dickinson, "Theodore Roosevelt: Press Agent," *Harper's Weekly*, September 28, 1907, pp. 1410, 1428; Scott M. Cutlip and Allen H. Center, *Effective Public Relations* (Englewood Cliffs, N.J., 1971), pp. 80–82.

18. Finley Peter Dunne, *Mr. Dooley's Philosophy* (New York, 1906), pp. 13–18.

19. The other three were Bernays, Jack Dempsey, and Upton Sinclair. Sinclair Lewis, *It Can't Happen Here* (Garden City, N.Y., 1935), p. 88.

20. Lloyd, *Introvert*, pp. xii, 3–17, 44.

21. Ibid., pp. 21–28, 76, 59. Edward L. Bernays worked for Hoover's President's Emergency Council on Employment during the Depression, and there is a melancholy postscript to Hoover's experimentation with public relations in the Bernays papers. In 1961, Bernays sent the former President a copy of a book entitled *Your Future in Public Relations*, which Bernays had just written. Hoover expressed his gratitude for the gift and observed, "I have read it with interest and detachment—as obviously its guidance is too late for me to be saved." Hoover to Bernays, November 10, 1961, Bernays papers.

22. James MacGregor Burns, *Roosevelt: The Lion and the Fox* (New York, 1956), p. 33.

23. Rollins, *Howe*, p. 22.

24. Ibid., p. 14.

25. Burns, *Lion*, pp. 52–53, 95; Rollins, *Howe*, pp. 205, 259–260.

26. Burns, *Lion*, p. 284; *Roosevelt: The Soldier of Freedom* (New York, 1970), p. 290.

27. Daniel J. Boorstin, *America and the Image of Europe* (New York, 1960), pp. 97–117; Boorstin, *Democratic*, pp. 474–476.

28. Brown, "Challenge," p. 1 and *passim;* George Wolfskill, *The Revolt of the Conservatives* (Boston, 1962), p. 127.

29. An example of the businessman's reactions to these remarks was the suggestions of F. N. Bard, President of the Barco Manufacturing Company and member of the Board of Directors of the NAM to the Association's public relations staff in 1937. He said it "should use certain stock phrases which, by their constant repetition, become fixed in the minds of the people as facts. . . . Some of our crazy politicians could be referred to as 'economic morons.' . . . 'Political exploiters of the people.' . . . 'Political royalists.'" ". . . [S]uggestions designed to lead to more effective public relations work," pp. 5–7, Drawer 1110, NAM papers.

30. Burns, *Lion*, p. 113.

31. Arthur M. Schlesinger, Jr., *The Politics of Upheaval* (Boston, 1968), pp. 302–324.

32. Philip J. Funigiello, *Toward a National Power Policy* (Pittsburgh, 1973) p.

105. I am indebted to Funigiello for much of this discussion. His treatment of Ross's role in utility public relations ranks with Albro Martin's study of Ivy Lee and the railroads in the Progressive era as among the most incisive considerations of public relations in historical literature.

For his services, Ross received $5,000 per month plus expenses. U.S. Senate, *Hearings* Pursuant to S. Res. 165 and S. Res. 184, Senate Special Committee to Investigate Lobbying Activities, 74th Cong., 1st sess. (Washington, D.C., 1935), p. 8 (cited hereinafter as Black Committee *Hearings*).

33. Funigiello, *Power*, pp. 107–110; Schlesinger, *Upheaval*, p. 314.

34. Funigiello, *Power*, pp. 108, 113.

35. Auerbach, *Labor*, p. 1.

36. Black Committee *Hearings*, pp. 7–8; Funigiello, *Power*, pp. 113–114.

37. Ibid., p. 119. Funigiello observed that the "lobbyists created an atmosphere in which sober-minded inquiry was difficult. . . . [T]hey . . . lacked confidence in the ability of an educated citizenry to make thoughtful judgments, which is the essence of democracy." The administration also used arm-twisting tactics, but its efforts at persuasion were made against the backdrop of a deeply held conviction that "once the public had the facts, it was capable of deciding the proper course of policy." This distinction, both in this instance and others in which business and government sought to influence public opinion against one another, strikes me as highly dubious. Pp. 98–99.

38. Robert James Bennett, "Carl Byoir; Public Relations Pioneer" (unpublished master's thesis, University of Wisconsin, 1968), pp. 160–180. This work is of particular value, for in its lenghty Appendix are published papers from the Byoir organization which are no longer available to scholars. Irwin Ross, *The Image Merchants* (Garden City, 1959), p. 114.

39. Scott Cutlip, *Fund Raising in America* (New Brunswick, N.J., 1965), pp. 357–358. Byoir persuaded Bernays to help him with his Lithuanian work. He later reminisced: "After the war, . . . [Bernays and I] started a little business— and believe me it was a little business—it was so little that . . . I decided to go into something more profitable." Bennett, "Byoir," pp. 70–72; Bernays, *Idea*, pp. 187–190. Even the worldly-wise Bernays was taken aback by the vigor with which Byoir exploited the postwar confusion.

40. Cutlip, *Fund Raising*, p. 358; Bennett, "Byoir," pp. 74–78.

41. Ibid., p. 115.

42. Ibid., pp. 116–117.

43. Evelyn C. Roat, "Current Trends in Public Relations," *Public Opinion Quarterly* 3 (July 1939), pp. 513–515.

44. Why the Hartfords selected Byoir is unknown, but he may have come to their attention because of a startling legislative turnabout he had recently been credited with. The Louisiana legislature had in 1936 passed, with one dissenting vote, a tax which would have cost the Freeport Sulphur Company dearly. Freeport hired Byoir, who organized third-party opposition to the tax and succeeded in having the legislature reduce it by 50 percent, despite the fact that Freeport was the only institution to benefit directly from this reduction. Bennett, "Byoir," pp. 194–196.

45. Ibid., p. 200; Andrew Hacker, "Pressure Politics in Pennsylvania," in Alan

F. Westin, ed., *The Uses of Power* (New York, 1962), pp. 336, 325. In 1956, Senator John McClellan expressed an opinion similar to Hacker's on the relative effectiveness of public relations compared to lobbying. Hill, *Making*, p. 127.

46. Bennett, "Byoir," pp. 241–242, 201; Roat, "Current Trends," p. 514.

47. New York *Herald Tribune,* September 15, 1938, p. 15.

48. Bennett, "Byoir," pp. 204–206.

49. Roat, "Current Trends," pp. 514–515; *United States* v. *New York Great Atlantic and Pacific Tea Company,* 67 F. Supp. 626, p. 673; *United States* v. *New York Great Atlantic and Pacific Tea Company,* 173 F. 2d 79, p. 89; Spencer Klaw, "Carl Byoir: Opinion Engineering in the Big Time," *Reporter,* June 10, 1952, p. 32; "Special Letter on the Channels of Communication," *Propaganda Analysis,* May 16, 1938, pp. 70–71. M. A. Adelman, a student of A&P, described the Byoir approach as "elaborately casual." *A&P: A Study in Price Cost Behavior and Public Policy* (Cambridge, Mass., 1959), p. 80.

50. Klaw, "Opinion Engineering," p. 33; Bennett, "Byoir," pp. 241–242.

51. Ibid., pp. 225–245.

52. 173 F. 2d 79, pp. 84–86.

53. Klaw, "Opinion Engineering," p. 33.

54. 173 F. 2d 79, pp. 89–90; see "Biggest Family Business," *Fortune,* March 1933, pp. 53ff. Byoir decided to accept the court's verdict, and he advised that his client should too. His view was that A&P should pay its fine, modify ACCO's activities, and continue to tell its story to the public. This the chain proceeded to do.

55. Bennett, "Byoir," pp. 260–268.

56. For Byoir's relations with Roosevelt, see Cutlip, *Fund Raising,* pp. 357–382.

57. George Felix Hamel, "John W. Hill, Public Relations Pioneer" (unpublished M.S. thesis, University of Wisconsin, 1966), pp. 1–5; Hill, *Making,* pp. 8–9, 16–20.

58. Ibid., pp. 36–37; Hamel, "Hill," p. 16. The partnership's headquarters remained in Cleveland into the mid-forties. At that time, Hill turned over his interests in the Cleveland branch to Knowlton and established a separate firm in New York City.

59. LaFollette Committee *Hearings,* Pt. 25, pp. 10493–10494.

60. Bernstein, *Turbulent Years,* pp. 475, 480–483; Louis Leotta, Jr., "The Republic Steel Corporation in the Little Steel Strike of 1937" (unpublished master's thesis, Columbia, 1960); Tom M. Girdler, *Boot Straps* (New York, 1943), pp. 164–182.

61. Hamel, "Hill," pp. 24, 18–19; Peter Bart, "What Will People Say?" *New York Times Book Review,* November 11, 1963, p. 58. Journalist Walter Goodman quipped that Hill had "never met a moneyed man he didn't like." *Book Week,* November 10, 1963, p. 8.

62. Hill, *Making,* p. 39; Hammel, "Hill," p. 161.

63. Hill, *Making,* p. 47.

64. LaFollette Committee *Hearings,* pt. 25, pp. 10310–10311, 10280–10281.

65. Ibid., pp. 10476–10478.

66. Eric Barnouw, *The Golden Web* (New York, 1968), pp. 34, 43, 89–91; Lewis, "Henry Ford," pp. 503–504.

67. LaFollette Committee *Hearings*, pp. 10310–10311. In Hill's defense, when he presented his public relations proposal to the Greater Akron Development Association he said he favored advertising "to a certain extent, as an advertisement is the most effective way of presenting a series of facts to the public in an attention-getting manner in exactly the form and sequence in which you wish them presented." He made no allusion to the possible effects such advertising might have on newspaper policy. Ibid., pp. 10476–10478.

68. Ibid., p. 10329; *Making*, pp. 57–59.

69. Ibid., p. 58; LaFollette Committee *Hearings*, pt. 25, pp. 10330–10331; Hamel, "Hill," p. 170.

70. Donald W. Rigle, "Hill and Knowlton, Inc." (unpublished Harvard Business School Case Study, 1966), p. 1; John W. Hill papers, State Historical Society of Wisconsin, Madison.

71. Bernays, *Idea*, pp. 288–289.

72. In addition to his promotional work, Bernays also serviced clients with government problems. But Bruno probably did not. For him, as for Benjamin Sonnenberg who became prominent in the 1950s, public relations meant "publicity, exploitation [and] sales promotion." There are good examples of his work in Vols. 3 and 10 of his papers, State Historical Society of Wisconsin, Madison.

73. Lillibridge, Adamson, and Kitchen, for instance, surfaced just long enough to announce that it provided both public relations and advertising services and then disappeared. *Tide,* June 1934, Box 47, Lee papers. A more serious attempt to branch out into the field was made by the nation's leading fund raiser, John Price Jones. Jones's experience dated back to 1919. During the Depression, he used the classic methods of establishing himself as a counselor: circulating a clip sheet and writing a book. Despite his work for the steel industry, his reputation in public relations never approached that of the major firms. He remained primarily a fund raiser. Cutlip, *Fund Raising,* pp. 169–188; John Price Jones and David McClaren Church, *At the Bar of Public Opinion* (New York, 1939) *passim;* "Original Plan" and "New Business Bureau," Vol. BB-1; "Publicity Plan . . . , July 15, 1938," Case 3, Box 3; "Public Relations Master Questionnaire," March 1, 1939, Vol. BE-1; "The Publicist," Case 2, Box 2, John Price Jones papers, Baker Library, Harvard Business School.

74. Stanley Kelley, Jr., *Professional Public Relations and Political Power* (Baltimore, 1956), pp. 39–66.

Chapter V

Public Relations During World War II

Pronouncements on public relations by counselors and by corporation executives had by World War II taken on the aspect of a litany. Oft-repeated choruses included, on the part of the former, an insistence that the corporation first clean up its own house and then go out and tell its story to the public. The latter would usually promise to do only good works and to raise the status of public relations. Both claimed that public relations had permanently outgrown the "space grabbing" stage, and both cautioned that unless public relations were vigorously pursued, labor unions and left-wing politicians would win the battle for public opinion with catastrophic consequences. And both agreed that the executive must bear the ultimate responsibility for the repute of his firm for it was he who determined whether or not to carry out public relations recommendations.

It is therefore essential in a study of corporate public relations to keep in mind the state of business sentiment as well as the development of public relations as a discreet field of activity which, like accounting, could be employed by labor unions, nonprofit organizations, and government. But what is "business sentiment"? The researches of such scholars as Robert Wiebe and Louis Galambos have demonstrated that business is not monolithic.[1] There are big and small businessmen; northerners, southerners, and westerners; shippers and manufacturers; etc. For our purposes, "business sentiment" has meant the opinions of those businessmen who have made use of public relations. These have usually directed the affairs of large, "impersonal" corporations with widespread interests or have been prominently associated with trade associations. Even this relatively exclusive group has been far from unanimous in its opinions and therefore its members have often pursued different public relations philosophies.

However, this corporate leadership never approximated unanimity more closely than in its oppostion to Franklin D. Roosevelt and his New Deal. This animus, which expressed itself through the public relations activities described in Chapters III and IV, had both rational and emotional roots. Businessmen disliked increased government restrictions, especially in the realm of labor relations, and they felt encumbered by such annoyances as the added paperwork which the New Deal required. They also bridled at their own precipitous decline in popularity and resented Roosevelt, who they felt was usurping their paternalistic role. During World War II, the high repute of business enjoyed a renaissance, and some businessmen were able to jettison their emotional defenses and to propose rational and practical measures which were incorporated into the conversion and reconversion processes.

Thus during the war we see the continued assertion of the conservative view through the NAM but also the growth of the more moderate approach of the Committee for Economic Development. In addition, we see a heightened sensitivity to the threat to worker loyalty posed by union activity. And finally we find a spreading awareness of the importance of routine public relations work, such as courteously answering letters and encouraging employees to present a smiling face to the community.

This chapter will survey the blooming, buzzing confusion of this array of activity by dividing it into four sections. The first is a discussion of the changed stance of government toward big business. The second is an examination of the responses of two important business organizations, the National Association of Manufacturers and the Committee for Economic Development, to this new environment. The third is itself divided into two parts, the first being an investigation of how businessmen hoped to use public relations to forestall unionization and the second a note on the difficulties which organized labor confronted in attempting to create a public relations establishment. And lastly, we have a discussion of the tactics involved in creating a favorable corporate reputation with the help of wage earners during years in which war-induced shortages caused problems in fulfilling consumer demand.

I

In his first inaugural address in 1933, Roosevelt had speculated that it might become necessary for him to ask Congress for a grant of "broad executive power to wage a war against the emergency, as great as the power that would be given to me if we were in fact invaded by a foreign foe." The analogue of war, so often employed by New Dealers, and for that matter, by Hoover and his aides before them, had its uses but was at bottom inadequate to help in coping with the problems of the Depression. The hope was that, in a nation in which "the sense of community is weak, the distrust of the state strong," the invocation of the selfless devotion to victory over the foe of the Great War would help garner support for administration efforts to deal with unemployment without the hindrances of disunity and domestic turmoil. Also for the sake of fostering national unity, the New Deal in its early days sought to squelch expression of antibusiness sentiment. The only thanks the administration received was the Liberty League and the public relations campaigns of the NAM and the Chamber of Commerce of the United States. The comparison to war, which seemed to promise the possibility of the acceptance of dramatic emergency action to alleviate the problems, steadily lost its impact as the Depression wore on.[2]

The Depression was a confused and confusing time when shibboleths were falling by the wayside and the conventional wisdom was proving never more inadequate. Total war for survival is not confusing. The outbreak of the war in Europe aroused deeply felt disagreements about the nation's world role, but "Pearl Harbor ended the debate between interventionists and isolationists."[3] The time for united action was at hand.

As the threat to the United States became ever more ominous at decade's turn, businessmen and Republicans began to accept service in the administration. William S. Knudson, of Du Pont-dominated General Motors and an alumnus of the Liberty League, headed the Office of Production Management upon its formation in 1941 and proved himself "utterly loyal."[4] Numerous others from equally conservative corporations did banner duty during the war as dollar-a-year men or in uniform.

> Thousands upon thousands of businessmen and lawyers who still harbored a suspicion of government came to Washington to help staff the war mobilization. As a social class these Americans had been basically conservative and Republican. During the war they learned of the unique exhilaration of public service. . . . Wartime Washington, they found, was a capital filled with practical people without noticeably radical inclinations. It was an educational experience for the elites of a capitalist society, and in the end a politically moderating one.[5]

When Roosevelt effected his celebrated switch from "Dr. New Deal" to "Dr. Win the War," he automatically earned the support of many nationalistic corporate leaders who had previously opposed him, at least for the duration. "Better Hitler than Leon Blum" may have been the chit-chat in some circles in prewar France, but no businessman of note publicly declared a preference for Hitler over Roosevelt.

America was to be the "arsenal of democracy" in a phrase with characteristic Rooseveltian sonority, and that meant that industrialists were called upon to tool up for the production of military material. The situation was even more critical than that which had prompted a World War I War Industries Board spokesman to lecture steel masters that "this is a crisis, and Commercialism, gentlemen, must be absolutely sidetracked."[6] Not unlike wartime declarations that "politics is adjourned," the desired abjuration of profit for the sake of the second great crusade did not materialize with the speed or to the extent that many wished. The pre-Pearl Harbor performance was especially disheartening; according to one observer, in fact, mobilization was then "faltering to the point of crisis."[7] Symbolic of the problem was the automobile industry. Devastated by the Depression, it was now enjoying the fruits of increased national wealth. Turning out cars and trucks at the rate of five million per year, it produced almost one million more cars in 1941 than two years previously despite increasingly severe shortages of rubber, aluminum, and steel.[8]

Businessmen were reluctant to convert to a war footing before Pearl Harbor for a number of reasons. They were finally making money after ten lean years and did not want to disturb relations with customers and suppliers. They feared losing their markets to competitors if they converted and competitors did not, and they faced with trepidation the specter of excess capacity after the war ended. They also recalled with discomfort the bad public relations suffered by World War I's "Merchants of Death" before the Nye Committee and recognized the possibility of similar treatment for those who profited from the present conflict. And the fissures of a decade of conflict did not heal overnight. New Deal veterans now manning war agencies occasionally chastised industrialists for their "business as usual" attitude while labor-management conflict threatened to curtail productive capacity if not cripple it altogether.[9]

Despite some grumbling on the part of veteran liberals, the Executive and Congress were extraordinarily responsive, some might say submissive, to big business and its fears and complaints. Eschewing charges of economic royalism and malfeasance of great wealth, the government facilitated corporate preparation and production for war by relaxing antitrust prosecution to permit pooling. Instead of charging a "strike of capital" when business was slow to convert, the government responded with such "mouth-watering incentives to operate at full throttle" as liberal plans for financing expansion and the cost-plus formula for filling defense contracts, which may have cost the taxpayer a considerable sum by war's end. The American fighting man might be called upon to sacrifice his life, but the American corporation was not going to be called upon to sacrifice its profits, which increased an average of about 65 percent from 1940 to 1944.[10]

A good example of the lengths to which the government was willing to go to develop and maintain good relations with business was its treatment of companies involved in war frauds. One investigator surveying seventy large corporations found them all guilty of at least one "war crime,"[11] and whether one accepts this judgment or not, the activities of at least two of the largest war contractors were indefensible. The Senate Special Committee to Investigate the Defense Program, usually known as the Truman Committee, was apprised of questionable practices of the Carnegie-Illinois Steel Company, a subsidiary of the largest firm in that most public relations-minded of industries, through a tip from a disillusioned employee. Investigation uncovered fraudulent inspection practices, which the Committee did condemn. Management claimed that these practices were unknown to it, a debatable point, and promised a cleanup, and the Committee declined to insist upon punishment. Indeed, it was "reluctant to place the blame and responsibility at the highest levels within [any offending] corporations"[12] after the fashion of the LaFollette, Nye, or Pecora committees.

Perhaps the most outrageous conduct during the war was that of Curtiss-Wright and the Wright Aeronautical Corporation, whose Lockland, Ohio, plant was the exclusive producer of an air-cooled airplane engine. The company was guilty of selling the government faulty products which were approved by a corrupt inspection system. Whenever an honest employee tried to put a stop to these practices, he was dismissed as a troublemaker and transferred. A large number of aircraft with Lockland equipment had crashed because of engine failure. The company defended its conduct to the last. In the age of public relations, major corporations were not caught unprepared when under investigation. The same day the Truman Committee's first findings were released, the company's president issued an emphatic denial and launched an institutional advertising campaign featuring his statement and citing (incorrectly) the company's contributions to the war effort. The cost of this campaign and future ones like it was borne by the government because of the company's tax position. The Committee pressed on and eventually won an apology, but Curtiss-Wright neglected inspection standards for the duration.[13]

All this is not to minimize the contribution of American businessmen to winning the war by their feats of production, nor is it to deny the coercive aspects of some legislation which included the right to seize plants and to force them into mobilization.[14] But it does illustrate that even under stern provocation, the government did not vigorously prosecute corporate wrongdoing. The Truman Committee, for example, operated on the premise that almost everyone wanted to win the war so much that in the case of a conflict between public and private interests, the business-as-usual mentality would naturally be abandoned. This was a concession that the administration did not make when considering the business attitude toward the New Deal's efforts to conquer the Depression. In both cases the administration's attitude was only partly justified. Its broad attack upon the "malefactors of great wealth" during the '30s served in a sense as a self-fulfilling prophecy. Finding themselves lumped together for the purpose of being vilified, more businessmen were no doubt more extremely anti-Roosevelt than they would have been if handled more gingerly. On the other hand, the examples of Carnegie-Illinois and Curtiss-Wright showed that, even with the nation *in extremis,* for some businessmen the company would always come first.

There are other noteworthy factors explaining the softening of the governmental attitude toward business. The government may have felt that alienation of the managerial class was a luxury a nation at war could ill afford. Moreover, excessive publicity for corporate chicanery had a dangerous potential for sapping the morale of the armed forces and defense workers. Propaganda was an important weapon of both the Germans and Japanese, who surely would not have failed to broadcast to American troops news of production failure.

Encouraged by the government, a rapprochement between business and the general public also developed during the war.[15] Dr. Claude Robinson, pioneer public opinion analyst and a frequent speaker before meetings of business public relations counselors during the 1940s, explained that "until the declaration of war . . . , industry was fighting an uphill public relations battle. It was tarred with bad symbols— unemployment, greed, lack of humaneness. It was on the defensive." Management, however, was handling the war skillfully. It was saying, "Tell us what to make, and we'll do it." Labor, on the other hand, was taking advantage of the fact that it was in great demand. "Labor unions are building up a public ill will," Robinson went on, "which is certain to crack down on them in the future. They have muffed their war opportunity badly."[16] He backed up these observations by citing the results of a poll his Opinion Research Corporation had taken early in 1942. It revealed 69 percent of the people questioned to be satisfied with the conduct of factory managers, 54 percent with government officials, and a scant 31 percent with union leaders.[17]

The public no longer followed stories critical of business with the avidity of years gone by. The Truman Committee, despite the generally favorable press it received, was criticized for its handling of industrial war frauds by a considerable number of articles which held that it "was hurting production or that its findings were bad for morale and should have been kept quiet."[18] A strange reaction indeed to corporate activities about which the objective observer could have but one opinion. The saga of Sewell Avery was yet another example of the changed climate. Avery was a cantankerous old fanatic whose efforts to sabotage the government-engineered labor-management truce of the war years resulted in his being bodily removed from the executive offices of Montgomery Ward. Perhaps because the photographs of this spectacle which appeared in newspapers around the country made him seem "frail and grandfatherly" or perhaps because his defiance appealed to an anarchic streak in Americans, he attracted widespread support. Sixty percent of those questioned in a poll approved of him. Meanwhile, polls taken the previous year yielded an 87 percent disapproval rating for John L. Lewis.[19] Times had indeed changed since the CIO campaigns of the mid-thirties.

In the dreadful Depression year of 1932, Carter Glass joked to a colleague that "one banker tried to marry a white woman in my state and they lynched him."[20] A mere four years previously, businessmen and all associated with the business world were being credited with leading the way to the millennium. And ten years later, businessmen were once again gaining respect because of their efforts toward defeating the enemy. It would seem that the reputation of the American businessman in the twentieth century has been largely a product of his ability to deliver the goods—the jobs as well as the products—to a demanding nation.

II

The problems of the '30s were the problems of failure: the staggering number of unemployed, the breadlines, the sidewalk apple peddlers, the stagnation and fear. The problems of the war years were the problems of success: wages and labor relations with manpower scarce, more customers than products, the new role of government which suddenly had become the major customer for many an important business. These new problems clustered around the issue of planning, specifically the implications which its successful use during the emergency held for the future organization of the American economy. The focus on planning was actually a new wrinkle to an old concern, the preservation of the prerogatives of private management from encroachment from government or labor.

During the '30s, in addition to their opposition to regulation and unionism, executives and their public relations men had pilloried administration attempts to plan the country out of the Depression (when, that is, businessmen were not allowed what they considered a sufficient say in the formulation of these plans) and the aims of those "social planners" who wished to redistribute wealth and power in the society. Much of the business community looked upon the Roosevelt of the '30s as a utopian. "Cartoons showed him as a bemused dreamer, attired in cap and gown and attended by crackpot professors, following wild intellectual theories. Business magazines drubbed him for his 'impractical theories.' " This picture constituted a serious misperception, as James MacGregor Burns has pointed out, for in fact, Roosevelt was "an eminently 'practical' man. He had no overall plans to remake America but a host of projects to improve this or that situation. He was a creative thinker in a 'gadget' sense: immediate steps to solve specific day-to-day problems."[21]

Roosevelt's intellectual sloppiness did not disappear with Pearl Harbor. He continued to run his administration through lieutenants whose authority was overlapping. Interagency competition was supposed to keep people on their toes and also to prevent the development of power centers independent of the President. Furthermore, Roosevelt saw danger in planning for postwar developments, because it might take minds off the immediate problem of victory. Nevertheless, a certain amount of planning and control was unavoidable. Most of the business community accepted the necessity for it, as it had not during the Depression. But there developed important disagreements among executives on the government's postwar planning role.

The stand of the conservative, NAM-oriented businessmen on this issue was nowhere better expressed than in a lengthy and thoughtful letter from Donaldson Brown, who had gone to General Motors from Du Pont and was at the time vice chairman of the board of the auto manufacturer, to President William P. Witherow of the NAM in mid-1942.

> We are now at war, and necessarily the rules by which we have lived in the past are changed for the duration. Unfortunately, the impact of a regimented war economy on American industry holds a threat not only to the efficiency of industrial management, but also to the whole system of free enterprise upon which this efficiency has been built.
>
> This threat lies in the fact that the public has not come to distinguish between the necessity of centralized planning and regimentation in time of war, and the exercise of corresponding functions on the part of the government in time of peace. The public is profoundly conscious of the "miracle of production" that industry is performing. Paradoxically enough, it is the very efficiency of our industrial system in turning out the goods re-

quired by the armed forces that endangers industry in the future through its threat to the system of free enterprise. Everyone knows that we are subject today to a high degree of governmental control, but too many may come to believe that the efficiency being displayed by industry derives from this war-time incident of centralized planning and administration, rather than the qualities inherent within industry itself.

It is understandable, in the circumstances, that those with ulterior motives should seize the occasion to contend that the war-time system under which industrial production has worked such wonders be extended and applied with equal benefit and effectiveness in the post-war economy. The fallacy of such a contention can be demonstrated, but unless it *is* demonstrated, in all those quarters where a lack of understanding exists, it is entirely possible that an unenlightened public may be led in its enthusiasm to hail a formula which has proved its necessity and worth in time of war as the formula that is needed for salvation also in time of peace.

The magnificent spectacle, Brown went on, of the efficient operation of the American industrial plant and private management's ability to meet the demands of the emergency had only been possible because of

long years of competitive effort, strengthened by the stimulus and incentive of the profit motive. It was the competitive spirit, tried and proven in the marketplace, that sharpened and toughened the managers of industry; it was the profit motive that drove them to the quest for greater and greater efficiency; it was the stern discipline of the objective laws of economics that brought those with maximum capabilities to the top.

The putative "New Order," government planning, would institute a "Tyranny of Incompetence." "God help the country if the American conception of political and economic freedom is destroyed and we are all of us required to become politicians!" The only healthy dictatorship, concluded Brown, who was certainly familiar with Adam Smith if not with administered pricing, was that of the consumer.

For Brown, the demonstration to the public of the superior efficiency of private management was an unavoidable responsibility of those astute enough to comprehend it. Witherow replied that he was in "complete harmony" with Brown's views and undertook immediately to discuss them with Walter Weisenberger. Here indeed was the public relations job of the war: to prevent industry's accomplishments from being used against it and to take such other measures as were necessary to insure the survival of private enterprise.[22] The issue of planning was to be, along with labor relations and such nuts-and-bolts problems as learning to found a plant newspaper and placating consumers frustrated by war-caused shortages of products, the central concern of the public relations forums which the NAM sponsored during the war.

The first of these forums took place late in 1942, shortly before the NAM's annual Congress of American Industry, in New York City. It was attended by 150 industrial executives and public relations counselors and was thought to be the first such assemblage to discuss "Industry's Public Relations." It was not, in fact, the first meeting of its kind, but its size and the prestige of its sponsor brought it attention, and the foreword to the published transcript may not have been far from right in asserting that "the occasion marked the coming of age of the profession of public relations."[23] There was another national conclave held during the war and a third soon after peace in 1945. In addition, regional conferences were held in Philadelphia, Los Angeles, Cleveland, Indianapolis, Salt Lake City, Seattle, and other cities. These meetings helped spread the public relations gospel and their transcripts constitute an important source for determining the opinions of business executives and public relations men in conservative circles.

On the issue of planning there was broad agreement. Centralized government planning, Thomas J. Ross told the first national convention, was the great threat for the future. The big question facing the nation was: who will get credit for wartime wonders, industry or government? He felt that the nation should be as proud of its businessmen as it was of its military heroes because free enterprise was making wartime production successes possible. Public relations had to convince the nation of this assertion—in Ross's words, "to get industry's symbols recognized as the symbols of what the people are for."[24] Fred Eldean, of General Motors, suggested the slogan, "Rationing Now, Yes. But How Would You Like to Be Rationed for the Rest of Your Life?" to drive home the potential problems of excessive government intervention in the economy.[25] A vigorous statement of the antiplanning school of thought came from J. Howard Pew, lord of Sun Oil and a "rugged individualist" of the old school:

> Industry's magnificent achievement in this war has laid the foundation for a better understanding of American business.
>
> Now we must undertake to get the American people to understand that industry was able to do this job only because individual initiative in this country remained unchained, and that despite the schemes of the bureaucrats and economic planners.
>
> Slandered and vilified as it was in the '30's, subjected to crushing regulations and restrictions, American industry retained its initiative to serve the nation and the world so well in this hour of peril.
>
> Had the advocates of state socialism succeeded, had the individual been suppressed in this country, the outcome of this war would be far different from the United Nations victories that are now indicated.[26]

It was up to Congress, declared the NAM's Public Relations Advisory Group, to protect the American people from "the ultimate loss of their freedom,"[27] and it was up to the business community to encourage it in this enterprise. It is significant, however, that in its next breath the Group wondered if individual businessmen "will submerge their own convictions and use material prepared for them."[28] For although the NAM continued to express the opinion of an important segment of the conservative business community, the spectrum of corporate feeling toward the President was becoming broader during the war years.[29]

Businessmen such as Pew and Brown and public relations counselors such as Ross and John Hill may have viewed the planning question in doctrinaire terms and believed it the entering wedge for socialists, but another organization was founded in 1942 which looked at the problem in a different light. Perhaps no issue better illustrated the diversity of views within the highest echelons of management as the New Deal faded into history and, concomitantly, the danger of accepting the NAM as the spokesman for all business than the planning controversy.

Months before Pearl Harbor, the Business Advisory Council of the Department of Commerce was expressing serious concern over the unemployment which it feared would reappear after the war's conclusion and the threat that would result to "our existing economic system."[30] The upshot of a BAC report on this matter was the Committee for Economic Development, which, with the blessings of Jesse Jones's Department of Commerce, set about to encourage businessmen both large and small to begin planning to effect high employment and production after the war. The CED encouraged positive thinking about the postwar economy. Secondly, through its Research Division, it educated the businessman about new economic theories. The Research Division was founded at the insistence of Studebaker's Paul Hoffman, the first chairman of the CED's board of trustees and the leading figure of its early years. Hoffman recognized that when it came to being economically illiterate, the American businessman was second to none.[31] Under his aegis, the CED became a public relations organization devoted to opening the mind of the businessman to such heretofore unmentionable possibilities as the necessity for the government to play a major part in insuring prosperity through Keynesean measures and also in improving the business image before the public.

There were certain similarities between the progressivism of the CED and the conservatism of the NAM. Both organizations had as their primary goal the preservation and prosperity of the capitalistic system. In order to promote this goal, both used the public relations technique of associating it with ideas that had widespread support. Thus in CED meetings, "The terms 'free enterprise system' and 'capitalist economy' were used interchangeably with 'free society' and 'democratic way of life'" while the NAM, in 1940, launched the "Tripod of Freedom" public relations symbol, referred to in Chapter III, designed to link private enterprise graphically with the First Amendment freedoms.[32]

Robert A. Brady, writing in 1944, was far more impressed with the similarities of the CED and the NAM than with their differences. He noted that such prominent members of the NAM as Fred Crawford, Walter B. Fuller, and Charles R. Hook were high in CED councils and that Eric Johnston, President of the Chamber of Commerce, was a member of the board of trustees. He also found what the CED stood for to be

> strangely indistinguishable from the content and outlook of the arguments of those who have long been pioneering methods of presenting the public relations case for giant politically and propaganda-minded American enterprise. All, or very nearly all—the exception is found in the postwar emphasis—is clearly in line with the public relations activities of Ivy Lee, Edward L. Bernays, T. J. Ross, Carl Byoir, Bernard Lichtenburg and other experts in opinion making. It is in line with the public relations activities of the N.A.M. under Walter Weisenberger after 1934, the National Machine Tool Builders' Association, the Machinery and Allied Products Institute, and with public relations campaigns conducted on their own by countless financial, manufacturing, and distributing corporations and business pressure groups from the middle '20's on.

Brady suggested that if the CED members "really mean what they say," they would "gain much by dropping the stilted clichés and the stock phrases of the public relations counsellor."[33]

To be sure, the CED did attempt to spread its findings to a broad business audience. Therefore, one of the three divisions founded in 1942 was "Public Information," and each of the 2,947 autonomous committees which were operating on the local level by mid-1945 under the general supervision of the Field Development Division was to contain its own public relations department designed to see that "all groups in the community hear about the practical 'grassroots' plan of business to provide jobs" at war's end.[34]

Nevertheless, the differences between the public relations philosophies of the CED and the NAM were important. Following a decade in which some businessmen were so anti-intellectual as to approach anti-intelligence, the CED resolved to exploit the nation's academic community. According to John D'Emilio,

> The frequently held joint meetings of the Research Committee, the Research Advisory Board and the economists preparing studies for the CED

were open and honest discussions of the topic at hand. The corporate executives of the Research Committee came to these discussions with their own prejudices, and often left with their opinions severely shaken by the onslaught of professionals. In the course of these meetings, preconceived notions changed substantially as the knowledge of professors was brought to bear....[35]

The CED's ideas about the place of government in the economy differed substantially from those current in the NAM. The CED favored as great a role as possible for the private sector in the planning that had to be done to preserve the country from another depression, but it recognized that government had an essential part—perhaps the major part, believed Paul Hoffman—to play.[36] Without government planning, business planning would be for naught. The CED strove to impress upon businessmen the potential of flexible monetary and fiscal policy to control fluctuations in the business cycle. To a group to which the balanced budget had been the most revered of sacred cows, the CED brought the news of Keynesean economics and in such a way as not to frighten businessmen into rejecting it. D'Emilio concluded that

> through their research into the broader questions of economic policy and government involvement in the economy, CED members found that government and business need not be antagonistic. They realized that the federal government had a large part to play in making the economy function smoothly. They realized that the government could expand its role in the economy while at the same time strengthening the economic system to which CED members were committed and from which they profited.[37]

Another CED historian wrote, "They [CED members] were not afraid of the power of the government but were determined to use it, on their own terms, to make the private enterprise system work...."[38] At last some leaders of the owning and managing classes were acting as they were supposed to. Gone was much of the irrational opposition of the thirties.

Robert Brady could not, of course, have known in 1944 that the CED would support the Full Employment Bill which was anathema to the NAM or that it would selectively support the continuation of price controls while the NAM was spending thousands of dollars propagandizing against the OPA after the war. But he should have been able to spot the differences in philosophy and public relations technique that were already apparent. While the CED was holding out the peace pipe to government, James W. Irwin, a public relations counsel and frequent speaker before NAM forums, was declaring:

There will be all manner of reasoning advanced at the conclusion of the war to prove that these [government-imposed] restrictions should continue, so that our bureaucrats will have opportunity to rebuild the world. We must watch this trend. If we don't, this country may be torn down rather than built up.

Let us organize. Let's adopt the tactics that the bureaucrats and the labor leaders have used. Let's be outspoken. Let's fight. For a change let us do some slugging and get in some of the first blows.[39]

At a time when the NAM was hoping that its members would submerge their own convictions and help distribute Association propaganda and when its public relations staff was proving *plus royaliste que le roi*,[40] the CED was encouraging questioning of old beliefs.

The public relations techniques of the two organizations also differed. The CED favored local publicity. When it did seek national attention, the medium usually chosen was the business trade journal, where articles were placed through the Business Publication Division whose chairman was also president of *Iron Age*.[41] An interesting clue to the difference in public relations approach was a remark Hoffman made in 1945 to the effect that "we did not subscribe to the idea that what helps business helps you, but rather what helps you and every other American, helps business."[42] These words were not randomly chosen. In 1937, the Chamber of Commerce with the cooperation of the NAM launched a public relations campaign whose theme was "What Helps Business, Helps You."[43] Hoffman's formulation symbolized not only a reversal of priorities, but also his desire to put daylight between the CED and the "rock 'em, sock 'em, let's battle the bureaucrats" attitude of the conservatives.

Unlike the NAM, the Chamber of Commerce, and the trade associations, the CED did not lobby for specific legislation, although it expressed its opinion when solicited. Its major purpose was to forestall a possible depression which might be brought about because so many people expected one. It comprehended that "businessmen have to act in accordance with the ideas they possess. . . ."[44] The task was to change those ideas through education. This the Committee helped to do, and its efforts contributed to the relative smoothness of reconversion. That Brady could see no difference between it and the NAM was a testimony to how scholars writing from a radical perspective could impose a "consensus" on the business community where none existed.

The CED put into practice some old public relations homilies. It was optimistic and assertive, not defensive. It was tolerant of the misconceptions of businessmen but worked to change them, while at the same time fostering the image of the corporate leader as the man who cared about employment and production and wanted to insure both. In a survey taken among "men in a position to view the conduct of public relations in wartime," Clark Belden, public relations director of the New England Gas Association, found that among the most constructive accomplishments was "the first organized business approach to the mass unemployment problem as reflected, for example, by the nationwide program of the Committee for Economic Development." The efforts of no other business organization were mentioned.[45]

None of the great names of professional public relations were prominently associated with the technical public relations chores of the CED or with its overall management. The CED executives were familiar with these names; Hoffman's own company, for example, had retained a well-known counselor. There are three possible explanations for the absence of these leaders. Practitioners had often advertised themselves as people who knew how to attract attention, and the CED was striving to keep a "low profile." Since the mere hiring of a counselor could be news (witness the reaction to A&P's retaining Byoir) and since more than one counselor had been known to err on the side of flamboyance, the CED may have felt that such men might have detracted from its "strictly business" air. Secondly, the CED tried to remain nonpartisan and apolitical. It may have feared that becoming associated with men who had spent most of their time bailing right-wing organizations out of trouble would have tarnished this reputation. (This consideration, however, did not prevent F.D.R. himself from approving the retention of Byoir and cooperating with him in his publicity work for the Warm Springs Foundation.) Lastly, the extensive use of well-known public relations talent may have lent credence to the suspicion that the CED was competing with the NAM and the Chamber of Commerce, an impression it strongly wanted to discourage.

III

Keeping the workingman loyal to his employer rather than to some organization operated by "outside agitators" and winning his loyalty even after unionization had taken place was an ongoing problem to which corporate public relations devoted itself. The complaint continued to be heard that labor leaders were driving a wedge between those natural partners, management and workers.[46] To this was added the new threat, especially to conservatives, posed by CIO support for greater social planning.[47]

Businessmen, pollsters, and public relations counselors gave one another contradictory pictures of the labor situation. Some of the tidings were encouraging. Pollster Claude Robinson repeatedly cited the results of his surveys as proof that in the battle for public favor labor leaders had fallen down badly whereas management "had catered to [the public's] mood with tremendous success." Laborers were part of this general public, and management's wartime performance had had positive effects on them.[48] ". . . [T]he workman is being subjected to the most thorough job of propagandizing in all history," explained James Irwin. "From theorists, buraucrats, self-seekers in Washington. From pressure groups of every color, stripe, and complexion. From that quasi-national administration made up of high pressuring labor leaders." (Irwin surprisingly did not include Nazi or Communist propaganda on this list.) But accomplishment was speaking louder than words. At last the worker was

> through with pap and nonsense about the sublime efficiency of the professors and social planners—after seeing them baffled, muddled, hopelessly inept in the face of their first man-sized emergency—the tough reality of war. He's all fed up with guff [one senses that it took considerable self-restraint on the part of Mr. Irwin to use this particular four-letter word] about "predatory interests" when he finds that the boss he was supposed to hate is the man who has suddenly emerged as the savior of Mr. Common Man and his wife and kids, of this country and all other democratic countries as well. . . .[49]

Frederick Crawford, president of Cleveland's Thompson Products Company and of the NAM in 1943 and long influential in the Association's public relations circles, gave as careful consideration to the labor problem as any other conservative big businessman in the country. As had other executives before him, Crawford believed that working conditions and wages were not as important as "the human approach." He once stated that "the worker doesn't care about his pay and plant conditions. It is what he thinks about the honesty and square-shooting and directness of the boss who is over the plant, and his ability to meet him and talk to him and know him." "The American workman," he declared, "is the best worker in the world." How was it, then, that the present collection of labor leaders had risen to their positions in organizations designed to represent him? Because he had "one great weakness—he was far too susceptible to emotional leadership." He was, in fact, a "sucker for any kind of leadership that comes along." The worker has "become greatly confused" because for the past ten years he has unfortunately had bad leadership from politicians, labor leaders, and industrialists themselves. "We haven't always been very smart. Has it ever occured to you, strange as it may seem, that the American manager can sell anything, any product he has got, but haven't we been dumb in selling simple ideas and truths?" "We have our workers for eight hours a day in our plants and shops and we pay them money. Some crackpot gets them for ten minutes as they go home, and takes money away from them. Who has the advantage? What more important job can management do?" The modern worker craved leadership that showed an interest in him and his welfare. If management did not fill the bill, Crawford warned, the worker would turn to someone who did.[50]

Crawford offered his own company as an example of how management could show its concern for the worker and thus win his allegiance. Back in 1928, Thompson Products had decided to acquaint every worker with the boss and other officers. The management would be "humanized," the long-emphasized goal of public relations, by showing the workers that the managers were, in fact, human. Secondly, the company made open and frank statements of its intentions, and it "adopted an open-door policy—anybody could come in and talk to anybody, on anything, at any time. . . . We tried to approach the subject in a man-to-man fashion." Thirdly, the company submitted financial reports to its workers in language they could understand as part of a general attempt "to remove all mystery regarding finances." And fourthly, the company sought "to merchandise this effort locally in our community" by communicating news of company meetings and financial information to the press.[51]

Crawford was most gratified by the results. The man on the Cleveland street supposedly had a high opinion of the company. Having conducted a survey employing some of the most obtuse questions in the history of opinion sampling,[52] he concluded that his employees understood the basis for the division of wealth among owner, manager, and worker. But the test was the fight against organized labor. In mid-1943, when the speeches from which the above quotations were taken were delivered, a union was spending $6,000 a month to organize the Cleveland plants, a goal of both the AFL and the CIO since 1939. The previous year, according to Thompson, the same union had called a strike and 97 percent of the workers rejected it "because the company's dealings are fair, and they know it. The strike effort was a dud. Our workers stuck with us."[53]

Beating the unions was not easy. Crawford became so well known for winning the fights by making workers loyal to him personally and for trying to eliminate conflict "by casting management as the benign but powerful 'father' figure" that in the 1950s his approach was referred to as "Crawfordism." Crawfordism was nothing but the old-fashioned paternalism of the small enterpreneur, but it is a commentary on Crawford's charisma and commitment to the open shop that he could make his system work in a company whose labor force grew from about 2,700 in 1938 to over 20,000 five years later.[54] No, it hadn't been easy. But Crawford insisted that the workers' loyalty could be won in other companies as it had been in his. Management had great natural advantages in the struggle; it had only to use them.[55]

There was, however, an opposing view, a strong impression that the corporate reputation was deteriorating during the war in the eyes of the general public and the worker. Summarizing the conclusions of his survey, Clark Belden stated that "unsound public relations policies and practices constitute the outstanding aspect of the public relations situation since Pearl Harbor." Of the thirty experts he questioned, only seven praised wartime public relations and even these were not unqualified in their endorsements. The respondents saw a number of errors: insufficient cooperation with the government, too much touting of the company's own contributions to the war effort, selfishness and the quest for profits instead of working for victory unstintingly, insufficient cooperation with labor, and a general neglect of public relations because of supposed insufficient need and the substitution of "stunts" and "smart ideas" for sound policies. One respondent asserted that the result of these errors would be to "put business, generally speaking, in the doghouse for some ten to twenty years."[56]

John W. Hill acknowledged in mid-1943 that the war was providing an opportunity for a better understanding of industry by the public. But in contrast to Crawford, he felt that the natural public relations advantages were with the opposition because union leaders and politicians had a freedom to be irresponsible which was not permitted management. Industry had been "out-generaled and outmaneuvered" in public relations by unions and government because the latter had learned to talk to the public in terms of its self-interest. Industry had to take a leaf from their book.[57]

Everett R. Smith also had disquieting things to say, specifically about the average worker's feelings toward management. The workers complained that industry was making too much profit, two or three dollars net, they believed, for every one dollar paid out in wages. They disliked foremen, who, they charged, were not selected on the basis of merit. (The last day on the job before being drafted, one West Coast shipyard worker announced to his supervisor, "I don't mind being drafted, but I hate like hell to fight for guys like you." Observed Smith, "Gentlemen, that is pretty bad labor relations.") They felt that management was graft-ridden and that they were being unfairly taxed. They were sick of boastful wartime advertising and frightened about the postwar employment picture. They felt that by "free enterprise," the managers really meant freedom to exploit the workers. Basically, Smith concluded, the men favored private management of industry but were getting mighty dissatisfied. "I can sum up the viewpoint in four words—they don't trust industry. . . . [A]nd because they don't . . . , they look to government. They believe that the unions and government are really interested in them and that we are not. . . ." Management had been making sincere efforts to show an interest, but those efforts had so far proven to be unsuccessful.[58]

The pessimists turned out to be wrong. The war did wonders for the reputation of American business, which certainly did not go through another "doghouse" phase for a decade. One would have thought that the pessimists would have been few, since most contemporary evidence, in the form of polls and public statements, indicated that the attitude of Depression America toward business was changing.[59] In fact, however, they were probably in a majority. One reason was the fear that at war's end depression would strike again, but another may have been that few businessmen would hire public relations counsel if they felt their reputation to be secure. The chances for landing a client were always better if he could be convinced that without expert assistance, he would be in trouble.

$$* \qquad * \qquad *$$

Very few people who promoted corporate public relations gave careful consideration to the natural liabilities with which their adversaries had to contend. Most seemed to believe, like Hill, that the opponent's job was inherently easier than theirs.

Most historians have disagreed with Hill. Students of strikes and labor organizations prior to 1933 have emphasized management's success at turning public opinion against the workers. The Knights of Labor, the International Workers of the World, the American Railway Union, and the Amalgamated Association of Iron, Steel and Tin Workers were all dealt severe blows by their loss of public support. During the Pullman strike, for instance, the great majority of newspapers and magazines supported management and exaggerated stories of union-inspired violence and vandalism. The General Manager's Association, with its own version of "the worse the better," apparently conspired to halt all freight and passenger service into Chicago to make the disruption appear more severe than it was, thus antagonizing public opinion at labor's expense and forcing federal intervention. Although not all reporters were prejudiced, the press in general "tried to promote a psychology of fear in the public mind," fear of the works of organized labor. Union leaders abhorred this bias but were unable to counter it.[60]

Management's natural advantages in the quest for public support thus included the backing of journals, which were big businesses themselves. In addition, management was often able to put the union in the position of aggressor. The unions consistently bore the blame for spreading the effects of a dispute beyond the bounds of a single business or industry. Management might initiate trouble by cutting wages, but this was an intra-company matter. When workers fought back by striking, the whole community felt the impact. Not only were unions perceived, fairly or not, as the aggressors, they were also tarred with un-Americanism. They violated the privileges of a businessman to run his own affairs and by positing working-class rights assaulted the belief in harmony and social mobility. The success of businessmen in winning public support and their appreciation of its importance is further testimony to the inadequacy of labeling the late nineteenth century as a "public-be-damned" era.

On the other hand, as Herbert Gutman has pointed out, the workers were not without resources. When strikes occurred in small towns, where the workers knew the merchants and editors and where they constituted a sizable percentage of the voters, middle-class sentiment often supported them. They were the friends, neighbors, and customers assailed by wealthy owners and tyrannical managers. The workers appeared here as the majority, "the people," whom the government was supposed to benefit. They won the support of the newspapers and the politicians, who opposed management's importation of strikebreakers. Businessmen were often forced to hire private police, Pinkertons, and appeal to state authority. A pro-worker public did not look upon such outside intervention kindly. To break strikes with public support, management depended upon the social atomization of big cities.[61]

During the 1920s, the decline of community combined with the touted successes of entrepreneurship to bring public support for organized labor to an all-time low. The situations where workers had a commanding position, as described by Gutman, diminished in number as the industrial ethos gained acceptance. Some union leaders accepted corporate hegemony and tried to sell themselves as adjuncts to the system. They seemed, however, monumentally irrelevant, weak and contemptible rather than weak and therefore deserving of support.

The Depression facilitated a shift in public opinion. The irreconcilable brute fact of the times was that the system had broken down. The promises of welfare capitalism were abandoned along with profits, and organized labor could hardly be blamed for the collapse. Such labor leaders as John L. Lewis and Sidney Hillman captured the imagination of the workers themselves, an essential first step to winning broad public support. The public, as Elmo Roper pointed out, favored the workingman,[62] but it would never favor the union until the worker himself did. The legalistic sideshows of the '20s continued with an increased intensity, but now they were accompanied by action. The federal government opened the door for organization with Section 7A of the NIRA, and labor leaders exploited every publicity device to promote their cause. They associated the movement with prestigious and popular symbols, claiming quite dishonestly that "The United States Government Has Said LABOR MUST ORGANIZE" and "The President wants you to join the union." They hired press relations specialists who saw to it that even if editorials denounced, the news columns would report accurately.[63]

"In 1934, everybody struck." And that year was just the beginning. Now the unions were viewed kindly as brave underdogs rather than as losers, and they reaped "public romantic support of an underdog group."[64] The benign countenance of the federal government supported this trend by exposing the transgressions of employers through the LaFollette Committee and restricting their actions through the Wagner Act.

The climax of organizing activity was the sit-down strike at General Motors early in 1937. Despite the radical nature of this tactic, Sidney Fine found "somewhat greater public support" for it than one should have expected. This resulted from the reservoir of good will of the preceding three years. But as the sit-downs spread, public opinion began to turn against them and the labor movement they were beginning to represent. So did politicians.[65]

Len De Caux, CIO publicity man and the first editor of *The CIO News,* blamed the public relations campaigns of Tom Girdler and like-minded industrialists for this turnabout. According to him,

> The anti-CIO public relations offensive was highly organized and extravagantly financed. Millions were spent on every device to guide opinion formation. Local business and civic leaders were bribed or bullied into "citizens committees." The press didn't need to be bribed; it let down the dams of all restraint. Anti-CIO propaganda flooded the land. . . .
>
> From professional experience, I knew how wealthy owners could use the mass media like faucets to turn "public opinion" on or off, to keep it under quiet control, or to make it a surging torrent for class or imperialist war. But never had I seen so sharp and sudden a switch of "public opinion" as that on CIO in the late spring and summer of 1937.[66]

As we have already seen, corporate opinion molders, although they can influence public opinion, certainly cannot turn it on or off like a faucet, De Caux to the contrary notwithstanding. The real reasons for the declining reputation of organized labor after the sit-down strikes relates to a phenomenon we have had occasion to mention before: suspicion of power.

For a half century preceding the sit-downs, "union labor benefited form the overestimation of union strength" because the movement was weak but had to convince potential members and adversaries that it was strong. After the 1930s, with the capitulation of even U.S. Steel, historic bulwark of the Open Shop, and with new statutory sanction, the unions began to seem powerful. The sit-down strikes added to this image. The unions did not understand that American middle-class opinion suspects power and insists on ritualistic disclaimers of its possession. These disclaimers were not forthcoming. The unions were turning out to be more powerful and less democratic than the public expected or wanted.[67]

John L. Lewis personified militant labor in the 1930s, and his image influenced the view of the union movement as a whole. Lewis had a keen sense for the dramatic gesture. The famous right fist which felled "Big Bill" Hutcheson at the 1935 Convention of the AFL was not thrown in passion or anger but rather was the result of cool calculation, intended to symbolize the irrevocability of the split between Lewis and his critics. It worked; the punch "resonated through the working class." Another example of Lewis's feel for what would impress the public was the pact unionizing U.S. Steel. Lewis actually made important concessions to Myron C. Taylor. Nevertheless, as his recent biographers, Melvyn Dubofsky and Warren Van Tine, point out, Lewis

> realized the importance of symbols and images, that what people believed to be true was often more significant than what in fact happened. When Myron Taylor, representing U.S. Steel, accorded recognition to organized labor in March 1937, newspaper columnists, public officials, scholars, and many labor leaders did not examine the terms microscopically. They were awestruck by news that the fortress of the open shop, the company that for four decades had used every weapon in its arsenal to combat trade unionism, had surrendered without a struggle to the CIO.[68]

Lewis also knew how to publicize himself. He assiduously cultivated newsmen and delighted them with his pungent news conferences. He was a superb orator, meticulously spicing up the speeches W. Jett Lauck wrote for him with biblical phrases which touched his working-class audiences. He was an accomplished platform orator and, unlike business leaders, very effective over the radio.[69]

But when he clashed with Roosevelt during the Little Steel strikes of 1937, his popularity began to wane, and during the war it disappeared completely. While executives were perceived as unselfishly working for the public good, Lewis appeared as selfishly pursuing his own ambitions. By 1943, he "was surely one of the most hated men in America"[70] because of what seemed to be his irresponsible wielding of great power. And this hatred rubbed off on labor because, although increasingly isolated within the movement, he continued to personify it to the general public.

The image of irresponsible power became the primary problem of unions in the 1940s. In the words of the editor of a union paper,

> A surprising number of Americans accepted the fiction that the employees of the nation's great business corporations had suddenly acquired greater power and greater resources than the owners of the corporations. That fiction was the basic excuse for the Taft-Hartley Act. And that fiction is today [in 1951] the Number One public relations problem of every international union.[71]

In its first convention in 1881 the American Federation of Labor acknowledged the necessity of influencing public opinion, yet not until the 1942 convention was a formal public relations department established. The Federation thus trailed the NAM by almost a decade. Commenting on the department three years later, Julius Hochman, vice president of the International Ladies Garment Workers Union and the man who proposed it, complained that very little had yet been done, "and I cannot help feeling that the problem has not received the consideration it deserves in labor's ranks."[72] He was right.

During the 1940s and even into the 1950s—when virtually all large companies had organized public relations programs, often with the counselor given a vice-presidency, when a score of experienced firms offered independent services, and when numerous trade associations, led by the NAM, made propaganda on a nationwide basis—the union effort was spasmodic and disorganized.[73] Loren Baritz found unions traditionally "either unaware of or indifferent to" the industrial use of the social sciences.[74] They were both aware of and concerned with corporate opinion manipulation but, for historic and institutional reasons, maladroit at coping with it.

Although we have seen how small-town newspapers often supported strikes, most major metropolitan dailies have been anti-union, many virulently so. Complaints about journalistic bias have pervaded union comment on the press. The movement developed an extensive press of its own, which members may have found satisfying but which influenced few outsiders. Some union leaders came to feel that "favorable mention in the general press was somehow a reflection on their militancy and dedication to the cause of working people." In order to maintain his militant credentials, the labor leader had to appear abrasive even when his actions were conciliatory (perhaps a better phrasing would be especially when they were conciliatory). Unlike the businessman, Daniel Bell has observed, "the labor leader is a politician, with a constituency. . ." The executive could make soft-spoken addresses full of reason and then work out his hostility in private, but the labor leader "carries out the performance in public." He must convince his union's members that he has not sold out to the boss, so if he doesn't lead them out on strike, "he had better give them a display of bristling menace." "Thus," according to Wilfred Sheed, "to please the members, it is often necessary to irritate the public. Bad public relations is built into the situation, although those grunts and snarls may not be aimed at you at all, but at the membership."[75]

John L. Lewis once again provides an example of this dynamic. In the midst of the GM sit-down strike, he picked a fight with Roosevelt. Most observers thought this was a serious gaffe, for the President seemed quite sympathetic to the cause of the CIO. His real purpose, however, was to encourage the strikers (and discourage Alfred P. Sloan, Jr.). Various friends encouraged Lewis to exchange his scowl for a smile and one business acquaintance suggested that he hire a public relations man to improve his image, but "Lewis replied that if he were going to fight for the coal miners, he was simply going to have to be disliked and disrespected by the majority of American people."[76]

By about 1950, despite all these handicaps, leading union journalists were beginning to forge a philosophy of public relations. They recognized the function as demanding more than superannuated warhorses cranking out flyers in a basement. It meant not only informing the public, but reforming the union when necessary. It called for expert advice, and unions were now "being eagerly sought as a clientele." It required the use of all media, and radio especially seemed promising because federal regulation curtailed bias.[77]

Nevertheless, the handicaps were not overcome. Unions were slower in developing a national public relations apparatus and by and large less efficient than management in dealing with local news. Newspapers maintained their antilabor attitude, and unions had less money than corporations to buy advertising space or radio time.[78] Worst of all, some union leaders felt that a good reputation with the general public would damage their authority within the union. This last was a difficulty no businessman had to face. These shortcomings helped create a climate of opinion favorable to Taft-Hartley and also contributed to the unpopularity of organized labor in the 1950s.

Crawford was right and Hill was wrong. The advantages in public relations lay mostly with management.

IV

We have already encountered numerous examples of how working men and women were made the objects of corporate public relations ictivity. Many public relations men, however, tried to do more than merely keep the employee from joining a union. Since the days when Anderson Pace was exhorting employers to "convert" their employees to ove of company, some have tried to persuade the worker into an active oyalty. This concern has shown both the liberalizing influence of the public relations movement and also its tendency to fasten an "organizaion man" mentality upon the employee.

"The petroleum industry," according to a speaker at the 1939 convenion of the American Petroleum Institute, "has nearly three-quarter million employees, counting those of the dealers, each of whom is either an ictive or a potential ambassador of good will. How quickly our public relations will improve if employers will act to improve the effectiveness of employees in building public good will!" In language reminiscent of NAM newspaper advertisements of earlier in the decade, he held that 'Employees are just as responsible as their employers to display a fair ind considerate attitude in promoting harmony within their company ind boosting it to the public. . . . Employees should recognize that their nterests and those of their employers are inseparable." But worker :ooperation was not bought cheaply; employers had to approach their vorkers with the same kind of care given to other important groups hrough a healthy employee relations program. Such a program began ind ended with fair wages and fair supervision but in between included uch progressive measures as

clear job classifications and equitable wage rates for each classification; fixed schedules of working hours and holidays; reasonable allowances for overtime work, vacations, emergency absences, jury duty, attendance at summer military encampments, etc.; comprehensive plans for health or income protection insurance, life insurance, and old-age security; and adequate programs for safety and health protection.

Workers were sensitive to style, so this program would have to be administered with a lack of condescension in addition to strict fairness.[79] At he General Foods Corporation, the employee relations program included some additions to this list. The company had a clear organization :hart available to every employee, one man whose specific responsibility vas personnel relations, standardized personnel records, a standard reruitment policy, a system for checking on the performance of supervisors, a method for getting the ideas of employees and also for handling heir grievances, and an employee newsletter to keep communication vell-oiled. The company said that the American worker was fair when reated fairly, but he steadfastly demanded "respect for his personality ind dignity." These and other employee plans show that welfare capitalism had not died with the great union drives of the 1930s. Public relations men helped keep it alive.[80]

Not only could the loyal employee act as an "ambassador of good will," especially at the local level, he could also be a better producer. Production and technology may be a source of pride now, wrote a counselor at the end of 1943, "but if two very human beings, the Big Boss and Joe, who works in the shop, can get so they really understand each other, there'll be production improvements never before dreamed of."[81]

Always the emphasis was on the natural harmony between employer and employee. Never was the possibility admitted that if employees learned the whole truth about employers and the system by whose authority they made such important decisions and earned such high salaries, conflict rather than harmony would be the result. Proof of the sincerity of this belief was that counselors repeated it in private as well as in public. Thus, before an off-the-record meeting of the National Industrial Conference Board in January of 1944. Du Pont's Theodore G. Joslin declared it axiomatic "that the better the public is advised about industry, the better the position of industry before the public."[82]

But what precisely did Joslin mean when he spoke of advising the public well? Did he mean telling the whole truth? Numerous public relations counsels have advised just that. Ivy Lee, with his doctrine that since business was right for America, the public could be trusted with the facts, became famous for persuading the Pennsylvania Railroad to tell the truth about a train wreck, and Du Pont itself had first established a press bureau in order to tell the truth about plant accidents because the truth was inevitably less gory than the rumors that otherwise followed such events. This support for straightforwardness persisted into the '40s and beyond. One advertising agency's public relations primer for 1943, under the heading "Riots, Strikes," advised, "Help newsmen, give facts, stress firm's effort to fix. Never try to suppress."[83] The usual reason advanced for this approach was that the truth would come out anyway, and it would usually be under more damaging circumstances than if the company volunteered it. Only rarely did a corporate counselor publicly advocate suppression of "information which, if revealed, would actually work to the detriment of the company's best interest."[84]

The amount of truth told by the nation's corporate public relations departments over the years is, of course, unquantifiable. The answer is probably a good deal more than the average intellectual would acknowledge and a good deal less than the average corporate public relations man would like to admit. A more interesting question is what happens to the concept of truth in the minds of men who have convinced themselves that what *seems* is more important than what *is*. One wonders, for exam-

ɔle, what to make of the following statement by Robert S. Henry, public
relations director of the Association of American Railroads, in 1944:
'We have used the ordinary means of communication; we have told the
story; we have tried to stay within the facts, and I think we have. We have
ɔught to create an *impression* of truth."[85] Truth may have been the goal,
ɔut lacking the genuine article its impression would do just as well.

The benefactions advocated by the petroleum industry and General
Foods, to cite just two examples, were not to be vouchsafed the worker
without some consideration in return. This was to take the form of cour-
tesy to outsiders, especially customers, and of speaking well of the corporation whenever the opportunity presented itself. Thus AT&T, as we
have seen, took special pains to educate operators in the proper way to
respond to telephone users. In reviewing a program which he had instituted for a railroad, a public relations man recounted an incident in
which a "minor employee" had words with the mayor of a town the road
served because he had parked his chauffeur-driven limousine in a reserved space when attending a civic ceremony commemorating the
launching of a new train. "Subsequently," according to the counselor, "it
was revealed that this employee's consistently belligerent attitude had
been creating ill will over a period of several years." The offender was
called to headquarters

> for a friendly talk with the president and general traffic manager. He was
> not threatened with discharge. He was shown how his attitude was building
> ill will. How ill will must inevitably result in loss of business, and how less
> business would ultimately affect his pay envelope. He was assured that
> repetition of such rudeness would result in drastic action.

(What form this action would take, if not the discharge with which we
were told the employee had not been threatened, was left to the imagination.) The employee was apparently appropriately impressed and left
the office "imbued with a new spirit of cooperation."[86] Mannerliness, to
be sure, is a laudable goal, yet it should be noted that companies sometimes adopt peculiar definitions of "belligerent attitude."

In addition to being polite, employees were urged to go out and make
friends for the company. Shell Oil, for example, sent a series of booklets
to workers containing such advice as:

> If every member of the Shell family will make just a few good friends, and
> will have a good word for his associates and his company, within a year the
> Shell family will have thousands of new friends and supporters. And a
> good, strong, well-liked company is a mighty fine guarantee of a good,
> steady job.[87]

The importance of making friends for the company and winning it supporters, as if it were running for office, pervaded the literature on public relations. When Paul Garrett, founder of the public relations department of General Motors, spoke before the third annual national public relations forum in 1945, he had to confess "just a little misgiving" because his company was in the midst of a strike. Nonetheless, he consoled himself with the observation that "if we are not making any cars I hope we are making some friends."[88] Another counselor suggested that, in order to make friends on the community level, "employees should always be encouraged—though not driven—to participate in community affairs, such as war relief, Community Chest, Boy or Girl Scouts, etc. It is not only good for the community—it is good for the employee as well."[89] As more than one white-collar worker was to discover, the line between encouragement and coercion could be a fine one indeed. The growing belief in the importance of keeping the corporation healthy in a political as well as economic sense was leading it to make concessions to its workers but also to demand that they not only do their jobs during working hours but give their hearts to their company's cause in other spheres of life as well.

*   *   *

Customer relations posed a unique set of difficulties during the war. In the Depression, corporations had not had a sufficient demand for their products. In wartime, the demand was no problem, but companies were often unable to fill it because of production for the military. "In a period when purchasing power is great and potential inflation is widely discussed, the businessman is left in a straitjacket with a pocket full of money."[90]

With the consumer either restricted or prohibited altogether from buying the products of so many companies, the disposition of the advertising appropriation became a pressing question. This problem contained a host of variables which each firm had to analyze for itself. It might at first seem that in cases where production for consumer use was greatly curtailed and existing inventories rationed, output would be sold without advertising. Therefore, perhaps advertising should be eliminated and profits thus increased. On the other hand, excess-profits taxes were so high that corporations could buy advertising for a fraction of its peacetime cost. The picture was further complicated by the question of what advertising expenditure the government would allow on cost-plus and fixed-price contracts. In the former case, consumer advertising was prohibited but not institutional advertising. In the latter, postwar price adjustment boards would take into consideration a "reasonable expenditure" for advertising. In this complex situation, businessmen were asking themselves some hard questions about the utility of nonconsumer advertising.[91]

James Scott, a student of this problem, listed five "promotional tasks for wartime advertising." The first was to aid dealers, as in the automobile industry, who no longer had new products to market. Chevrolet launched a campaign designed to publicize the service facilities of its dealers which could help keep a car, irreplaceable for the duration, on the road. The second was to maintain demand for a product line which, once forced to do without, the public might decide was not so necessary at all. The third was to maintain brand preference, which would especially be a problem if competitors continued to advertise. Promotion of conservation was another goal, which industry assumed in cooperation with government. And finally there was the desire to preserve public good will through institutional or public relations advertising, terms usually used interchangeably. Scott's primary interest in institutional advertising was whether it would encourage postwar sales, but he was also cognizant of the special political problems which the war posed, especially for larger companies. The public, for example, might react with disfavor toward a consumer goods corporation which made high profits during the war, and there were obvious "opportunities for public misunderstanding of the motives" of such organizations as Standard Oil of New Jersey with its patent arrangements with German firms.[92] Many executives apparently agreed. According to Paul West, president of the Association of National Advertisers, billings for institutional advertising increased from $1 million in 1939 to $17 million in 1943.[93]

In a business world becoming steadily more impressed with the public opinion survey, expenditures for institutional advertising were not made without such studies. One, commissioned by General Electric early in 1942, showed 90 percent of those questioned interested in learning from institutional advertisements how to make the products they owned last longer, 85 percent wanted information on products presently being sold, three quarters were interested in product development and work toward mitigation of the expected postwar unemployment problem, and only half wanted to know about the contributions of manufacturers to the war effort. People did not want to hear management blow its own horn.[94]

Authors of institutional advertisements looked for "newspegs" to make their advertisements more interesting. These might include awards and honors earned by product and company; news of new employees, products or equipment; customer comments on products; and case histories of personal success stories within the company. Coun-

selors were encouraged to investigate their company as if they were reporters writing a feature story on it and include in their institutional
advertisements details of its history and its operating procedures.[95]

Among the other ways to keep customers and potential customers
happy despite inability to fill orders was answering their letters. These
answers should be composed with "a little warmth [and] a little grace" for
those qualities were the "essence of sound public relations." Even if the
company's correspondent was not a customer, he or she might someday
become one. And even if no increase in sales resulted, the warm, genial,
and prompt response to mail would make "a favorable impression" and
also "some good friends."[96]

V

The government-business rapprochement made possible by the needs
of war led to a diminution of the name-calling that had characterized the
Depression era. Businessmen were able to work harmoniously with the
Democratic administration to an extent which probably surprised some
former Liberty Leaguers. The NAM continued to espouse conservative
principles, but with external pressures relaxed "unit thinking and unit
action" became more difficult to enforce. And a new organization, the
Committee for Economic Development, had begun to support more
moderate goals.

The American businessman of 1945 faced the postwar world with
mixed emotions. His productive achievements during the great struggle
had been recognized. Once again he was a figure to be admired, while
the prestige of his union adversaries had sunk to a new low. However
other nations which shared the form of economic organization under
which he had prospered seemed everywhere on the defensive. Even during the war, most public relations men were more concerned with competition from labor and government than from the enemy—in fact,
there were few references to foreign propaganda in their speeches and
articles, but the realization of this isolation must have been sobering. ". . .
[W]hereas fifty years ago, even twenty-five years ago, the system which
we call free enterprise was universal among all economically developed
countries," Walter Lippmann told the Association of National Advertisers in November of 1945, "today the U.S. is the only big industrial country now committed to the perpetuation of free enterprise." He warned
that advertising and free enterprise must continue to sell the system as
well as its products and concluded on a Schumpeterian note: "Let the
captains of industry be captains indeed, and go forward unafraid into
the days to come."[97]

The fact that public relations did not diminish in importance demonstrated that it was thought to do more than defend the corporation against direct criticism. Businessmen perceived public opinion as a long-term problem and stepped up attempts to deal with it. The answer of public relations to the threats from without and within the nation could best be summarized by the slogan of N. W. Ayer: "Keeping Everlastingly At It." Although advertising would now return to the moving of merchandise, public relations advertising, with its status "immeasurably exalted," could not and would not be neglected.[98] Employee relations and community relations programs were to be stepped up. The public relations professionals were to soar in numbers and in importance during the Truman years. The manner in which they approached the post-war corporate political needs and their attempts to dignify their vocation through the establishment of official organizations and codes of ethics will be examined in the following chapter.

NOTES

1. *Businessmen and Reform* (Chicago, 1962); *Competition and Cooperation* (Baltimore, 1966).
2. This discussion is based upon William E. Leuchtenburg, "The New Deal and the Analogue of War," in John Braeman, Robert H. Bremner, and Everett Walters, eds., *Change and Continuity in Twentieth Century America* (Columbus, Ohio, 1965), pp. 81–143. See also Otis L. Graham, Jr., *Toward a Planned Society* (New York, 1976), pp. 1–68.
3. Richard W. Steele, "Preparing the Public for War: Efforts to Establish a National Propaganda Agency, 1940–1941," *American Historical Review* 75, No. 6 (October 1970), p. 1652.
4. Burns, *Freedom*, pp. 194, 51.
5. Graham, *Society*, p. 81.
6. Quoted in Leuchtenburg, "Analogue," p. 85. One reason for the attraction to the analogy of war was the supposed efficiency of the War Industries Board, which efficiency, as recent scholarship has shown, was overestimated. See Robert D. Cuff, *The War Industries Board* (Baltimore, 1973), p. 149.
7. Burns, *Freedom*, pp. 192–193.
8. Ibid., p. 118; Richard Polenberg, *War and Society* (Philadelphia, 1972), p. 11.
9. Polenberg, *War*, pp. 10–11.
10. Ibid., pp. 12–13.
11. Donald H. Riddle, *The Truman Committee* (New Brunswick, 1964), p. 137; Edwin H. Sutherland, *White Collar Crime* (New York, 1949), pp. 164–175. Sutherland concluded that "profits are more important to large corporations than patriotism, even in the midst of an international struggle which endangered Western civilization." This proposition, he believed, was proven by evidence developed by congressional investigating committees. "This documentary evidence of the overt behavior of the corporation is generally in conflict with the verbal statements of the corporations." Ibid., p. 174.

12. Riddle, *Truman*, pp. 148–149.

13. Ibid., pp. 122–140.

14. A. Russell Buchanan, *The United States and World War II*, Vol. II (New York, 1964), p. 319.

15. An historian of the NAM observed that in 1940, "The government, to whom industry had been an errant child in need of discipline for eight years, overnight found the nation's manufacturing genius to be our only safeguard against possible destruction. The public, too, shared in the discovery." *NAM and Leaders*, p. 25.

16. Dr. Claude Robinson, "What the Public Thinks of Industry," *Industries Public Relations: Opportunities, Responsibilities, Problems and Case Studies*, New York, November 30–December 1, 1942 (hereinafter, *IPR*), pp. 16–20, Drawer #1110, NAM papers.

17. "Significant Quotes from the N.A.M. War Congress," *Sales Management* (December 15, 1942), pp. 26, 28.

18. This criticism was widespread but not universal. Riddle, *Truman*, p. 138.

19. Polenberg, *War*, pp. 171–175, 165.

20. Quoted in William E. Leuchtenburg, *Franklin D. Roosevelt and the New Deal* (New York, 1963), p. 22.

21. Burns, *Lion*, pp. 244–245. Roosevelt did show some early interest in planning, especially toward conserving natural resources. Graham, *Planned*, pp. 17–21.

22. Brown to Witherow, July 31, 1942; Witherow to Brown, August 24, 1942, Drawer #1111, NAM papers.

23. *IPR*, Introduction.

24. Thomas J. Ross, "Where are We Headed in Public Relations?", *IPR*, pp. 10–12.

25. *Proceedings* of the Second Annual Public Relations Conference, New York, December 6–December 7, 1943 (hereinafter, *SAPRC*), p. 50.

26. *Proceedings*, Philadelphia Executives Conference, Public Relations, October 19, 1943 (hereinafter, *Phila. PR*), p. 2.

27. "The Supreme Court, having embraced the theories of sociological jurisprudence, can no longer be counted on to protect our historic liberties. The policies of the Executive branch of the government will inevitably lead to the socialization of industry—despite the lip service that some of its spokesmen pay to private enterprise." NAM Public Relations Advisory Group (herinafter, PRAG). "Report of Meeting," October 21, 1942, p. 3, Drawer #1110, NAM papers.

28. PRAG, p. 2. The conferees apparently did not notice the irony in their wish that the rugged individualists whom they purported to champion "submerge their own interests." Here we have another illustration of sacrifices for the sake of "Unit thinking, unit action."

29. Indeed the NAM itself, showing a surprising open-mindedness, named a committee to study national planning for reconversion in 1943. Graham, *Planned*, p. 83.

30. John D'Emilio, "The Committee for Economic Development, 1942–1948"

(unpublished master's thesis, Columbia, 1972), p. 3; Kim McQuaid, "The Business Advisory Council of the Department of Commerce," in Paul Uselding, ed., *Research in Economic History,* Vol. I (Greenwich, Conn., 1976), pp. 184–185.

31. D'Emilio, "Committee," p. 9.

32. Ibid., p. 49; *NAM and Leaders,* p. 26; "Inarticulate Business Must Get Away from Its Dog House Complex," *Printers' Ink,* December 27, 1940, p. 17. See Chapter 3, Note 23, for the Tripod of Freedom.

33. "The CED—What Is It and Why?" *Antioch Review* 4, No. 1 (March 1944), pp. 21–46.

34. Karl Schriftgiesser, *Business and Public Policy* (Englewood Cliffs, N.J., 1967), p. 201; Brady, "CED," p. 27.

35. D'Emilio, "Committee," pp. 45–46.

36. Ibid., p. 43.

37. Ibid., p. 91.

38. Schriftgiesser, *Public Policy,* p. 13.

39. *Sales Management,* July 15, 1943, p. 46.

40. For example, in a paper prepared early in 1942, the NAM public relations staff expressed the same concern about the possibility that wartime dislocations and acceptance of government intervention during the emergency might trigger increased government influence in the peace-time economy as Brown had. But where Brown wrote in measured terms and in a relatively calm fashion, the staff was considerably more belligerent:

> At the moment, NAM's obligations to industry to continue, as vigorously as funds and facilities permit, to keep industry's record constantly before the public, are spotlighted by the crescendo of attacks on our performance in defense and war production.
>
> Witness the outpourings of such columnists as Lippmann and Clapper, the Truman Committee's report to the Senate, the Vinson Committee's "Profits" report to the House, the revival of the Reuther plan and the assorted attacks of others—officials and volunteers—too numerous to mention.
>
> These attacks from such varied quarters are probably not just coincidence or happenstance. Analysis indicates a clear pattern. The timing just after Pearl Harbor is convincing. This is the effort which N.A.M.'s program anticipated as early as September 1939—the attempt to shoulder off responsibility, for official lapses, material shortages and labor malingering and worse, onto private management to justify the first step toward socialization of our whole system.

"NAM's Public Information Program in 1942," Staff suggestions for consideration by the PRAG steering committee, January 23, 1941 [*sic,* should be 1942], Drawer #1111, NAM Papers. Freud once observed that it takes a high degree of sophistication to believe in chance. Primitive societies need devil theories to make the world comprehensible. So, too, did the NAM's public relations staff at this time.

41. D'Emilio, "Committee," pp. 33–34.

144 / *Keeping the Corporate Image*

42. Quoted in D'Emilio, ibid., p. 47.
43. John W. O'Leary, "The 'What Helps Business. . .' Campaign," *Public Opinion Quarterly* 2 (October 1938), pp. 645–650.
44. D'Emilio, "Committee," p. 38–42.
45. "Wartime Public Relations—A Survey," *Public Opinion Quarterly* 8 (Spring 1944), p. 97. Everett R. Smith, Director of Research for the Macfadden Publications, did extensive interviewing of workers during the war and reported the results to numerous public relations forums sponsored by the NAM. When he told the laborers of the work being done by the CED, he characterized the response as : "'Well, that's something that's swell. But,'" the workers complained, "'why don't they tell us about it? . . . And why don't they bring us into it?'" "What Your Workers Really Think," *Indiana Executives Conference: Public Relations*, April 14, 1944 (hereinafter, *Ind. PR*), p. 58, Drawer #1017, NAM papers.
46. For example, Charles R. Hook's comments in "Brass Hat Panel," *SAPRC*, p. 142.
47. Holcombe Parkes, "Tackling the Job at N.A.M.," *Proceedings* of the Third National Public Relations Conference, December 4, 1945 (hereinafter, 3NPRC), pp. 37–38. Drawer #1017, NAM papers. Daniel Bell has written that "from 1940 to 1947 CIO intellectuals were up to their ears in social planning." "Labor's Coming of Middle Age," *Fortune*, October 1951, p. 115.
48. "Let's Study Our Public," *Ind. PR*, pp. 4–5.
49. "Management Reports to Employees," *Ind. P.R.*, pp. 48–49.
50. *SAPRC*, pp. 85–88; *Ind. PR*, pp. 36–37. Steel executives, according to *Iron Age*, might have compromised with the strikers of 1919 had the issue been wages alone. But the Open Shop was the crux of the argument, and about that there could be no concessions.
   A study of the causes of work stoppages from 1927 to 1950 indicates that working conditions and union organization consistently caused more strikes than wages and hours. This finding supports Crawford's assertion that money was not the major labor issue. On the other hand, it is somewhat ingenuous to deny that an important reason for supporting unions was the promise of "more, more, more, now." Although money may not have been the proximate cause of the majority of strikes, it probably was the ultimate cause. Fleming, "Wagner Act," pp. 132–133; Brody, *Steelworkers*, pp. 242–243.
51. *Ind. PR*, p. 31.
52. For example: If a prospector goes looking for gold and a barkeeper "grubstakes" him, how should the gold be split? "The answers were overwhelmingly 'fifty-fifty,' and the majority of the workers said that the barkeeper should have more than half. Isn't that an astounding evidence of the value of educating the worker to understand the stockholder's relationship to business enterprise?" Ibid., p. 33.
53. Ibid., pp. 38–39.
54. Robert N. McMurray, "War and Peace in Labor Relations," *Harvard Business Review* 33, No. 6 (November-December 1955), p. 59; Baritz, *Servants*, p. 140. For a union organizer's reaction to Crawfordism, see ibid., pp. 151–153.
55. Ibid., pp. 31–38.
56. Beldon, "Survey," pp. 94–99.

57. "Where Are We Headed in Public Relations?" *Cleveland Executives Conference on Public Relations,* June 3, 1943 (hereinafter, *Cleve. PR*), pp. 6–8, Drawer #1110, NAM papers.

58. *Ind. PR,* pp. 54–60; "What Workers Are Thinking," *Proceedings* of the Southern California Executives Conference: Public Relations, October 3, 1944 (hereinafter, *Southern Cal. PR*), pp. 18–25, Drawer # 1017, NAM papers. Some executives came to feel that the adjective "free" when tacked on to "enterprise" was a public relations debit, for it seemed to imply that management and stockholders were getting something for nothing. As a result, when the NAM published its massive study of the economy, it chose the title *The American Individual Enterprise System* (New York, 1946). John Hill was a leading advocate of this semantic transformation.

59. Here, for example, are the results of a March 1941 Gallup survey asking "Which do you think is trying harder to help national defense production . . .?"

Labor leaders 10%
Business leaders 56
About the same 16
No opinion 18

In May 1943, Gallup asked war plant workers what they thought was the greatest mistake their company made. A remarkable 46 percent replied that there were no such errors. Only 8 percent complained of poor employer-employee relations and only 4 percent of lack of competent supervisors. These findings tend to contradict Smith. On the other hand they cannot be accepted unequivocally, for the Gallup polls on workers, management, and Roosevelt from 1937 to the end of the war are bewildering in their contradictions. George H. Gallup, *The Gallup Poll: Public Opinion, 1935–1971,* I (New York, 1972), pp. 271, 385.

60. Almont Lindsey, *The Pullman Strike* (Chicago, 1942), pp. 142–143, 315–317.

61. Herbert G. Gutman, "The Worker's Search for Power," in H. Wayne Morgan, ed., *The Gilded Age, A Reappraisal* (Syracuse, 1963), pp. 38–68.

62. Elmo Roper, "Public Attitudes Toward Labor Unions," *Labor and Nation,* (October, 1945), p. 33.

63. Bernstein, *Turbulent,* pp. 170, 41, 308; Schlesinger, *New Deal,* p. 139.

64. Bernstein, *Turbulent,* p. 316; Benjamin M. Selekman, "Trade Unions— Romance and Reality," *Harvard Business Review* 36, No. 3 (May-June 1958), pp. 76–86.

65. Sidney Fine, *Sit Down* (Ann Arbor, 1969), pp. 332–339; Bernstein, *Turbulent,* p. 481.

66. Len De Caux, *Labor Radical* (Boston, 1970), pp. 290–293.

67. Gordon H. Cole, "The Union's Public Relations," in J. B. S. Hardman and Maurice F. Neufeld, eds., *The House of Labor* (New York, 1951), p. 205; Sumner H. Slichter, "Public Reaction to Unions," in E. Wight Bakke, Clark Kerr, and Charles W. Anrod, eds., *Unions, Management, and the Public* (New York, 1960), pp. 626–629.

68. Melvyn Dubofsky and Warren Van Tine, *John L. Lewis* (New York, 1977), pp. 221, 273–277.

69. Ibid., pp. 447, 229.

70. Ibid., p. 424.

71. Cole, "Public Relations," p. 205.

72. American Federation of Labor, *Proceedings* of the First Convention, 1881, p. 6; *Proceedings* of the 62nd Convention, 1943, pp. 552–557. Julius Hochman, "Labor's Relations with the Public May Well Prove of Decisive Importance," *Labor and Nation* 1 (October 1945), pp. 43–44.

73. Ibid., p. 43; Barbash, *Unionism*, pp. 287–288; Elmo Roper, "The Public Would Not Do Away with Unions. . . ," *Labor and Nation* 1 (October 1945), p. 38.

74. Baritz, *Servants*, pp. 206–207.

75. Barbash, pp. 287–288; Daniel Bell, "The Language of Labor," *Fortune*, September 1951, p. 209; Wilfred Sheed, "What Ever Happened to the Labor Movement?" *Atlantic*, July 1973, p. 44.

76. Dubofsky and Van Tine, *Lewis*, pp. 264, 282; De Caux, *Radical*, pp. 292–293.

77. Hardman, "Union Communications," in Hardman and Neufeld, *House of Labor*, p. 173; Cole, "Public Relations," p. 207; and see Henry C. Fleisher, "Public Relations for Labor Organizations," in Philip Lesly, ed., *Public Relations Handbook* (New York, 1950), pp. 326–341. To judge from Edward J. Noble, founder of ABC, broadcasters were as antilabor as publishers. The NBC Blue Network was sold to Noble in 1943. His interrogation by the Federal Communications Commission's James Lawrence Fly showed that he intended not to sell time to labor organizations, despite his willingness to allow companies to broadcast institutional messages. Under FCC pressure, ABC finally relented, but it is noteworthy that while businesses had been using radio to sell their ideology as well as their products for almost twenty years, it took regulatory pressure to secure the same right for organized labor. Barnouw, *Web*, pp. 187–190. For comments on labor's problems with the general circulation press, see Liebling, *The Press*, pp. 156–173.

78. Cole. "Public Relations," pp. 206–207; Fleisher, "Public Relations," pp. 336–340.

79. H. H. Anderson, "Petroleum's Good Will Ambassadors," *Proceedings* of the Twentieth Annual Meeting of the American Petroleum Institute, Vol. 20 [1], 1939, pp. 83–86.

80. Verne Burnett, "A Public Relations Manager Looks at the Labor Relations Program," *Advanced Management* 8 (July 1943), pp. 4–8. Most of this article consisted of an interview which Burnett, General Foods' vice-president in charge of public relations, held with the company's director of industrial relations, Thomas G. Spates. It was Spates whose proposals these were, and it was he, apparently, who was the man at General Foods solely responsible for personnel. The fact that Burnett wrote this article showed that he approved Spates's measures and thought it would be good for the company's reputation to let others know what it was doing for employees. The frontier between public relations and industrial relations has historically been as ill defined as that between public relations and advertising. Their relationship will be considered in some detail in the following chapter.

81. Verne Burnett, "The New Frontier—Human Relations," *Advertising and Selling*, December 1943, p. 68.

82. *Proceedings,* 257th meeting, The Conference Board, January 20, 1944, p. 3. NICB transcript #89.27, Eleutherian Mills Historical Library, Wilmington, Delaware.

85. "Public Relations Primer," *Printers' Ink,* December 31, 1943, p. 68.

84. This remark was made by John P. Syme, whose title was director of industrial relations of the Johns-Manville Company. He made it with a complete lack of self-consciousness. *Ind. PR,* p. 32.

85. NICB transcript #89.27, p. 23. Emphasis added.

86. Thomas W. Parry, "Public Relations for a Railroad," *Public Opinion Quarterly* 3 (January 1939), pp. 154–163.

87. Paul B. West, "Needed Vitally: More Favorable Public Opinion of Corporations," *Printers' Ink,* September 14, 1945, p. 212.

88. "A Case Example in Public Relations," *3NRPC,* p. 77.

89. Dickson Hartwell, "Current Problems in Public Relations," *Public Opinion Quarterly* 6 (Summer 1942), p. 247.

90. Boyce F. Martin, "What Business Learns from War," *Harvard Business Review* 21, No. 3 (Spring 1943), p. 359.

91. James D. Scott, "Advertising When Consumers Cannot Buy," *Harvard Business Review* 21, No. 2 (Winter 1943), pp. 207–229; "Advertising When Buying Is Restricted," *Harvard Business Review* 21, No. 4 (Summer 1943), pp. 443–454.

92. Scott, "Consumers Cannot Buy," p. 226.

93. West, "Needed," p. 106. There was a shortage of newsprint during the war which forced publications to refuse some advertising. The result was a boom in institutional advertising on the radio. Barnouw, *Web,* pp. 165–168.

94. Scott, "Consumers Cannot Buy," p. 226.

95. McNutt, "20 Topics," pp. 19ff; Roland S. Neff, "Public Relations in Publicity—Or How to Handle Industrial News," *Industrial Marketing,* August 1944, pp. 41ff.

96. Donald F. Haggerty, "A Little Warmth, A Little Grace: Essence of Sound Public Relations," *Sales Management,* July 15, 1944, pp. 38–46.

97. "Business Faces a Challenge," *Advertising and Selling,* December 1945, p. 34.

98. Charles C. Carr, "Public Relations—Post-War Style," *Trusts and Estates,* May 1944, p. 467.

Chapter VI

Expansion and Attempts at Professionalization

I

The improvement in the reputation of American business which began with the wartime production achievement continued into the Truman era. When Henry Ford died in 1947, the press was "virtually unanimous" in its praise not only for him but for the economic system he was taken to represent. Enterprise and nation seemed securely linked.[1]

A 1951 study of public opinion conducted by the University of Michigan's Institute for Social Research showed 76 percent of the interviewees approving of big business with only 10 percent disapproving. The study found that the term "big business" had lost its "scare value." Interviewees were not without skepticism. While appreciating the contributions of large firms to high employment, productivity, and innovation, many mistrusted their power. A sizable minority also objected to the "impersonal and distant" attitude of managers toward employees, an attitude which public relations counselors had been laboring to change lo these many years. Despite the occasional negative note, most of the Institute's findings should have comforted the big businessman, who had been an object of such suspicion and ridicule during the '30s.[2]

There was, however, more than one way to interpret such findings. Claude Robinson's Opinion Research Corporation (ORC) conducted a public opinion poll for the American Petroleum Institute in 1946, and some of the results paralleled those of the Michigan study. People who thought of it at all were well disposed toward the industry.[3] From Robinson's data, one could have concluded that the industry did not need a

149

public relations program and that in fact such a program ran the risk of exciting negative feelings.[4]

Robinson disagreed with this analysis. He lectured the Petroleum Institute on the "principle of the 'unfilled vacuum,' or the advantage of getting your story across first." Many of the favorable opinions were weakly held and liable to change if exposed to the skillful propaganda of critics. The moral was "that you must get your word in first before someone comes forth with propaganda to fill the vacuum."[5] This the industry proceeded to do, with a big-budget campaign designed to convince the public that "petroleum is progressive."[6] During the period in which this program was being devised, the Labour Government of Great Britain was beginning its nationalization of major industries. One important reason for the takeover of the coal industry, according to *Fortune*, was that management "did not comprehend what the U.S. knows as public relations. [It had taken] the attitude that there is something a trifle underhanded about a planned campaign to sell people on an idea or product whose merits should be obvious."[7] The oil industry in America self-consciously set about to avoid a similar error.[8]

To be sure, American businessmen faced substantial problems in the postwar world. Some of them feared excessive government intervention in the economy and balked at the government's tardiness in eliminating such holdover war measures as price controls.[9] The inflation that affected every citizen was partly blamed on big businessmen. In 1948, the ORC reported that the public's demand for government regulation of big business was up to 46 percent from 35 percent two years previously and that acceptance of business was down to 70 percent from 77 percent in 1944. Respondents, the report concluded, felt that prices were too high and competition ineffective because of the activities of big business.[10] Severe labor troubles also persisted which reflected badly on both management and unions.

Despite these real problems, public opinion toward big business during the Truman years did seem to be generally favorable. Employment was high, real wages were climbing, trust-busting had lost its punch as a political issue, and agitation about the evils of a military-industrial complex or concern about the environmental implications of continued expansion of the industrial plant were not yet widespread. But businessmen remembered the '30s and looked abroad and were uneasy. As a result, corporate public relations experienced the most dramatic growth in its history. The field was flooded with new practitioners and budgets soared with expenditures for institutional advertising and for experiments with such "educational" devices as comic books and company-sponsored economics courses. More chief executives took a personal hand in public relations, and more counselors were attaining the rank of vice-president or assistant to the president.

Prior to the late '40s estimates of the growth of public relations must be based largely on impressionistic analyses of the writings of counselors themselves, the statements of business leaders, the complaints of opponents, and general comments in the business press. From 1945 on, however, numerous students of business took surveys of the function, so for the first time one can supplement impressionistic observations with statistical data.

Early in 1945, the National Industrial Conference Board found "an attitude of complete acceptance of industry's responsibility for developing and maintaining good public relations. . ." Twenty-two of the 89 companies replying to its questionnaire had in-house counselors, sometimes directing large staffs. Twenty percent of the sample employed outside counsel. Even those firms which did not have a public relations department were becoming "public relations minded." For example, a spokesman for a foundry explained, "We have no Public Relations Department. However, our key men are active in community affairs, patriotic, charitable, and political, and, in this way we are able to exert influences beneficial to our company." Although a small company in the iron and steel industry was without a public relations department too, "We have tried to give our employees a better understanding and knowledge of basic economic principles, and their application to our business, by talks, conferences and distribution of booklets and other printed matter from time to time." By a wide margin, employees were considered the major "public" of concern to corporate public relations. Following them, in descending order of importance, were customers, citizens of plant communities, stockholders, the general public, and government. Media used, again in descending order of importance, were newspaper releases, institutional advertising, house organs, stockholder reports, special booklets, personal contacts and community participation, radio programs, and motion pictures.[11]

In a 1946 survey, the Opinion Research Corporation (ORC) found "a great surge of interest" in public relations, with nine out of ten companies increasing their expenditures. Three reasons were advanced for this growth: the erosion of "the bond of confidence" between the front office and the shop, which had especially dangerous implications on the issue of collectivism; the "advance of statism"; and the "pariah label," a residue of the Depression. Forty-three percent of company chiefs polled wanted public relations to tell the public about their product. An equal number wanted it to achieve greater labor-management understanding and to tell the public the management side of the story. Twenty-eight percent wanted it to inform the public how business worked to serve the common good, with 14 percent seeking the related goal of selling the American system of free enterprise. Another 23 percent wanted it to combat government regulation. The function was most highly developed and most influential in the larger companies.[12]

The following year an ORC survey of 100 firms revealed a continued rise in public relations expenditures but also a tendency in some smaller firms to level off. Those companies with the most highly developed departments were expanding the most. The leading aims of the programs were to inform people of the "economic facts of business," to help sell products, and to promote harmony between management and labor. There was a growing movement to unite public and industrial relations; only 20 percent of the sample kept them separate. Within the organization, the public relations counselor was increasingly reporting to the chief executive or being given vice-presidential status.[13]

The year 1947 also witnessed a dramatic increase in public relations advertising. This method of reaching the public had the advantages of speed, wide circulation, and, unlike the press release which was reported in a newspaper article, guaranteed accuracy in the presentation of the message. Important components of that message were that management sought to be fair to employees and customers as well as stockholders, that business was efficient, and that productivity was the key to a higher standard of living. The outstanding aim was "to tell the facts about profits," i.e., refute the charge that they were excessive.[14]

According to the ORC, public relations continued to grow in importance, though not at a steady rate. Reviewing the developments of five years, the 1951 report found:

Table 1. Public Relations Expenditures of Selected
Companies from 1947 to 1951

Year	Increased	Decreased	Unchanged
1947	59%	9%	16%
1948	56	6	24
1949	41	14	38
1950	52	24	17
1951	38	38	8

Source: Opinion Research Corporation, *Public Opinion Index for Industry,* "Growth Trends in Industry Communications," Vol. 9, No. 10, p. 37.

Companies exploited a wide variety of avenues to the public:

Table 2. Media Used by Public Relations Department
of Selected Companies in 1951

Medium	Used by % of Sample
Employee publications	59
Annual reports for stockholders	38
Pamphlets, brochures	34
Newspaper advertisements	34
Meetings for supervisors	33
Speeches by officials	29
Plant tours	26
Management letters for supervisors	23
Management letters for employees	23
Annual reports for employees	17
Economics courses for supervisors	17
Motion pictures (internal)	17
Company publications (external)	16
Meetings for employees	16
Motion pictures (external)	14
Economics courses for employees	11
Radio, television	11
Misc.	10

Note: 22% of the sample was not working at economic education.

Source: Opinion Research Corporation, *Public Opinion Index for Industry,* "Growth Trends in Industry Communications," Vol. 9, No. 10, p. 57.

Fifty-nine percent of the sample had specific publics in mind as targets for their media efforts. Table 3 shows which targets predominated. The ORC concluded its 1951 study by observing that "the dominant problem of this business age is to win and hold public support for competitive capitalism in practice."[15]

These surveys and others indicated that expansion rather than innovation was the keynote of the postwar public relations effort. Since the Progressive era, railroads and utilities had recognized the importance of "converting" the employee because he could do such effective "missionary work" for the corporation. Since at least the steel strike of 1919, corporations had experimented with institutional advertising to deal with labor unrest.[16] The multi-media approach had been familiar since Ivy Lee, but the prejudice formed during the Depression in favor of print over the electronic media persisted. The plant tour and community relations programs were not new either; General Motors instituted its own "Ohio Idea" (a community public relations program for Dayton) as early as 1934. In the late '40s, however, such plans were being further refined and more companies were using them.[17] Another important continuity was the bifurcation in general business propaganda between the NAM and the CED which had begun during the war.

Table 3. Targets of Companies with Public Relations
Programs Concentrating on Specific Audiences in 1951

Group	Primary Audience	2nd	3rd
Employees: supervisors and rank and file	31%	13%	3%
Customers	13	7	4
General Public	5	1	4
Press	4	2	1
Thought Leaders	3	6	5
Stockholders	1	7	4
Community residents	0	5	3
Suppliers	0	1	2
Dealers	0	0	2
Employees' families	0	1	1

Source: ORC, "Growth Trends," p. 60.

New attitudes and actions among businessmen, which public relations activity had always portended, developed with the heightened sensitivity to public relations. The counselor's emphasis on the importance of community support and employee loyalty increased the significance of the manner in which managers conducted their private lives. Large firms encouraged personnel to be civic-minded, to serve on local committees for community betterment and to contribute to local charities. The neighborhoods and towns in which executives lived became a matter of concern. Junior managers could excite charges of snobbery if they forsook the plant community and commuted from another town. Executives' wives were sometimes requested to minimize news of their social activities in the local papers to save the company from accusations of overpaying their husbands.[18] The attitude of wives toward the firm was becoming an increasingly important consideration in the promotion of their spouses.[19]

The salaried man was at least as important a good-will ambassador as the wage earner. Thus International Harvester's Dale Cox declared in 1949 that

all the public relations men serving all American business . . . can't do the job [of selling business] alone. It is too big. It has, therefore, to be the job of everyone in business, especially those in managerial capacities. . . . [We] must use . . . the educational process with all the managerial people we can reach. . . . So, in our company, we are devoting as much attention now to the indoctrination and training of these managerial people in public relations as we do to the day-to-day operations of our [department] in direct work with the public.[20]

The work of counselors inevitably served to increase management's concern about public opinion and to encourage activities which would foster a benign atmosphere. More counselors were basing their work "on the solid foundation of extensive and careful opinion research."[21] In its 1950 public relations survey, the ORC found over half its sample saying that getting information from employees was at least as important as getting it to them. Although communication from the bottom up has never been as well developed as the reverse trip, progress was being made.[22] Sensitized to the feelings of underlings and outsiders, management did take concrete steps to curry public favor.

A journalist highly critical of the efforts for free publicity of the more flamboyant public relations men reported a case in point. A company was "cordially hated" by the community despite its big weekly payroll. The counselor conducted a survey which revealed townspeople unhappy over a number of "prinpricks." Employees took all the parking spaces for blocks around the plant; the company paid by check, and workers expected local merchants to carry large sums of money to cash them; the plant discarded rubbish in a nearby vacant lot which was an eyesore and a breeding ground for rats; etc. At the public relations man's suggestion, the company cleared a parking lot, cleaned up its rubbish, arranged to have checks cashed conveniently, and worked out a traffic-control plan. Favorable newspaper articles resulted without the necessity of writing releases or buttonholing editors.[23]

Public relations should be viewed as both a cause and result of the ascendance of the managerial attitude over the classical one.[24] As W. Howard Chase of General Foods put it in 1949, ". . . [N]o economic system, American or otherwise, is a natural law. Everyone is man-made—just as legal systems or political systems are man-made. Consequently, the system we live under today is neither inevitable or necessarily permanent."[25] It was up to public relations to defend it. In this context, the NAM was not the bastion of the classical creed which some have supposed. Holcombe Parkes said that his real goal was to stimulate action by management which would win the active good will of the American people.

> Internally, this means the education and inspiration of management to the point where overwhelmingly the resulting policies and actions of manufacturing industry will be automatically and consistently identified with the best interests of the country and all its citizenry.

Such an attitude would require a departure from the single-minded pursuit of profit in favor of the ideology of service. This is the "gospel" which Parkes, in his first 17 months on the job, "preached" before 10,897 businessmen in 24 cities in 15 states.[26]

A petroleum trade journalist asked of the American Petroleum Institute's public relations program in 1946:

> ... [I]sn't it a fact that the existence of this program ... will put more of a spotlight on the conduct of the companies, so that the companies will be inclined to watch their conduct more carefully? This program will educate the top executives to that fact, and give them a realization that we newspapermen ... are just reporters of facts. We can't report falsehoods. Therefore, when we report their conduct, they will want to see to it that their conduct is good—or they won't get pretty pieces in the paper![27]

For all the corporate pressure on the press, for all the sympathy of big journalism with other big businesses, and for all the rumored successes of public relations men in putting a good face on a bad situation, the simple dynamic described by this journalist was not without long-run significance. Claims that counselors liberalized policy should be approached with caution, but the vocation's reforming influence should not be discounted.

II

As they had during World War I, the armed forces employed a host of public relations personnel during World War II. One observer estimated that the military employed 75,000 men and women in public relations capacities who were "looking with longing eyes toward the day when they can return to civilian life and enjoy some of the 'lush pickings' which they think await them in public relations. . . . Long since past the stage of youthful gamboling, [the profession] is launched upon a wild expansion."[28] This influx of personnel was one reason for an increased interest in the establishment of professional standards and associations, since one function of the panoply of professionalism is to combat overcrowding through exclusive accreditation.[29] Professional organization would also bolster prestige within the business world by giving the impression that public relations encompassed a technical body of knowledge requiring careful study and by showing that practitioners were willing to fight shoddy or unethical conduct.

Professional associations dated back to before the First World War,[30] but the first really important steps toward the development of a professional *esprit* were taken by Bernays in the 1920s. Unlike Lee, who believed public relations would die when he and Bernays did, Bernays foresaw the growth which has taken place. His efforts to dignify public relations through his insistence on the title "counsel"; through his writings, in which he held that for reasons of professional ethics the counsel should decline to serve unworthy clients; through his course at New York University; and through his advocacy of state licensing have been outlined in Chapter II. In 1927, he spearheaded an attempt to build a formal association "similar to the American Medical Association to clear up evil practices," but the effort came to naught.[31]

After false starts, permanent steps toward the creation of a professional association were taken during the Depression. In his study of the trade association movement in the cotton textile industry, Louis Galambos discerned three stages of professional development. The first saw the growth of dinner clubs, which were little more than meeting places for informal discussion about the industry. Their income was minimal and their ideology weak, and they were nonbureaucratic. The second was reached with the service associations, which boasted a substantial income and a permanent staff. These could assemble data, lobby for the industry, and perform various other services. The third stage consisted of the creation of a national organization of greater financial resources with a larger and more talented staff and a well-articulated ideology whose aim was to shape policy for the industry as a whole.[32]

The trade association movement in public relations took the first two of these steps in the 1930s and 1940s. The two outstanding early dinner clubs for corporate counselors were the National Association of Accredited Publicity Directors, Inc., founded in 1936, and the Wise Men, founded two years later, both based in New York City. Members of the first organization bore "lightly [its] rather overpowering name," which was changed in 1944 to the National Association of Public Relations Counsel. Its purpose was to study "the publicity profession" and to interpret it to businesses, public, and press. Meetings consisted of luncheons or dinners at which members talked shop or listened to guest speakers. In its early years, the organization presented awards for skillful publicity work to such diverse individuals as William O. Douglas and Walter Weisenberger.[33]

The Wise Men were a group of prestigious counselors who met monthly at exclusive clubs or private homes in the New York metropolitan area to discuss their field and related topics. Members were public relations directors for large corporations or conservative independents who have "good clients and keep them over a period of years rather than operating a constantly revolving clientele."[34] Unlike the National Association, with its vice-president and fifteen directors, the Wise Men had no bureaucracy. It did not undertake to present awards or interpret public relations to the outside world. Its meetings were the occasion for "some very interesting discussions on the subject of public relations, [which], as usual on that subject . . . got nowhere."[35] It was, however, at a meeting of the Wise Men that Paul Garrett made a suggestion which eventually resulted in the annual National Conferences of Business and Public Relations Executives sponsored by the NAM in the 1940s.[36]

The name most conspicuously absent from the Wise Men's roster was that of Edward L. Bernays. Despite his advocacy of professionalization, Bernays has never been active in any society of counselors. (In fact, he never even belonged to one until the Public Relations Society of America made him an honorary member on his eightieth birthday.) His relations with a number of the Wise Men were distinctly cool. He never shared their devotion to big business or their conservative politics. Symbolic of his ideological distance was a remark he made at a convention in 1945. The customary words of criticism had been directed at unions when Bernays asserted that the record would not be clear "if we didn't say a few words about the strategy of the revolutionary employer. I think we all know men who are revolutionary in their attitudes and actions to kill off the labor unions." "Oh, no, no, no, no!" moaned George Kelley of Pullman in reply. "Don't speak of them in that way."[37]

For their part, conservatives viewed Bernays and such flamboyant liberals as Benjamin Sonnenberg[38] as mere publicists rather than bona fide policy advisers. Bernays was accused of inability to keep clients because he kept forgetting who the client was. In other words, he was said to be excessively interested in publicizing himself. Thus the man who represented public relations to many outside the field, who was, as even one of his critics admitted, the vocation's "window on the world,"[39] was isolated from its other leaders as professional organizations jelled.

The formation of the American Council of Public Relations in San Francisco in 1939 represented a step from the dinner club to the service association. Its president, a lecturer in education at Stanford named Rex F. Harlow, stated that its purpose was one of "education and scientific research; of finding facts and making them available for all who can use them constructively."[40] The Council sponsored one- to two-week courses on public relations featuring addresses by experts in opinion polling, labor relations, and the consumer movement. The courses were given all over the nation. In the eighteen months following their inception, they were attended by 1,572 people.[41]

In the confusion caused by the influx of people into the field after the war, counselors recognized the need for at least one good professional association. "At present there are four or five," one lamented in 1946, "none of them well recognized or to any extent influential."[42] The formation of the Public Relations Society of America from a merger of the American Council on Public Relations and the National Association of Public Relations Counsel on February 4, 1948, was an attempt to answer this call. Holcombe Parkes was enthusiastic,[43] but leading Wise Men were reserved. James Selvage told Hill that he had "never been much of a joiner but everyone kept telling me that this was something that I should do, so I suppose you should too." Ross, too, joined and advised Hill to do the same. Replied Hill,

> If you are willing to take a chance on being blackballed, I am too. I am sending in my application and hoping for the best. Seriously, I think that if a few of the folks of some substance in this business join and take an active interest in the society, some good may come of it. A number of my associates here are joining also. At least it's worth the effort.[44]

The PRSA has grown into a service association of some note. It has adopted a code of ethics and taken disciplinary measures against member agencies that have violated it. It maintains a staff, which, among other duties, dispenses funds for the study of public relations, and an office where information about the field may be obtained. It also supervises the publication of two professional journals.[45] The PRSA has not taken and probably will never take the step from service association to policy-forming organization. Its membership is too limited and the effect of its censure too uncertain for it to take the lead in directing the development of the field.

Public relations education also blossomed after the war. One study in 1947 found 30 colleges and universities offering 47 courses labeled "public relations" and other schools offering courses in related topics. The same year, Boston University founded its graduate school of public relations. The basic problem in developing a curriculum has been the inability to arrive at a generally accepted definition of what the field involves. As a result, some of these courses restricted themselves to the mechanics of obtaining publicity while others encompassed wide-ranging speculation about "the crowd" and "the public mind."[46]

Indicative of the intellectual difficulties surrounding attempts at professionalization was a speech Thomas J. Ross delivered to the New School in 1950. Ross, who had had a quarter century's experience and had learned his trade at the foot of the master, quoted Lee to the effect that good public relations meant "merely applying common sense to the obvious." "Assuming this to be true," said Ross, "and I think it is, then if public relations is to become a profession, some way must be found to determine who possesses 'common sense' and some method devised to measure the individual's capacity to apply it effectively." There is no field of human endeavor that would not be enriched by such a procedure. Later in the talk, Ross asserted that "a public relations man should know many things. He should know something of economics; sociology; history; labor relations; labor unions; corporate organization and finance; stockholder relations; newspaper, magazine and radio practices—to say nothing of human nature."[47] Something more, it would therefore appear, than the mere possession of common sense was required.

The drive toward professionalization should be seen within the context of similar efforts among other business auxiliaries and indeed in the society in general. The twentieth century has witnessed a steady increase in the proportion of the work force engaged in services. The accomplishments of those thus engaged are sometimes intangible. This is particularly true of public relations. The counselor works to better a firm's reputation, but the improvement can rarely be satisfactorily measured. How can an executive calculate the proper expenditure for persuading people to like his company? How can he be sure the job is being done properly? In addition to limiting competition from those hoping to enter corporate service after public relations work for the army, professional codes of ethics and rules of standard practice could increase the counselor's prestige within the firm. They could aid him in what was still his number one problem: "selling the boss" on the validity of his work.

For some counselors, selling the boss simply meant convincing him to renew the contract by producing a stack of complimentary clippings. For those with dreams of molding business policy to satisfy public desires, selling the boss meant convincing the client to act in accordance with their estimate of public opinion. It meant educating the client to ask "What about the public?" before making major decisions and taking their advice[48] because they were masters of special techniques for dealing with public opinion.

Franklin Waltman of Sun Oil asserted that in 1942 selling the boss was a major dilemma, but by the war's end the problem had been solved. He was, however, overly optimistic. In 1945, Holcombe Parkes was still complaining that ". . . we, as craftsmen, have failed in too many cases to reach the first of our 'publics'—those in positions of authority—our own bosses."[49] Most of his colleagues agreed.

If selling the boss was a major problem for the leaders, many of whom had outlooks similar to their employers', it was a yet more severe dilemma for the less established man, who was often a newcomer with more liberal ideas than the veteran. Sociologist Leila Aline Sussman found that nearly all of the 132 public relations men she studied in the late 1940s had difficulties with their clients who didn't want to hear what counselors felt obliged to tell them. The counselors, she concluded, saw themselves as liberal moralists dealing with conservative businessmen who persisted in questioning their judgment. According to Sussman, the popular conception of public relations men, which still tended to link them to the ballyhoo press agents of the 1920s, and the client's conception of them as "word mongers" suffering from "professional retardation" both inhibited the achievement of a policy-making role. Counselors stood on shaky ground when they disagreed with their employers.[50]

No doubt professional trappings would have raised the stature of the public relations man within the corporation. But for all the college courses, trade journal articles, books, and endless speechmaking, public relations was far from being a profession in the late 1940s and still is today.

To be a profession an occupation must first of all seem to be one, and public relations does not. Professionals have a realm of authority in which their expertise is generally recognized and accepted. Yet as counselors themselves admit, their decisions and opinions have often been overruled by their clients. They therefore lack that "extensive autonomy in exercising [their] special competence" that is one of the hallmarks of professionalism.[51]

Aspiring lawyers and doctors must satisfy strict requirements, but anyone could call himself a public relations counselor. (There is an ancient joke in the trade that one Chicago prostitute claimed to be in "public relations.") There was some talk after the war, predictably stimulated by Bernays, of state licensing, but many feared this as a threat to the right of self-expression.[52] Efforts have been made from within the vocation to promote ethical standards. The PRSA now has exacting qualifications for membership, including an accreditation examination. But charlatanism pervaded public relations at mid-century, even within the most established firms, and it is by no means absent today.[53]

Members of a profession are supposed to have fraternal feelings toward their colleagues, with whom they work toward overcoming problems important to society in addition to pursuing private gain. Counselors have often professed a belief in the social utility of their work. Bernays saw his as invigorating the competition of ideas in the marketplace, which was "an essential democratic process, for then the public can make its own choice." He believed that public relations diminished conflict and fostered the peaceful adjustment of opposing views through increased communications.[54] Hill and other conservatives saw their mission as helping to preserve the free enterprise system, which was beneficial to the nation but threatened by the brickbats of radicals and politicians. In his view, the trade opened minds and was thus the reverse of propaganda which closed them.[55] Ivy Lee has been defended on the grounds that his activities helped to open channels of communication to misrepresented institutions.[56]

As for fraternity, however, public relations has not been noted for it. Parkes, among others, tried to encourage it. He exhorted a 1947 public relations convention to rise above the adolescent pastime of throwing cabbages at each other. We've got to learn to cheer our fellow practitioner as long as he is producing results and moving in the right direction, regardless of whether or not we happen to like his methods or his style or the cut of his hair. We've got to learn to use the sealing wax of silence if all we can come up with is destructive criticism. In short, we've got to demonstrate a real pride in our profession—as a profession; the pride that is expressed by tolerance and sympathetic understanding, if we are ever to measure up to the challenge we face.[57]

Sussman's impression from her interviewees was that such friendly camaraderie was still far off. She found public relations rife with cynicism as well as "fierce competition, mutual mistrust, jealous secrecy, low standards, and low prestige."[58]

Addressing a convention in 1943, Colby Chester declared ". . . I am speaking to a professional group of men. I am not talking to people who get out publicity." He told his listeners to "drive harder" and "make your presence felt" in the corporation.[59] Some did strive to assume this role. Whether they could or not depended largely on the outlook of the client. If a firm's decision makers did not appreciate the counselor's technique, little could be done to change their opinion.

*   *   *

In the mid-term elections of 1938 and 1946, conservative public relations men saw evidence of the country's "returning to its senses," only to be disappointed in the presidential elections that followed. They detected those same hopeful signs in 1950, and two years later their hopes were finally satisfied. Shortly after the election, Hill observed that many elements contributed to the happy election outcome, "And I would like to think that some of the work that business has been doing in explaining itself over these years had a part in it."[60]

At least one business journalist denied this claim of effectiveness. William Whyte asked "Is anybody listening?" to "the Great Free Enterprise Campaign" and answered that "it is not worth a damn." Political and economic ideas could not be marketed like concrete articles such as toothpaste and frozen food. The "American way of life" could not be "sold" to an American; it was his by definition to do with as he pleased. The economic facts so often publicized by the likes of the NAM were usually really conclusions, and their advertisement was not aimed at true education but rather at political victory for the Republican party. The result was pretentious, insulting to the intelligence, ineffective, and, in a word, stupid.[61]

What is more, said Whyte, many executives agreed with him. Of 84 businessmen to whom he spoke about the NAM's efforts, 43, including some prominent members of the Association itself, "were almost violently anti-NAM." "Everytime I see the big shots of the NAM in white tie and tails having dinner at the Waldorf and posing for newspaper photographers," said the president of an aircraft company, "I retch." Why, then, did the campaign continue? Although perhaps in the majority, the businessman holding this view was likely to fear its being labeled heretical "when convention time comes." "Since the man next to him, and the one next to him, entertain the same fear, all too often they respond to the expected ritual." This analysis was strong stuff indeed, especially coming as it did from the pages of *Fortune,* which had boosted the public relations movement since the Depression. (Whyte did, however, manage a kind word for the educational efforts of the C.E.D.) In all, Whyte believed that the mania for "communication" was almost a complete waste of the $100 million it was estimated to cost each year.[62]

For whatever reason, and Whyte's explanation for the continuation of economic education programs seems a little too convenient, expenditures for economic education and for more intimate community relations programs continued to increase into the 1950s. The ORC answered Whyte's question by citing its finding that 70 percent of the companies in its sample believed that "companies as a whole are making headway in building economic understanding" and that "Large majorities also feel that employees believe information supplied them, and that information changes attitudes."[63] Few if any major companies were willing to face the second half of the twentieth century without the help of advisers whose specific task it was to organize and dispense news, to coach executives in their public statements, to harmonize community relations, to keep management informed of trends in public opinion, and to contribute to an overall effort to popularize capitalism and business leadership. Some businessmen might "retch" when faced with these efforts, but unlike their nineteenth-century ancestors, they were careful to do their retching on a "not for attribution" basis.

The public relations movement had helped to alter permanently the public vocabulary of business. Flexing of economic muscle would henceforth be sugarcoated for public consumption. It had also provided sincere business leaders with potentially invaluable tools for discovering and satisfying—rather than damning—the desires of the many "publics" their activities affected.

NOTES

1. Lewis, "Henry Ford," p. 526; Sigmund Diamond, *The Reputation of the American Businessman* (Cambridge, Mass., 1955), pp. 142–175.

2. Burton R. Fisher and Stephen B. Withey, *Big Business as the People See It* (Ann Arbor, 1951), pp. 20, 57–58, 43, 76. Elmo Roper, "The Public Looks at

Business," *Harvard Business Review* 27, No. 2 (March-April 1949), p. 165; Burleigh B. Gardner and Lee Rainwater, "The Mass Image of Big Business," *Harvard Business Review* 33, No. 1 (November-December 1955), pp. 61–66.

3. Claude Robinson, "Address," *Proceedings* of the 26th Annual Meeting of the American Petroleum Institute (cited hereinafter as API), Vol. 26 [1] (1946), pp. 11–30.

4. This last point was made by John D. Gill of the Atlantic Refining Company in some of the most trenchant yet calm criticism of public relations anywhere. API, Vol. 26 [1] (1946), pp. 136–139.

5. Robinson, "Address," API, Vol. 26 [1] (1945), pp. 23–24.

6. Robert T. Haslam, "Progressive Public Relations for the Progressive Petroleum Industry," API, Vol. 26 [1] (1946), pp. 31–35.

7. "The British Coal Industry," 34 (October 1946), p. 121.

8. Haslam, "Progressive," p. 35.

9. Some, but not all. The NAM's anti-OPA campaign met with considerable resistance within the Association itself. For some devastating comments: Memo, T. M. Brennan to Holcombe Parkes, March 2, 1946; Memo, William Dalton to E. J. Sherman, March 6, 1946, Drawer 1134, NAM papers.

10. ORC, "Big Business on the Spot," *The Public Opinion Index for Industry,* August 1948. This survey and all others in the *Public Opinion Index* (cited hereinafter as *PO Index*) preceding 1950 were made available to me through the kindness of Mr. Fred Mason of the ORC in Princeton. Surveys after 1949 are available through University Microfilms.

11. "Industry's Public Relations Job," *The Conference Board Business Record* 2, No. 3 (March 1945), pp. 75–79.

12. ORC, "Public Relations in Industry—1946," *PO Index, np., p. 17.*

13. ORC, "Trends in Industry Public Relations—1947," *PO Index,* September 1947, np., pp. 9–10.

14. ORC, "Trends in Industry Public Relations," *PO Index,* January 1948, np.

15. ORC, "Growth Trends," pp. 3–6.

16. Interchurch World Movement, Commission of Inquiry, *Public Opinion and the Steel Strike* (New York, 1921).

17. Helen A. Winselman, "Industry's Community Relations," NICB *Studies in Business Policy,* No. 20 (1946), p. 12 and *passim.* By 1947, GM's community relations program in Dayton touched all the bases. See Frank C. Lyons, "Public Relations at the Community Level," *Proceedings* of the Fourth National Business Public Relations Executives Conference 1947 (cited hereinafter as 4PRC), 8-31, NAM papers, Drawer #1017.

18. Winselman, "Community," p. 7.

19. William H. Whyte, *Is Anybody Listening?* (New York, 1952), p. 183.

20. "Techniques of Promoting Understanding—Externally," *Proceedings* of the Fifth National Conference of Business Public Relations Executives, 1948 (cited hereinafter as 5PRC), p. 105, Drawer #1017 NAM papers.

21. Parkes, "Tackling," p. 36.

22. ORC, "Industry's Communication System," *PO Index,* Vol. 8, No. 10 (October, 1950), p. A-35. Methods of obtaining information from employees included, in descending order of importance: suggestion systems, supervisory

channels, general "Open Door" policy, departmental meetings, letters to company publications, surveys, conferences and training program, grievance system, and personal interviews, Ibid., p. A-14.

23. Eugene Whitmore, "Public Relations—A Two-Way Street," *American Business,* May 1946, pp. 49–50.

24. The distinction between the "classical" and "managerial" philosophies was made by Sutton, et al., in *The American Business Creed* (New York, 1956): "The classical strand centers around the model of a decentralized, private, competitive capitalism, in which the forces of supply and demand, operating through the price mechanism, regulate the economy in detail and in aggregate. The managerial strand differs chiefly in the emphasis it places on the role of professional managers in the large business firm who consciously direct economic forces for the common good." Pp. 33–34. The authors were contradictory in their view of which philosophy was predominant. See pp. 34, 263.

25. "Profits," 5PRC, p. 59.

26. "Tackling," pp. 35–36; "The Public Relations of Public Relations," 4PRC, p. 47.

27. API, Vol. 26 [1] (1946), p. 135.

28. Rex F. Harlow, "Public Relations at the Crossroads," *Public Opinion Quarterly* 8 (Winter 1944-1945), pp. 552–553.

29. Leila Aline Sussman, "Movement," p. 131.

30. The Financial Public Relations Association, now the Bank Marketing Association, was founded in 1915. Cutlip and Center, *Public Relations,* p. 676.

31. *Editor & Publisher,* April 2, 1927, p. 9.

32. *Competition and Cooperation,* pp. 34, 55, 90. My discussion of professionalism has drawn heavily on Pope's comprehensive treatment of the same question in advertising. See Pope, "Advertising," pp. 249–346.

33. Cutlip and Center, *Public Relations,* pp. 674–675; William H. Baldwin, "Association of Publicity Directors," *Public Opinion Quarterly* 1, No. 4 (October 1937), pp. 139–140; "Publicity Group to Honor Weisenberger," Drawer #1110, NAM papers.

34. James Selvage to Hill, January 23, 1951, Box 37, Hill papers. A membership list of the Wise Men in the mid-1940s (with affiliations where I have been able to determine them) included: Bronson Batchelor, independent; Allen Brown, Bakelite; Verne Burnett, independent; Charles C. Carr, ALCOA; Ralph Champlin, Ethyl; Northrup Clarey, Esso; Norman Draper, American Meat Institute; Pendleton Dudley, independent; Paul Garrett, GM; John Hill, independent; James Irwin, independent; Chester Lang; John Long, Bethlehem Steel; J. Carlisle MacDonald, U.S. Steel; Frank Mason; Arthur W. Page, AT&T; Robert S. Peare, GE; G. Edward Pendray, independent; Dr. Claude Robinson, ORC; T. J. Ross, independent; Herbert W. Smith; John P. Syme, Johns-Manville; Walter Trumbull; Gordon Wasser; James Selvage, independent. Box 38; Hill papers. Membership was constantly in flux, so that some well-known names not present on this list, such as that of Harold Brayman of Du Pont, would later appear. It may be noteworthy that in a profession in which Jews have been overrepresented, most if not all the Wise Men have been Gentiles.

35. Hill to Dudley, January 29, 1945, Box 7, Hill papers.

36. Interview with Harold Brayman.

37. 3PRC, p. 66.

38. For Sonnenberg, see Croswell Bowen and George R. Clark (pseud.), "Reputation by Sonnenberg," *Harper's,* February 1950, p. 42, and Geoffrey T. Hellman. "Profiles: A House on Grammercy Park," *The New Yorker,* April 8, 1950, pp. 40ff. For Hill's opinion of Sonneberg, see Hill to Ross, January 31, 1950. Box 37, Hill papers.

39. J. Carroll Bateman, review of *The Engineering of Consent, Public Relations Journal,* March, 1970. p. 30.

40. Rex F. Harlow, "The American Council on Public Relations," *Public Opinion Quarterly* 4, No. 2 (June 1940), p. 324.

41. Benjamin Fine, "New York Course on Public Relations," *Public Opinion Quarterly* 5, No. 1 (March 1941), pp. 111–113; and see "The Short Course in Public Relations: Summary of Lectures and Discussions," August 14–25; August 28–September 9, 1939, Bernays papers.

42. Stephen E. Fitzgerald, "Public Relations: A Profession in Search of Professionals," *Public Opinion Quarterly* 10 (Summer 1946), p. 199.

43. Parkes, "Public Relations," pp. 50–51.

44. Selvage to Hill, September 13, 1948; Ross to Hill, September 13, 1948; Hill to Ross, September 14, 1948, Box 37, Hill papers.

45. Cutlip and Center, *Public Relations,* pp. 672–677.

46. Alfred McClung Lee, "Trends in Public Relations Training," *Public Opinion Quarterly* 11 (Spring 1947), pp. 83–91.

47. "Some Comments on Public Relations Today and Tomorrow," May 3, 1950, copy of speech in Bernays papers.

48. William G. Werner to Hill, January 19, 1949, Box 39, Hill papers.

49. 5PRC, pp. 5, 43.

50. Sussman, "Movement," pp. 127–130.

51. Kenneth Henry, "The Large Corporation Public Relations Manager: Emerging Professional in a Bureaucracy?" (unpublished Ph.D. thesis, New York University, 1970). pp. 323 and 306–388 *passim.*

52. Hill, *Making,* 39; Major General Philip B. Fleming to James Gerard, January 31, 1946; Frederick R. Gamble to Gerard, January 31, 1946, Bernays papers. Financial public relations is the only branch subject to state regulation.

53. Cutlip and Center, *Public Relations,* pp. 660–673.

54. Quoted in Cochran, *Business in American Life,* p. 253. "Adjustment" is a key word in the Bernays lexicon. See the interesting and engaging anecdote in his autobiography, *Idea,* pp. 710–711.

55. Hill, *Making,* p. 6. One of Hill's employees who had been discharged knew the effective way to appeal to his chief to save his position:

> I had hoped in time to be able through this association with you to render a service to all American industry in helping it to get off the defensive hook upon which it is now so uncomfortably hanging and thereafter aiding it to regain the psychological initiative. This must be done if economic freedom is not to perish; it can be done. Until it *is* done, our enemies will continue to beat us, propaganda-wise and every other-wise, at every turn.

Hall Griffith to Hill, April 17, 1952, Box 26, Hill papers. This appeal may have won the day. At any rate, Griffith was still employed at Hill and Knowlton six months later.

56. Hiebert, *Courtier,* p. 318.

57. "Public Relations," p. 50.

58. Sussman, "Movement," pp. 130–131. She believed these characteristics to be common among young professions and predicted that public relations would outgrow them. Oddly enough, transcripts of public relations conventions indicate very little conflict. The aforementioned argument of Bernays and Kelley stands out as an almost unique exception.

59. *SAPRC,* p. 144.

60. Hill to Walter S. Tower, November 5, 1952, Hill papers.

61. Whyte, *Listening?,* pp. vii–xii, 1–20. If Republican victory was the true goal of the free enterprise campaign, the election of 1952 showed that it was at least not wholly counterproductive.

62. Ibid.

63. ORC, "Growth Trends in Industry Communications," *PO Index,* Vol. 9, No. 10 (October 1951), p. 26.

Chapter VII

The Public Relations of Public Relations

As the mongoose loathes the cobra, as the herring fears the shark, as the flapper dodges "lectures," so do editors shun the machinations of a species whose villainy is (to editors) as plain as the nose on your face and as hard to clap your eyes on.

Time, 1926[1]

We have no list of "responsible" press agents nor are we acquainted with anyone who has. . . . [R]esponsibility in a press agent is a flat contradiction in terms. His whole stock in trade is the ability to impose upon editorial carelessness by means of a false pretense, and a man who is hired to deceive others may be relied on sooner or later to swindle his own clients.

Printers' Ink, 1922[2]

The preceding chapters have shown how the image of public relations improved in the eyes of executives. Businessmen who would never have taken a flamboyant, hard-drinking press agent seriously were, by 1950, according some respect and devoting a lot of time and money to the systematic cultivation of a benign image with the help of public relations counseling.

We have also sampled the reaction to public relations among advertising agents, journalists, and intellectuals. The attitude of these three groups toward the vocation is important and deserves more attention than it has heretofore received. It will be the purpose of this chapter to provide a summary of how public relations has been viewed over the years by representatives of these three groups, each of which has had a definite impact on the way businessmen have viewed public relations and on the self-image of counselors as well.

I

The early attitude of advertising agents toward public relations can be easily characterized: vehement condemnation. To the outsider, especially of today, this strife must seem like a family quarrel. Both advertising and public relations men have historically worked to promote the wares of private enterprise, both have extolled the benefits of social harmony accomplished through mass communication,[3] and both have wrestled with the problem of finding the proper balance of emotion and reason to achieve maximum persuasiveness. In fact, for the forty or so years prior to Ivy Lee's Declaration of Principles, the two trades seemed inseparable. Advertisers demanded reading notices as a matter of course. Until as late as World War I, the terms "advertising" and "publicity" were often used interchangeably.[4]

The question which naturally poses itself is why the public relations function was not annexed to the advertising agency. From the end of the Civil War to the turn of the century, the advertising business had shown itself remarkably flexible in responding to the changing demands made upon it. Agencies had worked primarily for advertisers, for publishers, and/or solely as middlemen during this period,[5] and they had transformed the character of the service they provided from that of simply purchasing space and inserting an announcement to actually making an effort through clever copywriting to sell the product.[6] Why couldn't the agencies have expanded one step further to manage all the news, whether reaching the public eye through paid space or not, about their client?

Some did. Such prestigious agencies as J. Walter Thompson, Lord & Thomas, and N. W. Ayer and Son appeared on the American Newspaper Publishers Association's 1915 list of agencies which demanded free publicity along with the advertising their clients bought.[7] Ayer established its own publicity bureau in 1920 and began public relations work in 1930.[8] In 1934, McCann-Erickson did public relations work for the Industrial Association of San Francisco. In addition, some outstanding advertising agents made their mark as public relations men, including Don Francisco of Lord & Thomas and the redoubtable Bruce Barton.[9]

Nonetheless, most advertising men feared and disliked public relations from the advent of Ivy Lee at least up until the stock market crash. They expressed their disapproval against a backdrop of confusion concerning the nature of publicity and public relations, the differences between the two (if any), and the relationship that they should bear to advertising and journalism. And as befitted a profession which claimed so many sons of clergymen, this animosity was often couched in moral as well as practical terms. Thoughtful advertising men rejoiced, wrote one observer, when public relations counselors attempted to dissociate themselves from the advertising business.

> The man who is hired to use his specialized training as a writer, as an artist, and as a judge of good typography to present the merits of a definite product over the signature of the manufacturer or seller of that product, and solely inside of advertising space which has been bought and paid for by that manufacturer or merchant, is certainly enacting an open role which is very different from that of the man who remains behind the scenes and manipulates various stage devices for purposes best known to himself and those who employ him.

As long as seller sought buyer, the role of the advertising man would at least be tolerated. "But with his public relations cousin, that super-off-stage person who juggles with the League of Nations in one hand and with millinery and cosmetics in the other, I fear the accountability is different." Such a man was "useful whenever and wherever skillful and intelligent manipulation is needed to accomplish an end that cannot be disclosed."[10] Another author theorized that advertising may have been the child of publicity, but

> The parent has become a parasite for it frequently engaged in activities bordering on commercial blackmail. . . . Advertising commands attention through attractive display, through frank statement, through brevity, through positive appeals to economy, vanity, comfort, luxury, or service in some form very decidedly expressed. All this is denied publicity.[11]

Publicity was reprehensible because it involved getting something for nothing[12] and took people by surprise, while advertising helped support the medium that carried it and included a frank declaration of its source. But there were also practical reasons to avoid publicity. When an advertiser bought space, he could be absolutely certain what message appeared therein. When he hired a publicity man to concoct a stunt, he could not be sure whether or how the papers would carry it.[13] Furthermore, when the costs of the publicity man's fee and the expenses he incurred were totaled, his services were often found more expensive than paid advertising would have been.[14] Such important public relations counselors as John W. Hill and Carl Byoir were impressed by the first argument. Thus their clients who wished to make lengthy statements to the public, such as the AISI and A&P, did so through advertisements. Even Edward L. Bernays, perhaps the most reluctant of early public relations men to pay for space, placed advertisements on occasion.

The second argument, the higher cost of public relations, was not conceded and was impossible to prove or disprove.

The industry's principal torchbearer in the crusade against press agentry was *Printers' Ink*. No issue seemed complete without some reiteration of the charge that public relations, usually referred to as press agentry, publicity, or "space grabbing," was some compound of "Trickery, Fraud, Hoax and Bunk."[15] The 1920s witnessed the height of the magazine's outrage, but virulently antipublicity articles continued to appear into the mid-thirties. It is difficult to judge how many advertising agents shared *Printers' Ink*'s views, but indications are that many did. One who did not was Herbert Everett, whose complimentary letter to Ivy Lee following his reading of *Publicity* in 1925 indicated that he was an exception:

> I have read your book and agree with it and your point of view 100%. I fully realize that many advertising men will look upon me as violating the advertising point of view with regard to publicity.
>
> I heard a discussion the other day among a group of six or eight men who are prominent in advertising and I was amazed at their resentment based upon misinformation concerning you and your work. . . . As a result of my comments, two of the men present felt that I was treasonable to my profession.[16]

Another observer at the mid-point of the '20s noted that "the general impression amongst advertising men is that publicity consists of advertising that is not paid for."[17] The competition for the disposition of corporate funds for sales promotion was at the bottom of many an advertising man's objections.

On the other hand, even in the '20s, there were indications of an ambivalence toward public relations on the part of advertising agents. When Ivy Lee was applying for membership in the Advertising Club of New York, he was assured by its president that the club had not given "any thought whatsoever of ascertaining the attitude of any in the club, whether or not a so-called press agent should be excluded or dropped from our membership rolls. If for any reason such action was undertaken we would lose some very valuable members, friends and counselors." Whether such a discussion had taken place or not, the necessity for a disclaimer was noteworthy. Two days after it was written Lee was granted membership,[18] but his triumph must have been somewhat dulled by having himself referred to, even with kindly intent, as a "so-called press agent." Yet more intriguing was the fact that advertising agencies sometimes suggested that their clients retain public relations men. Thus the Blackman Company referred Procter & Gamble to Bernays in 1923, and the George Harrison Phelps agency turned to Bernays to help promote the Dodge Victory Six automobile through radio in 1927. Bernays kept the former account until 1953.[19]

There was serious discussion of the nature of publicity work in business and advertising trade journals other than *Printers' Ink* in the 1920s. Sometimes advertising men even spoke up for publicity. In 1924, the *Advertising Club News* took exception to a *New York Times* writer's condemnation of all free publicity. "There is publicity and publicity," it explained, and that which was newsworthy should not be rejected along with the "puff" and "dog stories." An observer writing in *Advertising and Selling* in 1929 understood full well that "the circulation of publicity by the organization which undertakes space buying leads to a logical fear that the advertising appropriation will be used as a club to 'suggest' the publication of publicity." Although this coercion was undoubtedly an abuse, it was nevertheless necessary to recognize that there was a legitimate need and place for publicity. The important question was who should prepare it: the advertiser, the professional publicity organization, or the advertising agency? He concluded that the time had come for advertising agencies to staff their own publicity departments.[20]

A strong current of antipublicity sentiment persisted into the Depression. In 1936, advertising man Bernard Lichtenburg announced his entry into public relations, and the reactions of his former colleagues were in large part unfavorable. The industry had been hit hard during the '30s, and advertising managers, provoked by the defection of one of their own and no doubt fearful of a further loss of revenue, were irate. Charles M. Pritzker, advertising manager for Gillette, charged that "most public relations counsels talk a lot better than the service they render." Gillette had used public relations men in the past

> but we have never been able to trace any real benefit from them. Public utilities, railroads, refrigerator industry, radio industry, etc. subject themselves to the dangers of ill will and fickleness of public opinion from time to time and to a much higher degree than our commodity or company is subjected to.
>
> We have a very alert selling organization—we subscribe to the Nielson service for reports on market trends and maintain quite a large staff for sales research work—all of which with the right kind of coordination enables us to carry on satisfactorily. The day has passed when publicity to educate people to shave can be considered a matter of importance.

Elmer T. Wible, advertising manager of the Pittsburgh Steel Company, was "surprised" and "disappointed" by Lichtenburg's move. "It seems to me that Public Relations Counsel activities as usually practiced are 'insidious propaganda and specious hokum. . .'" Such activity could only be justified on the grounds of fighting fire with fire, wrote Wible, who hoped Lichtenburg's practice would be conducted on a higher plane.[21]

The '30s, however, saw important changes in advertising attitudes toward public relations. Public relations had indeed threatened advertising expenditures when it was used primarily for sales promotion, but an equally, if not more, important service it provided was aiding corporations in coping with political problems. Never before were such problems as severe as they were during the Depression, and as business turned to public relations for help, public relations turned to paid advertising, often written and placed with the assistance of established agencies. Institutional advertising, promoting the good works of a corporation, an industry, or the economic system as a whole, was coming into its own. Its advent meant increased revenues for advertising agents and public relations counselors alike. Ivy Lee's assertion of the previous decade that ". . . I stimulate more actual advertising than do most of the men who are called advertising agents" was being borne out. When a public relations man purposely avoided paid advertising, the old objections reappeared.[22]

This change in attitude was evidenced by some of the other reactions to Lichtenburg's change of profession. "Work of this kind," wrote a member of *The New Yorker*'s advertising department, "has a perfectly legitimate place when done in the right way." John Benson, president of the American Association of Advertising Agencies, commented that Lichtenburg was well qualified to fill his new role and even promised to steer clients his way. He also remarked that "the value of this kind of work, of course, depends on how you do it, and I am taking for granted that you are going to do it in the right way."[23] By "the right way," these correspondents presumably meant the use of plenty of paid advertisements and the avoidance of "space grabbing." The astute Herschel Deutsch of the Lawrence Gumbinner Advertising Agency noted that agencies were doing a steadily increasing amount of publicity work. There was, he believed, "a definite, if gradual, tendency to divert advertising money to publicity work, or at least to include publicity in the advertising and promotion plans." Agencies were establishing publicity departments because of client demand.[24]

Competition between advertising and public relations for the corporation dollar continued into the 1950s, but its intensity was mitigated by the fact that an ever greater number of advertising agencies were providing publicity services of some kind to clients and at least one major public relations firm, Hill and Knowlton, acquired status as an advertising agency. Interagency competition there surely would be, but advertising men were unlikely to oppose public relations on principle if their own agencies provided such services. By the mid-1940s, according to *Advertising Age*, seventy-five of the larger agencies were doing public relations work.[25]

Perhaps the best indication of the change in outlook was that *Printers' Ink* itself hired Edward L. Bernays in 1951. In a 1952 editorial inspired by the publication of Bernays's *Public Relations*, C. B. Larrabee, the president and publisher, wrote that although some public relations men had not yet passed the publicity stage, "It must be encouraging to people in public relations to see . . . more and more broad-gauged young people with good cultural backgrounds attracted to public relations."[26]

And yet, despite the cordiality, the advertising world has never ceased being somewhat ill at ease with public relations, and vice versa. Albert Lasker, a seminal figure in the development of modern advertising, "hated" public relations, while Bernays once said it was "anathema" to hear himself referred to mistakenly as an advertising man.[27] Scott Cutlip and Allen Center, leading scholars of public relations, wrote that "most advertising agencies have found it difficult to determine what public relations services to offer, how to effectively organize the function, and how to sustain it apart from the advertising relationship. . . . Few agencies are adequately equipped to offer broad-gauge public relations counseling."[28] Most, that is, look at it as a supplement to sales promotion rather than as an opportunity to offer "two-way street" advice about corporate policy.

Considering the historic differences between advertising and public relations, it is odd that almost no speculation has been offered in the trade press about the possibility that these two seemingly similar activities might attract different personality types. In 1935, Herschel Deutsch did observe that double service in advertising and public relations rarely worked, "perhaps because of the psychological separation between the practitioners in the two fields. The publicity man's business is news; the advertising man's is sales."[29] In one view, these two functions should operate in tandem for maximum efficiency. Dempster Mac Murphy, vice-president of the Middle West Utilities Company in Chicago, wrote in 1932 that "intelligent advertising, planned with an eye to the future, can create new popular interests which in time make topics similar to those dealt with in the advertisements a matter of news interest. All advertising to the extent that it heightens popular interest in the utility industry has the effect of giving added news value to any news facts given out by the publicity department of a corporation."[30] Recent studies have buttressed Murphy's point of view, predicting the emergence of agencies which will "cut across artificial boundaries" to offer a "complete marketing service."[31] However reasonable this prediction may seem, such agencies have been launched in the past and have failed. And perhaps a reason for that failure is the basic difference between the "news" and "sales" point of view and the issue of the ombudsman function, so basic to the public relations rationale but largely ignored in pure advertising.

II

Since the first press agent demanded a puff for a client, the problem of public relations has caused controversy in the world of journalism. Public relations, especially as practiced in the first third of this century, posed a challenge to every aspect of running a paper, from the garnering of revenue to the determination of what is news and what is not.

R. C. E. Brown captured many of the complaints of reporters and editors in a 1921 article in the *North American Review*. He wrote that potential journalists were forsaking a noble craft in favor of special pleading and foresaw "the growth of a race of mere retailers of ready-made intelligence, and the turning of the newspaper more and more to distribution, less of news than to what somebody wishes to be considered news." To a degree greater even than during the heyday of the party newspaper, the American press was "taking things at second hand and allowing artificially stimulated sentiment to appear as the expression of natural public opinion." To the reply of the publicity man that he provided positive news which offset the journalist's natural inclination to accentuate the negative, Brown replied, "That news that is too retiring to meet the reporter unchaperoned by the press agent . . . is too good to be true." The only remedy was a boycott—"Nothing but the absolute refusal to recognize the press agent, or to publish news that is not prepared by the editorial staff and its disinterested agents." Brown was joined by many others, such as Marquis James and Silas Bent, who added that public relations also posed the threat of making good reporters lazy. Investigative journalism seemed to be on the wane as reporters simply collected releases and were then denied any further access to news sources.[32]

Brown's stand was nothing new. Initial disquiet in both advertising and journalism had broken into open warfare against the press agent menace back in 1908. That year the American Newspaper Publishers Association initiated a campaign to abolish it. The ANPA stated in 1910 that progressively fewer papers were printing publicity. Many other statements of the imminent demise of "space grabbing" were to follow this one—all, needless to say, premature.[33]

As early as 1920, the *New York Times* reported an unprecedented increase in the number of press agents trying to attract editors' attention. Not only businesses, but nonprofit organizations such as churches, universities, and social service organizations of every stripe were turning to public relations to aid fund-raising drives and to increase their status. And the use of publicity and public relations in government administration and politics was also on the rise.[34]

These organizations were hiring reporters away from their papers by the lure of vastly increased salaries and with the hope that their former connections would enable them to influence news coverage. The Washington Bureau of the Associated Press alone lost six or seven men to publicity in the six years following World War I. The superintendent of the Washington office issued a circular to employees in 1924 speculating on the motives of the fallen journalist:

> . . . there is a certain innate embarrassment which we all feel in having a
> man of this staff join a corporation, particularly one of those which is
> under fire in the Congressional investigations. For that and other reasons
> all of us need to be very circumspect in our relations with these men. . . .
> [When a reporter leaves his post to go to an institution] of an entirely
> different kind, and for the purpose of whitewashing a corporation, or
> popularizing a commercial venture or a line of merchandise, he invariably
> finds that it is impossible to maintain his influential contacts.

He gave no thought to the claims of a Bernays or a Lee that the public relations man helps humanize corporations by making them more responsive to the public will. The practitioner performed one of two functions: whitewashing or promoting sales. And he took his new position for one reason only: ". . . we know that the motive is entirely one of money."[35]

Money was also the issue for the publishers, although they were not as exercised by the fact that their reporters were being hired away (not that this was a welcome development) as they were by the threat that press agentry could so reduce their income from advertising that they would go out of business. One estimate had it that if the press agent could deliver equal linage to an advertisement at one-third the cost of paid space, advertising would end and with it newspaper revenue and reader confidence. The free publicity problem "goes more thoroughly into the guts of the newspaper business than anything else," S. E. Thomason told the 1927 ANPA convention. "There is no subject closer to our belts than this one." The Association accordingly decided to expand the anti-press agent crusade, adopting a proposal to set up a monitoring service to warn papers of press agent activity.[36] At the bottom of these bulletins appeared in bold type the question "WHY DON'T THEY PAY THE

PUBLISHERS FOR IT?" In 1930, *Editor & Publisher* came to the dubious conclusion that publicity in New York was indeed on the decline, not because of the diminution of the amount being sent out but because less of it was being printed. Almost simultaneously, Stanley Walker wrote that "The publicity business is thriving. . . ."[37]

The newspaper trade journal, *Editor & Publisher*, filled the role for journalists that *Printers' Ink* did for advertising agents as far as public relations was concerned. It ridiculed the desultory attempts at professional organization of press agents, led by "Dr. Ivy Lee" and "Professor Edward L. Bernays," in the 1920s. There were evils, it explained, inherent in press agentry which no amount of policing could expunge. "Our view is that press agentry, both high and low, is on the wane," it stated in 1927, in yet another example of wishful rather than thoughtful analysis. "The encouraging fact, in our view, is that newspaper managements are coming more and more to understand that the press agent is getting the advertising dollar that belongs in the till. When they organize against this abuse something important will have happened." The publication's leader in the fight was Marlen Pew, an editor and regular columnist. He lost few opportunities to lampoon New York's "ballyhoo boys" "whose business it is to short circuit legitimate advertising and irresponsibly monkey with public opinion for paying clients. . . ."[38]

However, as was true of the advertising agent, the journalist viewed public relations with a curious inconsistency. When Standard Oil hired Joseph I. C. Clarke as its publicity director in 1906, *Editor & Publisher* itself hailed the move as "another victory for the newspapers" because it proved how much big business valued the good opinion of the press. Ten years later, the New York *Herald* congratulated Du Pont for establishing a similar department:

> Here is an industrial enterprise . . . which, after due consideration, has decided that for the public to draw closer to it it is necessary for it to draw closer to the public. No better evidence of the "power of the press" can be dreamed of than this change of policy. . . .

Editor & Publisher concurred. It noted that several newspapermen had competed for the position, which finally went to a reporter on the Philadelphia *Ledger,* and concluded that "publicity of this sort is not only an absolute necessity with important organizations, but it is a valuable and welcome service to newspaper editors." Although such figures as James, Bent, Nunnally Johnson, and Ernest Gruening often expressed their dislike for press agentry, many journalists were grateful for the fair treatment and important information they had received from counselors.[39]

Editor & Publisher's rival trade journal (until purchased by *E&P*) was *The Fourth Estate,* which took a moderate position on the publicity issue. It gave *Crystallizing Public Opinion* a short but favorable review and tried to draw a distinction between "the true counsel or director of public relations" whose job was of undoubted importance and the old publicity man who merely tried to get something for nothing and "is about passé."[40]

Bernays has suggested that Marlen Pew's opposition to him and his trade was something less than genuine. According to Bernays, Pew once told him that *Editor & Publisher*'s attacks "were not personal, that, in fact, they were a good way of promoting *Editor & Publisher.* It made him and his journal an adversary against someone portrayed as an outside enemy."[41] Thus there is the possibility that the journalistic outcry against press agentry was contrived to move merchandise. The attack on publicity men, in other words, may have been nothing but a publicity stunt itself.

It is not necessary, however, to resort to so farfetched an explanation for the inconsistency of journalism's response to public relations. The fact is that both sides were right. Public relations could be used to seal off sources, twist information, and push propaganda.[42] It could lead to lazy journalism and perhaps threaten the income of papers (although this problem was surely exaggerated). On the other hand, it could promote better reporting because the public relations department of a company had more time to assemble the correct data than did the harried reporter, it could bring to the attention of an editor newsworthy stories which he otherwise would have no way of finding out about, and it could and did supply news-hungry newspapers with something to print in the news columns. The rules proposed by R. C. E. Brown and *Editor & Publisher* for the disposal of publicity releases unread were as inadequate a solution to this complex problem as the abject subservience of some business trade journals in the face of publicity releases from companies in the trade they served.[43] Public relations was a living part of the world of news and could not be dealt with in a rigid fashion.

Historian of journalism Alfred McClung Lee has asserted that anti-press agentry activities by publishers increased during the Depression and especially after 1935. There are convincing indications, however, that the reverse was the case. To be sure, individual journalists, such as Elmer Davis, continued to complain that press bureaus were being staffed "with ex-newspapermen by the infamous expedient of offering them more than newspaper owners will pay them" and that the publicity function on balance "has indubitably made it harder for newspaper men to get at the truth." Professors of journalism also voiced such sentiments, and *Editor & Publisher* continued to print many a nasty word on the press agent. And some publishers, suffering from a loss of revenue caused both by the Depression and the rise of radio, entered into local agreements to curb blatant free publicity and the "business office must" stories submitted by advertisers. But Harry Donald Knight, a student of press criticism of government public relations, has noted that in the pre-World War II period, *Editor & Publisher* began running straight stories about opportunities for newspapermen in government publicity. It also acknowledged the importance of government public relations in an article in the August 6, 1938, issue. This article was significant because it marked the first instance that government public relations men were given that title without quotation marks around it and without being lumped together with press agents.

This changed attitude was the result of the growth in the complexity of government and the resultant inability of the newspaperman to cover events without some assistance and also the growth in esteem for public relations in general. These same factors were operating with regard to the journalistic opinion of corporate public relations as well. More and more reporters, some of them with distinguished careers behind them, were leaving newspapers for news sources. If publicity were actually "a type of prostitution to which we have given a form of dignity," newspaper work was proving an excellent background for high-class harlotry.[44]

"I trust that your long experience with advertising will insure a place at the top of any program you may evolve for paid space in newspapers," wrote William A. Thompson, director of the ANPA's bureau of advertising, to Bernard Lichtenburg on the occasion of the latter's announcement that he was forsaking advertising for public relations. "Public relations projects and press-agentry are still synonymous in a good many quarters, but I feel that the modern councillor [*sic*] recognizes the vast superiority of an advertisement signed by the advertiser himself over a story in which an editor has been persuaded to see 'news value.'"[45] Circumspect though this note was, one need merely compare it to Ben Mellon's diatribe against the proposed publication of *Crystallizing Public Opinion* to see how the atmosphere was changing.

In the 1940s perceptive journalists were less prone to blanket condemnations or endorsements of public relations than they had been in previous years. The managing editor of the *New York Times*, for instance, acknowledged that Bernays was "at the top of his profession" but appealed to him to explain his art to some of his less acceptable colleagues. A member of the New York *Daily News* editorial board was willing to trust those public relations men with whom he was personally acquainted but was skeptical about others "because of a series of unfortunate experiences." The general manager of the New York *Sun* said that Bernays's work "has helped greatly make management more fully appreciate its responsibilities," and the managing editor of the Buffalo *Courier Express* asserted that the reversal of the old public-be-damned attitude was at least partially due to the work of the public relations man.[46]

Edward L. Bernays's seventieth birthday celebration in 1961 provided an occasion for the many well-known prople who had dealt with him over the years to evaluate him and the vocation for which he was such an untiring publicist. Bruce Bliven wrote that the public relations man was now "a solid citizen, respected because he is respectable" and making so much money that journalism students seemed to want to move into the field en masse. Even Philip N. Schuyler, who had written some of the most critical articles under the aegis of Marlen Pew for *Editor & Publisher* in the 1920s, told Bernays that "as an early attacker of you, I am proud I learned to praise." In all, of the 175 encomiums which Bernays received from personages of note, 42 were from people who either were then or had been associated with journalism.[47]

One need only peruse coverage of the Watergate scandals, however, to discover that old suspicions remain. Liberal journalists, usually without bothering to define the term, used "public relations" to symbolize the prevarications of the Nixon administration or more loosely simply as an antonym for truth, despite the fact that no public relations counselors were directly involved. There remain institutional frictions between the public relations man and journalist which have not been eliminated by fraternal celebrations. Public relations work, Bernard A. Weisberger has held, presents

> a major threat to the role of the newspaperman, and by its very nature would always remain one. The "independent" newspaper had broken away from mercantile and party control in order to assume a pose, at any rate, of presenting the news in the interest of the public at large, not simply one portion of it. The basic premise of objective journalism was that news *happened,* that the press presented it impartially, and that the people had the facts at their disposal to render a free judgment on the performance of their institutions. The creator of public images in the public relations firm, however, worked on the assumption that news was *managed,* in order to create an impression.[48]

Oddly enough, historian Weisberger's assessment lacked historical perspective. The public relations man of the twentieth century was not the first to create events in order to manage news. As Weisberger himself recounted, nineteenth-century newspapers, even after the demise of the party press, produced numerous hoaxes and other "pseudo-events" because of the pressure to print exclusives which would add to circulation. (What easier way to score a scoop than to make up a story?)[49]

Nonetheless, Weisberger's complaints had great merit. Steadily throughout the course of this century, reporters have needed increasing amounts of news with which to fill their pages and television programs. And the news has had to be reportable, to have taken place accessibly and with proper allowance for cameras and lights and traffic jams. As a result, the number of events specially staged for public consumption seem indeed to be increasing. The interview, the press conference, and the press release should be included in a list of such events. The contrast between the unthinking acceptance of the bland pronouncements made through these sources and the harsh, dangerous truth was dramatically illustrated during the Watergate scandals.[50]

III

Public relations has attracted some attention from observers outside of the business community, especially academicians. The main theme of their pronouncements has been denigration, sometimes contemptuous and sometimes light-hearted. Bernays's *Crystallizing Public Opinion* has always been a lightning rod for sentiment about his vocation, and Stow Persons saw it as a fine illustration of "the cynicism of the new profession." The counselor promoted his client's interest by subtly manipulating public opinion through careful association of his products with favorable stereotypes and by playing on public prejudices. Objective considerations of value and truth were irrelevant to the public relations man's world. What counted was public acceptance. "The only test of truth was the power of the idea to get itself accepted in the marketplace." Persons dismissed Bernays's attempts to achieve professional status for the vocation through the enunciation of a philosophy. His transformation from the publicity man to the public relations counsel was "[h]is greatest publicity stunt."[51]

Alan R. Raucher's *Public Relations and Business, 1900–1929*, the only book-length scholarly treatment of its subject, was consistently critical and skeptical. Public relations counselors, he found, were simply not able to deliver on the grandiose claims of power they advanced. They were not the shrewd and clever men they portrayed themselves as being. Ivy Lee had probably not even read the numerous works he recommended to young men starting out in the field, and Bernays's methods as outlined in *Crystallizing Public Opinion* were "exhaustive but long familiar to

other publicity men." As for his social psychology, it was "jabberwocky."
Public relations was a new name for an old routine, and its practitioners
were rarely able to perform the higher functions, those of the ombudsman, to which they aspired.[52]

Economist Robert Heilbroner, in a 1957 article in *Harper's,* referred to
public relations as "the invisible sell" and wrote that "whereas one may
not particularly like what is being sold, it is hard to get much worked up
over the salesmanship." He conceded that public relations firms had
scored their share of coups and he also allowed that perhaps one-tenth
of public relations activity had nefarious goals. But he did not deal excessively with the evil doings of opinion manipulators. "The really important question about the power of public relations is whether it can influence what men *think.*" Perhaps under certain favorable circumstances,
with limited and specific goals, public relations could change people's
minds. But the biggest programs, those, for example, of the American
Iron and Steel Institute and General Motors and the great campaign to
sell the United Nations to a typical American city (Cincinnati was
selected) in 1947, showed meager results when not actually negative.
The populace, it appeared, was not very impressed with the programs
designed to influence it. Neither, in their more sober moments, were
public relations counselors themselves.

It was, Heilbroner believed, the business community which was most
enthusiastic and self-deceiving about its public relations efforts.
Businessmen, he thought, had even sought to live up to the images their
public relations departments had created for them, with the result that
"good conduct *is* more prevalent on the business scene, and public relations can rightly take much of the credit." It was a "weapon whose recoil
is greater than its muzzle blast." Heilbroner thus nicely reversed
the normal critique of the vocation, which would grudgingly acknowledge that the public relations man could put something over on the
naive citizenry but rarely succeeded in getting his boss to live up to his
press notices. In his view, the public relations counselor made a poor
salesman to the populace but a most effective one to the executive.[53]

Other scholars have not been willing to dismiss the vocation in so
blithe a fashion. Historian Richard Abrams has turned to it as the possible answer to a critical problem of twentieth-century American history:
"[H]ow corporate capitalism has managed . . . to employ the presumably
outmoded rationale of proprietary capitalism to justify its own institutions and practices." How has it survived for so long "*without* an intellec-
tually respectable claim to legitimacy?" The celebrationist would explain
its survival on the grounds of its having produced the greatest good for
the greatest number. But Abrams insisted on noting that business had
acquired "remarkable skills in 'public relations.'" Has the public really

been satisfied or have clever public relations men hoodwinked it into thinking it has been?[54]

This is a question that needs asking. It would be easy to answer, as Heilbroner might, that numerous failures prove that public relations is not powerful enough to accomplish such a gigantic task. However, we shall never know what depths of public displeasure these organizations would have been confronted with during crises had the long-term programs not been carried out.

Public relations seemed sufficiently effective to the professors who founded the Institute for Propaganda Analysis (IPA) in late 1937 to merit scrutiny. The Institute saw a conflict between two creeds, that of the dictator, whose first aim was to create a propaganda machine through which he could control the populace, and that of the democrat, whose belief was in the consent of the governed freely given and based on honestly provided and thoughtfully considered information. The chief danger of public relations propaganda was that "it appeals to emotion, and decisions made under stress of emotion often lead to disaster when emotion crowds out cool, dispassionate thought."[55]

The IPA published a newsletter called "Propaganda Analysis: A Bulletin to Help the Intelligent Citizen Detect and Analyze Propaganda." The bulletin reported on the activities of Don Francisco and Carl Byoir for A&P, of Hill and Knowlton for Little Steel, and of Bernays for the "United Brewers Industrial Foundation." One issue was devoted solely to "The Public Relations Counsel and Propaganda." It was

> not intended to indict the business of public relations. Our society is run by public opinion.... What other people do poorly, the public relations counsel does well. If his methods seem rather shoddy at times—and they do—the fault lies not so much with him as with the conditions that make those methods efficacious: the willingness of the press and radio to cooperate with the public relations counsel, the readiness of the average man or woman to get on the band wagon, the fact that we often let our biases and prejudices, rather than our minds, think for us.[56]

This emphasis on the superiority of reason to emotion in problem solving characterized much of the criticism by intellectuals of the public relations function. The public relations man accepted emotion as being the central component of decision making and was willing to take advantage of it. The problem was not solely that he used emotion. Many intellectuals also would have agreed that emotional appeal is essential to effective communication. But the counselor was viewed as using it not to make the truth more comprehensible but to make the worse appear the better argument. He used it not in conjunction with reason but as a substitute for it and not in the cause of social justice but to screen the depredations of big business.[57]

The IPA found his methods particularly insidious, because although paid advertising also appealed to the emotions, it at least was easily recognizable as special pleading. The public relations man "attempts to slip propaganda into the press as news," thus making special pleading appear as objective reportage. He also concocted bogus institutes and foundations, the third-party groups, for essentially the same reason. He knew how to conceal his client's motives, which was fortunate for him because "with few exceptions those motives are never altruistic." However, the public relations man was not invulnerable; to unmask him was to render him impotent. Sounding a call familiar from the time of Ray Stannard Baker's pioneering muckraking efforts, the IPA explained that "if special pleading is recognized for what it really is, then it loses much of its effect."[58]

This solution to the public relations problem did indeed seem rational, but it did not succeed consistently. These propaganda analysts made the same error of critics from Baker to Otis Pease, who in *The Responsibilities of American Advertising* took advertising to task for "circumvent[ing] the process and operation of rational thought in a free society."[59] Since reason rather than emotion should be the basis for decision making, it was assumed that it could and would be if those who profited from the manipulation of emotion were forced to desist by being exposed for the special pleaders that they were.

The fact is that on numerous occasions Americans have chosen to be duped even though they were aware of the facts.[60] In the words of P. T. Barnum, "[T]he public appears to be disposed to be amused even while they are conscious of being deceived."[61] How else explain the continued popularity of professional wrestling, or the desire expressed in some quarters to see television quiz shows brought back to the air even after they were unmasked as frauds. The American public, it would seem, has sometimes preferred being victimized by the confidence man to sitting at the feet of the expert to hear lectures on the beauties of reason.

IV

Our topical review of the attitude of three groups—advertising agents, journalists, and observers outside the business world—has revealed, in the cases of the first two groups, a similar pattern. Spokesmen changed from a qualified rejection to a qualified acceptance of the vocation.[62] They felt less threatened by it and more willing to enlist its aid in fighting the New Deal and selling the corporation to the public. This change in attitude took place during the Depression, when many public relations men leavened their search for free publicity with a healthy dose of paid advertising. The danger of short circuiting the communications process was thus reduced. Publishers, advertising agents, and public relations counselors learned during the Depression that they could all make money together as long as public relations was practiced in "the right way."

Like journalists and advertising agents, observers outside the business community also began with opposition to public relations. In their case, however, that distaste has, if anything, intensified over the years.

One of the most distressing aspects of the critique of public relations from outside the business community has been the paucity of serious analysis. There have indeed been exposés of wrongdoing, and a number of writers have taken exception to the philosophical underpinnings of public relations, especially as expressed in Bernays's formulation of the vocation as "the engineering of consent." There have been some full-scale works as well. But none of these have offered extended discussions of public relations within a sufficiently broad context.[63]

An important reason for this dearth of scholarship has probably been the distaste felt by many educated people at what the public relations man does (or at least their image of what he does). The charge that his work has led to the "debasement of communication," or to borrow Bernard De Voto's description of advertising, that it is "a torrent of mendacity, imbecility, and bilge" has often been repeated.[64] Be that as it may, public relations has also spread throughout major institutions in every corner of our society and has affected and continues to affect both the tone and content of the information which reaches the public. Questions concerning the reasons for its growth and the nature of its impact are surely worth more attention than they have thus far received.

NOTES

1. *Time,* February 22, 1926, clipping in Bernays papers.

2. "A Contradiction in Terms," *Printers' Ink,* June 1, 1922, clipping in Bernays papers.

3. "By showing that advertising was 'a necessary element of social solidarity,' advertising men were seeking a recognition of the legitimacy and respectability of their occupation." Pope, "Advertising," pp. 330–332; Ewen, *Captains, passim.*

4. Pope, "Advertising," pp. 320–327.

5. Ibid., pp. 225–233; Ralph M. Hower, *The History of an Advertising Agency* (Cambridge, Mass., 1949), pp. 13–58.

6. Gunther, *Flood,* pp. 57–59; Pope, "Advertising," p. 413.

7. Ibid., p. 361.

8. The difference between publicity and public relations from Ayer's point of view was, according to Hower, that "publicity relates chiefly to the product itself. Public relations is concerned with the attitude of the public toward the company and includes the subject of industrial relations—the promotion of satisfactory

relations between the company and its employees." By 1937, the firm's president was singing the praises of public relations. Hower, *Agency,* pp. 286–288.

9. Francisco lectured advertising men on the importance of public relations in a 1937 article, "Business Must Make Friends," *Advertising and Selling,* July 15, 1937, p. 22.

10. "Through Many Windows," *Advertising and Selling,* clipping in Bernays papers.

11. Franklin Russell, "The Parasite: A Truth or Two About So-Called Publicity," *Printers' Ink,* June 12, 1924, pp. 137, 145.

12. Daniel G. Evans to Lee, April 29, 1925; A. L. Higgenbotham to Lee, April 8, 1925, Box 8, Lee papers.

13. Ernest Elmo Calkins had a quaint cautionary tale to illustrate this point:

One of the most pathetic incidents in the history of advertising was implicit in a story which appeared on the front pages of New York newspapers a few years ago, and, as a further indication of its news value, duly surrounded with boxed rules. It told of a sky writer in a Southern city whose plane crashed into a tree while making a landing, throwing the aviator out and causing his death. His name was given and all the attendant circumstances—in fact, every detail but one.

"He was engaged," the account said, "in advertising a cigarette."

The pathos did not lie in the sudden death of the aviator. That was lamentable enough, but not unexpected in his hazardous calling. But an advertiser hoped to buy a large measure of fame by having performed the unusual stunt of writing the name of his product in letters of smoke across the blue sky of heaven, and Fate assisted and gave the enterprise the most dramatic ending conceivable—and the dispatches omitted the name of the product the aviator lost his life to advertise! The advertiser got only what he paid for, and not a groat over, and all his enterprise in employing so daring a method did not avail to get his cigarette named in the news story of the sky writer's death. (*Civilizer,* pp. 88–89.)

14. James True, "Two Press Agents Tell About the High Cost of Free Publicity," *Printers' Ink,* March 12, 1925, pp. 41ff.

15. For example, James True, "Trickery, Fraud, Hoax and Bunk—The Press Agent's Tools," *Printers' Ink,* March 19, 1925, pp. 104ff.

16. Herbert Everett to Lee, May 29, 1925, Box 8, Lee papers.

17. Harry N. Field to Lee, April 26, 1925, Box 8, Lee papers.

18. C. C. Green to Lee, March 3, 1926; Green to Lee, March 5, 1926, Box 27, Lee papers.

19. Bernays, *Idea,* pp. 342–355, 403–418. R. J. Compton, Jr. of the Blackman Company explained that Bernays was retained because the agency believed that Procter & Gamble could be helped if the public were reached through news columns. "There were certain states of mind which we wished to bring about which could hardly be brought about through the medium of regular paid advertising." R. J. Compton, Jr. to Horace B. Cheney, February 28, 1923, Bernays papers.

20. "Free Publicity," *Advertising Club News,* June 23, 1924, issue in Box 7, Lee papers; Edgar H. Felix, "Organizing Broadcasting and Publicity Bureaus in Advertising Agencies," *Advertising and Selling,* February 20, 1929, 25ff.

21. Pritzker to Lichtenburg, February 3, 1936; Wible to Lichtenburg, March 17, 1936, Vol. 15, Lichtenburg papers. Lichtenburg answered that business is constantly criticized but not constantly defended. The public relations man does more than seek free publicity; he also maintains relations with "stockholders, employees, dealers, etc." Naturally his would be no "shyster" practice but rather "studied, careful, and as scientific as possible," Lichtenburg to Wible, March 19, 1936, Vol. 15, Lichtenburg papers.

22. Lee to Herbert Everett, June 2, 1925, Box 8, Lee papers; S. H. Walker and Paul Sklar, "Foundation Trouble," *Printers' Ink,* July 8, 1937, pp. 29ff.

23. Ray Bowen to Lichtenburg, February 13, 1936; John Benson to Lichtenburg, February 19, 1936, Vol. 14, Lichtenburg papers.

24. "Publicity and the Advertising Agency," *Advertising and Selling,* February 28, 1935, p. 26.

25. Cutlip and Center, *Public Relations,* p. 34. In a 1951 survey of 100 firms, the Opinion Research Corporation found that of thirty-eight making use of outside public relations help, ten received this help from advertising agencies. "Industry's Communications Systems—1951," *PO Index,* Vol. 8, No. 10, p. 32.

26. In 1951, Larrabee wrote to Bernays that "we at *Printers' Ink* are finding our relationship with Edward L. Bernays as stimulating as we thought and hoped it would be. In fact, far more." September 19, 1951, Bernays papers. In the 1960s, the American Association of Advertising Agencies retained Hill and Knowlton during a controversy with the Department of Justice about the effects of advertising. T. A. Wise, "Hill and Knowlton's World of Images," *Fortune,* September 1, 1967, p. 98.

27. Gunther, *Flood,* p. 154. Bernays's remark was made in conversation with the author.

28. *Public Relations,* pp. 34–35.

29. "Publicity," p. 52. Clever formulations such as this must be approached gingerly. Albert Lasker once said that all good advertising is news. Boorstin, *Image,* p. 210.

30. "Advertising vs. Publicity," *Electrical World,* January 30, 1932, pp. 231–232.

31. Cutlip and Center, *Public Relations,* pp. 35–36.

32. R. C. E. Brown, "The Menace to Journalism" *North American Review,* November 1921, pp. 611ff; Atherton Brownell, "Publicity—and Its Ethics," *North American Review,* February 1922, pp. 188ff; Brown's reply to Brownell, *North American Review,* February 1922, p. 198. Knight, "Press Criticism, pp. 25–26; 59. An example of how public relations could stifle journalistic initiative was the regime Ivy Lee instituted for John D. Rockefeller. He persuaded his boss to give out no exclusives. This, according to his biographer, "appealed to the newsman's sense of fair play and allayed his fear of being scooped by the opposition." It also provided a convenient excuse to deny individual interviews. When Rockefeller met the press, it was at a press conference. When Lee discovered that an individual reporter had independently uncovered newsworthy information,

he released it to the rest of the press as well in order to avoid the appearance of favoritism. Thus the utility of using initiative to score a scoop was obviously greatly diminished. Hiebert, *Courtier*, pp. 118–124.

33. Pope, "Advertising," pp. 359–362; Edwin Emery, *History of the American Newspaper Publishers Association* (Minneapolis, 1950), pp. 127–129.

34. *New York Times*, February 20, 1920; Cutlip, *Fund Raising*, pp. 168–187, 233–238, 244–253, 268–271.

35. "Associated Press Is Checkmating the Space Grabber," *Printers' Ink*, April 10, 1924, pp. 77–80.

36. Philip Schuyler, "A.N.P.A. Launches New War on Press Agents," *Editor & Publisher*, March 29, 1930, p. 15.

37. "Publicity in New York Is Decreasing," *Editor & Publisher*, March 29, 1930; Stanley Walker, "Men of Vision," clipping in Box 46, Lee papers.

38. "Holding Hands," *Editor & Publisher*, April 9, 1927, clipping in Bernays papers; "Shop Talk at Thirty," *Editor & Publisher*, June 11, 1933, p. 40.

39. Lee, *Newspaper*, p. 442; "Du Pont Decides to Establish New Publicity Bureau," *New York Herald*, February 23, 1916; "Du Pont Powder Company Sees New Light," *Editor & Publisher*, February 26, 1916, clippings in Box 6, Lee papers; Nunnally Johnson, "And Now a P.R.C. Is Added to H.C. of L.," Brooklyn *Eagle*, clipping in Bernays papers; Johnson, "Why We Are Mere Putty in the Hands of Press Agents," New York *Post*, July 6, 1928, clipping in Box 7, Lee papers; Ernest Gruening, "The Higher Hokum," *The Nation*, April 16, 1924, p. 450.

Joseph Dorney, railroad editor of the Cincinnati *Enquirer*, wrote in 1917 that "it wasn't so many years ago that a newspaperman was as welcome in the office of a railway official as a secret service agent in the cabin of a moonshiner." But all that had changed. "About the time railroad officials woke up to the fact that their clam-like proclivities were not doing their companies any good, came the press agent or publicity man, and these needed additions to the staffs earn their salaries many times over." *Railway Age Gazette*, May 4, 1917, p. 560. Charles K. Weston, the Philadelphia *Ledger* reporter who got the Du Pont publicity job in 1916, wrote that he and his colleagues on the paper did not at first trust communications from Ivy Lee, but "it was not long before we could depend upon the information sent us by the railroad." "Du Pont Sees Light." Herbert L. Matthews of the editorial board of the *New York Times* wrote that when he was a reporter of Latin American affairs, he could always get the straight and honest story from Bernays (who at the time was retained by the United Fruit Company). Matthews to Bernays, November 17, 1966, Bernays papers. When Harry A. Bruno asked Joe King, boating editor of the New York *World-Telegram*, whether he wished to continue receiving Bruno's weekly motor boat bulletin, King replied that he did "most emphatically." "I find the information contained therein of great value in arranging our motor boat columns, especially as the bulletin acts as a clearing house for the sport throughout the country, a scope which is usually beyond the power of the individual newspaper to accomplish." (A most impressive testimony indeed.) King to Bruno, Blythe and Associates, April 13, 1933, Vol. 10, Bruno papers.

Even in the 1920s, at the height of antipublicity sentiment among newspaper-men, Arthur W. Page questioned the sincerity of this animus. In mid-1927, he told his colleagues at AT&T that there used to be much objection to publicity handouts, and some such prejudice lingered among reporters. "But they don't mean it, and for this reason, the information which they print is so various that they haven't got the staff to collect it." "What Publicity and Advertising Can Do to Help Operation," General Operating Conference, May, 1927, Vol. 5, Page papers.

40. *The Fourth Estate*, March 8, 1924; May 5, 1923, clippings in Bernays papers.

41. Bernays, *Idea*, p. 288.

42. Knight, "Criticism," p. 9, listed these as the major complaints against public relations in government.

43. Business trade journals were always less averse to publicity than the general circulation press. From prior to the First World War, the *Electric Railway Journal* and the *Railway Age Gazette*, among others, were urging their readers to explore the possibilities of publicity, and Bernays's *Crystallizing Public Opinion* received for the most part a kinder reception from them than from the general circulation press. Most trade journals apparently used corporation publicity as a matter of course in their own columns. As the *Heating and Ventilating Magazine* remarked, they "have lived on publicity, which in turn they have provided." "Publicity from the Standpoint of the Technical Journal," *Heating and Ventilating Magazine*, November, 1923, pp. 84ff.

44. Lee, *Newspaper*, p. 470; Emery, *Association*, p. 130; Knight, "Criticism," pp. 108, 127–128, 141–142, 78. The low wages and harsh working conditions which drove some journalists from reporting to public relations are described in Daniel J. Leab, *A Union of Individuals* (New York, 1970), pp. 4–9.

45. Thompson to Lichtenburg, February 17, 1936, Vol. 15, Lichtenburg papers.

46. Ed James, managing editor of the *Times*, added, "If you could see the number of bone-headed stunts pulled by publicity people as they drift into newspapers, you would realize the force of what I am saying." James to James W. Gerard, January 26, 1946; Lowell M. Limpus to Gerard, February 23, 1946; Edwin S. Friendly to Gerard, January 29, 1946; John H. Tranter to Gerard. January 31, 1946; Harry C. Withers to Gerard, February 1, 1946, Bernays papers. See also Wayne L. Hodges, "Newspaper Coverage of Labor-Management News," *Industrial and Labor Relations Review*, 8, No. 1 (October 1954), pp. 90–97.

47. Benjamin Fine to Bernays, November 13, 1961; Bliven to Bernays, October 28, 1961; Schuyler to Bernays, November 20, 1961, Bernays papers; Philip Schuyler, "Ed Bernays Honored; PR for a Paradox," *Editor & Publisher*, December 2, 1961, clipping in Bernays papers.

48. *Newspaperman*, p. 200.

49. Ibid., p. 135.

50. See Carl Bernstein and Bob Woodward, *All the President's Men* (New York, 1975), pp. 21, 247, 344–347, and *passim*.

51. Persons, *American Minds,* pp. 379–380.

52. In at least two instances, Raucher took his criticism too far. He claimed that the social sciences could not be applied to the practice of public relations and that Bernays knew it. Were this true, it would relegate Bernays's talk of the social sciences to just another example of the devices he employed to draw attention to himself and to dignify his vocation. Whether Bernays really applied his theories to his practice, or whether he merely used a veneer of academic language to justify his hunches, is a question worth considering, but there is simply no doubt that the social sciences have been applied to public relations, advertising, and marketing. Raucher also questioned whether the public relations man could interpret public desires better than those who were institutionally assigned to do so. If America's political and economic institutions operated perfectly, there would probably be no need for an ombudsman from outside the organization. But as they do not, outside opinions certainly could be and have been helpful. See Chapter 3, note 49.

53. *Harper's,* June 1957, pp. 23–31.

54. Richard M. Abrams, Introduction to Louis D. Brandeis, *Other People's Money* (New York, 1967), pp. xlii–xliii.

55. "Propaganda Analysis" (Institute for Propaganda Analysis, October 1937–October 1938), Vol. I, p. iii of Preface and Announcement for issue No. 1.

56. Ibid., Vol. I, No. 11 (August 1938), pp. 61–64.

57. J. A. R. Pimlott has asserted that the root cause of the unpopularity of public relations has been its association with big business. The problem was not methodology but sponsorship. *Public Relations and American Democracy* (Garden City, N.Y., 1951), p. 206.

58. "Propaganda Analysis," Vol. I, No. 11 (August 1938), pp. 61–64.

59. (New Haven, 1958), p. 203.

60. Pop sociologist Vance Packard concluded his best-selling *The Hidden Persuaders* (New York, 1957) by asserting, as so many others had, that unmasking the persuader would render him relatively powerless. This would not, however, put an end to irrationability. It would simply enable people to be irrational in their own ways. Pp. 226–229.

61. Harris, *Humbug,* p. 25.

62. A similar change occurred with corporate lawyers. They first tended to view public relations men as interlopers in the corporate arena, and tried to block their access both to the public and to executives. By the 1950s, however, lawyers were suggesting that the American Bar Association itself could use a public relations program to dispel the Hollywood-inspired image of the lawyer as shyster. Hill, *Making,* pp. 24, 47–50; Lloyd Wright, review of Edward L. Bernays's *Public Relations,* American Bar Association *Journal,* November 1952, p. 942.

63. The most noteworthy of these is the Raucher book. The author unfortunately tried to restrict himself to a study of men actually using the term "public relations" to describe their work. As a result, he tended toward an antiquarian search for the term, while neglecting the onset of public relations-mindedness in this century. Although his book is rather brief, one reviewer observed

that the topic did not seem to merit book-length treatment at all. The problem was not as much the topic as the context in which it was placed. See C. B. Cowing, review of Raucher's *Public Relations and Business, 1900–1929,* in *Journal of American History* 56, No. 1 (June 1969), pp. 163–164.

64. Bernard De Voto, "Why Professors Are Suspicious of Business," *Fortune,* April, 1951, p. 114.

Chapter VIII

Conclusions

How often it fails to work! How often we fail to do what we set out to do!
Public relations counselor
Earl Newsom, 1951[1]

Public relations is the curse of our times. It could be the sign of a very deep disease.
Mark Van Doren, 1967[2]

I

Public relations has promised two benefits to business: increased sales
and protection from unpopularity which could lead to detrimental governmental or regulatory agency activity. Improving sales has been a goal
of the function from its inception, when advertisers insisted upon reading notices as a reward for the space they bought. The attention-getting
stunt also dated back to at least the nineteenth century. It was refined to
a high level of sophistication by Bernays, who christened it the "created
event," in the 1920s. He combined a shrewd sense of news value with
careful research to attract publicity for his clients in news columns.
Counselors have also contended that improved sales would be a natural
by-product of public approval of corporate conduct, for consumers
would prefer the products of companies they liked.

Sales promotion has persisted as a demand which companies have
made of public relations. In 1946, the Opinion Research Corporation
(ORC) found 43 percent of the corporate chief executives it polled ex-
pecting public relations to tell the public about the company's products,[3]
and this expectation continually appeared at or near the top of ORC

studies. A 1950 study at the University of Illinois found over a half a sample of 84 companies also seeking increased sales from the function.[4] During the 1950s, in a notable throwback to the reading notice practice, at least one agency promised to obtain seemingly spontaneous "plugs" to promote products on television shows. This practice caused serious embarrassment to the networks when it was publicly revealed during the quiz-show scandals in 1959.[5] "Payola," or paying disc jockeys to favor certain records on their radio programs, is also in this tradition.[6]

Advertising and public relations have often worked in tandem, especially when a manufacturer has attempted to diminish sales resistance rooted in custom. In his campaign to overcome the taboo against women smoking in public, George Washington Hill, president of the American Tobacco Company, retained Lee, Bernays, and advertising man Albert D. Lasker. Lasker composed and placed copy while Bernays solicited opinions from a psychiatrist on the best way to conquer this prejudice and staged events such as the "Torches of Freedom" parade of socialites smoking cigarettes as they strolled down Fifth Avenue.[7]

In rejecting Bernard Lichtenburg's new business solicitation, Gillette's advertising manager observed that "the day has passed when publicity to educate people to shave can be considered a matter of importance."[8] Educating women to the use of Kotex, on the other hand, was a delicate merchandising problem which Albert Lasker solved by acting both as an advertising and a public relations man. To introduce this product, he not only advertised, he mailed circulars to outlets explaining how sales could be made with a minimum of embarrassment to the customer. He also inspired an article in the *Ladies' Home Journal* on menstruation "and systematically organized a campaign to inform school boards and other organizations all over the country about the product, and to explain how teachers could perform a valuable public service by instructing girl students about elements of female hygiene."[9]

No firm has been more successful in winning free sales publicity than the Ford Motor Company. Ford made front-page news all over the country when it announced in the spring of 1927 that it would produce a new car. Henry Ford recognized that, left to its own devices, the press would speculate endlessly about the forthcoming vehicle. Even editors who had long fought to exclude names of products and firms from their news columns were defeated by the very lack of information the company gave out and were forced to give publicity to "the most arrant space poacher in the world." "The mystery and suspense surrounding the new Ford [which was to be the Model A] was greatly dramatized by the Ford Company's 'golden silence.'" Ford adopted the same approach three decades later when it introduced the Edsel. The public relations director at that time released a few facts about the car prior to its unveiling, and journalistic exuberance became so widespread that the advertising company wrote low-key copy because it could not top the adjectives reporters were using.[10]

Public relations has unquestionably helped the sales of certain products through publicity, especially those in entertainment, fashion, and the arts. It reached the apex of its importance in this regard in the 1920s, when it was an exciting innovation. During the '30s, however, product promotion by publicity waned in relative importance. The political problems of the decade virtually preempted the attention of many counselors, and stunts and gambits were growing stale.[11] Americans were slowly becoming educated in the ways of persuaders. Today, public relations for sales promotion persists, but it is of marginal import. In the standard text, increasing sales is not among the problems set out for student exercises.[12]

The arguments that sales increases would be an ancillary benefit to improvements in the corporate image were succinctly summarized by Gerry Swinehart, president of Carl Byoir and Associates in 1953:

Good labor relations or good stockholder relations . . . definitely help sales where these policies are made known to prospective buyers. . . . When A&P ran its nationwide advertising, telling its side of the story against antitrust charges, there was a marked increase in sales—a by-product of the public relations advertising that in this instance was not primarily intended to affect sales.

Public relations frequently brings a new dimension to selling. The longer-range public relations approach can provide the means for creating a friendlier and more cooperative attitude on the part of the company salesmen, the jobbers and retailers. This gives added impetus to the immediate product-sales activities. . . .

Perhaps the general proposition is clearer . . . in the negative: bad public relations adversely affect sales; therefore, good public relations positively help sales.[13]

This seemingly sensible assertion was contradicted by a popular public relations cliché: "The public can buy the shelves clean of your product in the morning, but vote you out of business in the afternoon." In this view, there was no direct correlation between a person's opinion of a company in his role as consumer and as citizen. In other words, a firm could have a bad reputation but good sales, and vice versa. In 1944, for example, an Elmo Roper survey disclosed that while people loved the Ford Motor Company, most of them preferred General Motors products (a finding with interesting implications for the question of the emotional versus the rational bases for the purchase of automobiles). Four years later, Roper asked in a general opinion poll which company the public would least like to see go out of business. Ford won easily, but was still being outsold by its principal competitor.[14]

The demise of the corner grocery store in the face of competition from the supermarket chain is another example of the divergence between emotional preference and buying habits. The small businessman has occupied a place in the American pantheon beside that of the yeoman farmer, but he has nevertheless been evicted from his shop on main street by the suburban shopping center. Indeed, to cite Swinehart's own example against him, the Byoir organization discovered after being retained by A&P that most people preferred to shop at the chains despite their support for anti-chain legislation. Therefore although common sense would lead to agreement with Swinehart, there are enough examples of a disparity between opinion about a business and preference for its product to call his assertion into doubt. At best, the equation between these factors is not a simple one.

II

It is not as a sales device, however, but as a method for protection against the political consequences of a hostile public opinion that corporate public relations has been most influential. If it had been restricted to sales promotion, public relations might have been absorbed by advertising departments and could have been dismissed as a footnote to business history. Instead, it grew into a tool for dealing with many publics, including residents of plant communities, employees, suppliers and dealers, and politicians as well as customers. Increased sales were of course welcomed, but except in the entertainment industry[15] they were usually the result of activities designed to "make friends" for the organization.

Public relations, then, grew as an institutional response to the problem of managing the business reputation. This response has taken place on two levels: within individual firms and in concert through trade associations.

On the company level, public relations has been most conspicuous when statements were necessitated by direct public criticism. Thus we find Ivy Lee retained by the Rockefeller interests during Ludlow, Carl Byoir by A&P during the chain-store legislation controversy, and the Wright Aeronautical Corporation placing public relations advertising after exposure before the Truman Committee. By itself, however, response to public criticism is an insufficient explanation for why the function developed in so many firms, even those which were not suffering image difficulties or were, like Ford before World War I, actually quite popular. The answer lies in the drive for more efficient internal organization which has been a hallmark of American business since the railroads began to grow too large for chief executives to supervise the details of their management.

It is no accident that public relations began with the railroads. The first of America's big businesses, their policies affected localities far removed from the central office. As early as the 1830s, they were giving free passes to ingratiate themselves with leading citizens along the route. They were, furthermore, the first businesses in which ownership and management became separated. Executives began to lose that sense of public acceptance which might have been theirs without effort if they owned a small factory in the town in which they lived. Public acceptance would now have to be cultivated by dealing with a press not always favorably disposed to absentee managers. Careless remarks by men like Jay Gould could have severe effects on a firm's reputation, worker morale, and stock prices. Rumors about slipshod management invited government interference. And with increased literacy rates and magazine circulation, these remarks received unprecedented attention. As the *Railroad Gazette* observed during the controversy over William H. Vanderbilt's alleged "public be damned" gaffe, "[W]hen Mr. Vanderbilt talks to a reporter, he makes a speech to the entire nation. . . ."

Often criticism and growth, especially if it was sudden, coincided, as in the cases of United States Steel and International Harvester during the merger movement at the turn of the century. The bankers and executives who masterminded these mergers knew they were changing the rules of the economic game. The talk was of a "new competition," which was in fact centrally directed corporate cooperation resulting in ever fewer men making decisions affecting progressively larger numbers of people. Unorganized segments of the middle class resented this new power, and their attitude was reflected in and stimulated by muckraking exposés. To deal systematically with this discontent, many of these new firms made special provision for public relations. Even after the resentment abated, however, and after journalistic treatment of big business became more bland, public relations remained because the companies remained large. Had it not been for bigness, businessmen would have continued to respond to criticism as they had in the past, in an ad hoc fashion.

Along with the growth of business came the scientific management movement and other techniques aimed at eliminating hunch and bringing precision to business administration. A publicity or public relations department of some kind began to appear on the new organization charts which innovative firms were drawing up.[16] The leading company in the field in the 1920s was AT&T. Management encouraged Page's work not because it was being publicly criticized but because it recognized that an organized and prudent public relations program could make important contributions to a firm with such wide interests.

In the work of Page, Lee, and Bernays in the 1920s and 1930s, we see how corporations began to use public relations not just as press liaison but also to learn about their environment. One of the chief problems "of this era of bureaucratization," Louis Galambos has written, "was that of maintaining contact with and power over the organization's external environment. . . . This task involved communication as well as control. The organizations needed a steady flow of information from their immediate surroundings if they were going to stabilize or—even better— manipulate their environments."[17] In order to serve as the ears of management, public relations men conducted their own public opinion surveys and cultivated the acquaintance of various "opinion leaders." They also commissioned independent opinion research and market research firms to poll the public. These independent organizations date from about 1910, but it was not until mid-Depression that businessmen turned to them seriously to diagnose their image problems. The public opinion poll became such a valued tool that even the flamboyant misjudgments of the 1948 presidential election failed to discourage business in its use. Public relations thus became a mechanism for absorbing as well as dispensing information.

But has public relations been effective in manipulating the attitudes of significant publics? If so, is it because it has persuaded great corporations to take the two-way-street idea seriously enough to mold their policies to fit public desires? Have public relations men become "keepers of the corporate conscience," as many have sincerely wished to be?[18] Or has it succeeded because of the effectiveness of its sometimes mendacious propaganda?

These are questions which have been asked and begged more than once in this study. Satisfactory answers are, unfortunately, impossible to arrive at because there is simply no way to assess the impact of factors having nothing to do with the function.[19] A brief analysis of the history of public relations at Du Pont, a firm for which there is more information available than most, will illustrate this difficulty.

Du Pont was stigmatized for war profiteering during the Nye Committee Hearings in 1934; its executives were labeled "merchants of death." A shrewd program to win back a good name began the following year, when the company began its sponsorship of the radio show *Cavalcade of America*, a series of thirty-minute dramatizations of American history broadcast over a forty-three-station network. The company hoped to con-

vince the public that it was primarily a chemical, rather than merely a munitions, manufacturer and that its real goal was progress. The advertisements were soft-spoken institutional messages, designed to tell the lis-
tener about the company rather than sell merchandise. Their theme was
"Better things for better living . . . through chemistry," and they did not
directly respond to the Nye charges. The programs themselves emphasized humanitarian achievements:

> Though international struggles were occasionally mentioned—they were
> difficult to avoid—battle scenes were not permitted. The sound of a shot
> was taboo. Even explosions were for many years forbidden. The atmos-
> phere was pacifist and highly idealistic.[20]

Du Pont had had a publicity office since 1916, but its duties had been
restricted to dispensing routine information and product publicity. In
1938 it was renamed the public relations department, and in 1942
Harold Brayman became its director.[21] A graduate of Cornell who had
extensive experience as a Washington correspondent and who had been
president of both the Gridiron and National Press Clubs, Brayman attracted a skillful staff which produced brochures, newsletters and films,
sponsored conferences with educators, gave painstaking consideration
to the problems of those affected by plant closings, and participated fully
in policy discussions about matters which could affect the firm's reputation. Three years after the Nye Committee hearings, Du Pont commissioned a public opinion survey which showed that 47 percent of the respondents held a favorable opinion of the company, 16 percent an
unfavorable opinion, and 37 percent no opinion. Twenty-one years later, the final survey in this series showed 79 percent favorable, 3 percent
unfavorable, and 18 percent no opinion.[22]

Standing alone, these data would indicate as successful a public relations effort as any firm could wish for. But how much credit should the
function be given? During these years, Du Pont produced such popular
synthetics as nylon, and war material became a progressively smaller part
of its operation. After Pearl Harbor, manufacturing armaments came to
look a good deal more patriotic than it had a few years earlier anyway.
Furthermore, business as a whole enjoyed a steadily increasing popularity.

It does seem probable, however, that public relations has made a
noteworthy contribution. A brief exercise in counterfactualism can illustrate this proposition. Even if they had not been public relations-
minded, Du Pont executives would have been wounded by the Nye
characterizations and the subsequent bad publicity. Instead of respond-

ing with the subtle device of *Cavalcade of America,* however, they would have maintained a sullen silence or perhaps have issued a truculent declaration that it was God's will that they manage their firm as they pleased. In place of careful consideration of the needs of workers and local citizens, they would have closed plants without any attempt to cushion the impact. Instead of issuing statements concerning plant accidents, they would have tried to conceal news of them altogether, thus fostering rumors. Rather than mending fences with journalistic and academic critics through annual conferences (or junkets), relations would have been strictly formal when there were any at all. Instead of making their opponents look ridiculous by a legitimate and very clever journalistic coup during the Du Pont divestiture case in the late 1940s, they would have strolled through the halls of Congress with fists full of dollars, trying to buy legislators outright after the manner of Jay Gould and risking an avalanche of disastrous publicity. It is indeed difficult to believe that this firm would not have had considerably less public approval without public relations. This unpopularity could have led to unfavorable legislation, poor morale within the company, and perhaps loss of sales.[23]

The keys to a successful company public relations program are sensitivity to the public, publicity for this sensitivity, and "keeping everlastingly at it." Continuous effort is essential. In general, people have not been volatile in their opinions of companies. Unpopular firms cannot change their reputations overnight through stunts or advertising. When quick results have been achieved, the goals have been specific and short-range. Thus when Byoir fought antichain-store legislation, he did not try to win popularity for A&P, which would by necessity have been a long-term operation. As he put it, he made "no appeal for the chain store as such." Instead, he opposed taxation through third-party organizations, seeking to convince the public, or more accurately, to convey to legislators the impression that the public had been convinced, that the proposed taxes were not in the public interest.

The reverse of the above proposition also holds: popular businesses do not forfeit good reputations immediately because of bad publicity, as the history of the Ford Motor Company demonstrates. Henry Ford's innovativeness, his fight against the Selden patent, his post-World War I price cut to stimulate the faltering economy, and the reliability of his product enabled his company to accumulate such a store of good will that his later, gratuitous blunders did not tarnish it. Polls showing public affection for the firm in the 1940s have already been mentioned. In 1937, the Curtis Publishing Company asked respondents to rate the policies of twelve leading corporations. Ford ranked first in labor and pricing policy despite the fact that at the time it was having severe labor trouble and was hiking prices $15 to $35 on its models, thus paving the way for industry-wide increases.[24]

How far were executives willing to go to propitiate public opinion? Most saw the necessity of guarding carefully their public statements and insisted that employees do likewise. But how far would they go to insure that private business was operated in the public interest? At the suggestion of their public relations departments, manufacturers cleaned up their plants, railroads installed high-quality glass in their passenger cars, and all kinds of firms increased communication with employees and entered into community activities.

Even among companies with a professed concern for public relations, however, examples of the limitations of the function are numerous. When Ivy Lee was preparing W. W. Atterbury, chief executive of the Pennsylvania Railroad, for his testimony before the Commission on Industrial Relations, he knew Atterbury would be asked about the large stock of weapons the company kept in a Philadelphia warehouse. The two men worked out what they considered a satisfactory response: the company had a duty to protect its property and its patrons. A statement to this effect was issued to the press prior to Atterbury's appearance before the Commission and "it effectively cut the ground from under Chairman Walsh's feet."[25] Lee apparently did not feel it his duty to encourage serious exploration within the company of the propriety of a private firm maintaining an arsenal of 5,000 rifles. That level of policy discussion was none of his affair.

This pattern of the essentially peripheral influence of public relations can be traced down to the Watergate scandal, in the course of which it was revealed that numerous major corporations had illegal political slush funds from which they had made surreptitious donations to the Committee for the Reelection of the President. Probably all, certainly most, of these firms had large public relations departments, which helped draft statements of corporate contrition after executives were trapped into confession. But where were these departments when the slush funds were established?

There is a difference between educating executives about new techniques to solve problems and attempting to reform a company. It is sometimes true that genuine reform has been an ancillary result of policies motivated by public relations advice. Those counselors, however, who have self-consciously set about to reform their employers as the first order of business, and there seem to have been quite a few of these who entered the vocation after World War II, most likely met with failure more often than success. Public relations has helped to bring business and public closer together, but in many, if not most cases, this rapprochement has been achieved by selling the corporation to the public rather than the other way around.

*   *   *

In addition to the activities of individual corporations, public relations has been active on the trade association level. In fact, trade associations, especially the National Association of Manufacturers, were instrumental in educating smaller firms and uninitiated larger ones about the function in the 1930s and 1940s. In these cooperative public relations programs, the aim was to convince the public either of the rectitude of an industry, as with the campaigns of the utility executives and the American Iron and Steel Institute during the Depression, or, more generally, of the beneficence of the system of free enterprise and private property and of the qualifications of business leaders to make their decisions about allocation of national resources. During the Depression, some executives felt their leadership jeopardized by what they considered syndicalist union leaders and socialist politicians. They called upon the public relations arm of such organizations as the National Association of Manufacturers to "sell the American way of life to the American people."

Scholars from various disciplines have discerned a movement away from physical force to persuasion as the chief method for social control in twentieth-century America. Public relations can be seen as part of this movement. Indeed during the 1930s its proponents in the NAM were explicit in their assertion that it was more effective than bullets, tear gas, and espionage in getting workers to do what management wanted. Yet a more important target than the workers was the middle class. Trade association propaganda taught that business leadership would insure the sanctity of property and equality of opportunity. Just as the development of organized public relations departments within individual firms is indicative of the rationalization of the administration of these growing bureaucracies, such trade association programs as the NAM's show how business sought to rationalize the living world outside the factory and office and impose a social order favorable to doing business.

Let us ask the same questions of public relations aimed at selling the system as we did of that intended to make friends for individual firms: Has it worked, and if so, how?

In his recent study, Louis Galambos found a secular trend in the improvement of the image of big business from 1880 to 1950, with cyclical downturns during such periods as the Great Depression. But neither he

nor Richard Hofstadter, who noted the same trend, assigned any importance to public relations in the process.

Galambos approached the business image from a different direction
from that of this study. He was concerned with the external response to
it rather than the business self-image and based his findings upon
exhaustive content analyses of selected periodicals which he believed
represented the views of elements of the middle class. The explanation
for the improved reputation of business lay not in the conscious efforts
of corporate leaders to sell the system but in the fact that Americans
came to accept the existence of large bureaucratic organizations as part
of modern life. Business pioneered in building such organizations, but
by World War II numerous groups, such as workers and farmers, that at
the turn of the century had felt atomized and naked before corporate
power, had developed impressive organizations of their own to represent their interests before the broker state. As early as 1920, these bud-
ding new organizations were fostering "a new approach to the large corporation, one that stressed emulation over antitrust, cooperation over
class conflict." Hofstadter's explanation is essentially similar. People have
become more concerned with carving out a life "within the corporate
framework" than breaking the corporation down into smaller units.[26]

From this analysis it would seem that criticism of big business diminished more or less automatically, as a by-product of acquiescence in
bureaucratic life rather than as a result of public relations efforts to convince the public that business organizations themselves were beneficial.
In one particualr way public relations may have been harmful. Galambos
asserted that the impersonality of corporate bureaucracy actually facilitated public acceptance. When citizens could single out an individual
villain like Gould or Rockefeller, they could focus their discontent more
effectively. Public relations advisers, on the other hand, had always tried
to "humanize" their clients. This attitude is clearly evident in the conduct
of Frederick Crawford, who expended much effort in making his personal presence felt.

Perhaps, then, there was some justice in William H. Whyte's complaint
that the "Great Free Enterprise Campaign" was a waste of time and effort, an assessment shared by some executives.[27] It does seem striking
that after all the work and money expended, the associations came up
with such banal slogans as "Prosperity Dwells Where Harmony Reigns"
and "Petroleum Is Progressive" and such vague symbols as the "Tripod
of Freedom." Such bland banners resulted from the need to avoid step-
ping on members' toes, which the associations did anyway.

Trade association public relations offered two justifications for the
business system. The older one, championed primarily by the NAM,
based its appeal on the free market and social mobility. The newer

rhetoric of social responsibility, associated with the CED, had, however, superseded the more traditional argument by the 1960s.

This new rhetoric presented problems of its own. It did not convince skeptics of the left, who saw it as a sophisticated attempt at "the legitimizing of privilege, differential reward, and life chances brought about by the existing institutions."[28] Ideologues of the right labeled the "acceptance by corporate officials of a social responsibility other than to make as much money for their stockholders as possible" a "fundamentally subversive doctrine." Business executives were a self-selected private elite. They had no mandate to make basically political decisions. What qualified them to serve an undefined and indefinable social interest? How were they to recognize it, and how was the stockholder or the public to limit their activities? The introduction of the social responsibility rationale to private enterprise, a development much stimulated by public relations counselors, had the defects of its virtues.[29] If executives were no longer "soulless," they could now exercise their whim in a vastly enlarged realm.

As intellectual justifications for the nation's "mixed economy," classical and managerial philosophies are both unsatisfying. The forms of modern business institutions were designed for a world of vigorously competing small entrepreneurs. However, the classical creed, which justified those forms, has ceased to describe reality. As for the social responsibility ethic, the conservative criticism of it carries the day. It fails to provide a justification for the lack of control over businessmen acting in their role of social statesmen. Essentially, the rhetoric of social responsibility is a stopgap to fill the breach created when the classical creed collapsed.

General business propaganda has tried to sell an idea, to convince the customer to change his attitude, rather than a tangible product. Despite Whyte's criticism and Galambos's neglect of it, trade association public relations probably did make some contribution to gaining public acceptance for the system, although as with company public relations its precise impact cannot be measured. This assertion is based upon a number of factors previously discussed. First, big businessmen themselves were sufficiently convinced of its effectiveness to provide continuous funding for trade association public relations programs since the Depression. Some executives seem to have been dissatisfied, but they expressed this dissatisfaction privately and by their ongoing financial support they showed they were not willing to take a chance on being wrong. Second, whether or not trade association public relations was able to create the reality of broad public support, it definitely helped create the appearance that such support existed for the business point of view, a key asset in modern political and economic struggles. Third, it educated executives to the importance of not boasting of their influence, because the public suspects power. By the post-World War II period, labor unions were complaining that the public far underestimated corporate power and thus supported legislation prejudicial to them. Lastly, by making executives conscious of public opinion, trade association public relations helped discourage the use of violence in quelling labor unrest, a traditional tactic prior to the Depression. Strong-arm tactics would doubtless have become progressively less acceptable to the middle class. By providing businessmen with an alternate method of influencing events, it helped them to avoid tarnishing the system's image. As for Galambos's speculation that executive impersonality led to diminished dislike of business leaders, it is noteworthy that, according to the University of Michigan study of 1951, many people objecting to big business singled out the "impersonal and distant" attitude of executives as being offensive.

III

The public relations of public relations counselors among intellectuals has deteriorated steadily since the days of the watchdog activities of the Institute for Propaganda Analysis. The central complaint has been that practitioners have used half truths, meaningless slogans, and false-front organizations to bamboozle the public at the behest of special interests. They have, it has been charged, dealt with image and neglected or purposely disguised substance. Thus, it was not surprising to see John Ciardi blame "The Public Relations Mind" for the most remarkable created events of the 1950s, the television quiz shows. "The basic trait of that mind is that it accepts public appearances as the basic test of principles and that it cannot in fact distinguish between appearance and principle."[30] By the early 1970s, the term "public relations" was being widely used in liberal journals as an antonym for truth. "The time for lies, cover-ups, public relations posturing, and cute maneuvers is over," thundered the *New York Times* in a Watergate editorial in April of 1973. "The time for truth is at hand." The blame for Watergate was repeatedly laid at the door of public relations maneuvers and mentality, despite the fact that no professional public relations counselors were among Nixon's entourage.[31]

Except for those few fortunate enough to be retained by perfect clients, public relations counselors do engage in creation of an image different from reality. The raw material for this image is usually genuine fact. The counselor selects which facts to publicize and which to conceal and accentuates them to the advantage of his client. This editing of the truth has drawn constant complaint. In an open letter to Bernays in 1958, Irving Kristol remarked that he would not visit a United States

Information Service exhibition in London on "Kalamazoo and How It Grew" because "frankly, I don't trust it. Is it the *whole* truth about Kalamazoo—including the truths, say, that John O'Hara would tell? Not likely. . . ."[32] Public relations always turned out to be "somewhat—but not entirely—misleading."[33] Nothing but the truth, perhaps; but not the whole truth. Disaffected public relations man Alan Harrington defined the craft as that of "arranging the truth so that people will like you." He asserted that it "invariably involved altering the truth in a nice way, if only by withholding unpleasant news."[34] Unlike Hitler, counselors shun the big lie forcefully stated for the non-lie. The technique is therefore more difficult to expose. Ellery Sedgwick, editor of the *Atlantic,* understood this dynamic perfectly when he wrote to Bernays in 1934, ". . . You see life like a billiard table. Direct strokes are barred, and your nimble ball caroms continually off the cushion of circumstance, affecting the situation not at first, but at second, hand."[35]

Counselors have been acutely conscious of their low repute. In fact they have probably exaggerated its extent and have responded both with reasoned argument and with bitterness. To be sure, a reputation for Machiavellian opinion manipulation could attract clients, as Bernays discovered in the '20s, because it at least posits effectiveness. On the other hand, it could also be damaging, for a prospective client could be pardoned for speculating about how a counselor could improve someone else's reputation if his own press notices were so poor. It is also fair to assume that, like the Standard Oil executive of the Gilded Age, public relations men have thirsted for "a place in the good will, honor and affection of honorable men."

To the charge of being persuaders for profit, they have pleaded no contest. They have insisted that this is an honorable function in a democracy, and they have also asserted that they persuade the client as well as the public, with society as a whole benefiting by a lessening of tensions. The problem of how far to go to persuade has caused real soul-searching. "To what extent does a business have a responsibility to tell the truth to the public—about prices, labor policies, and so forth—and to what extent can it afford to dissimulate?" asked counselor David Finn. His answer: "In public relations, truth is a hard word."[36] One recalls the railroad public relations director "creating the impression of truth." Is it truthful to send out press releases without identifying their origin, as the Publicity Bureau did in the Progressive era? Or to identify them to the journalist but then see them published without their source being identified to the public? Is it honest to write statements for executives who then deliver them as if they had written them?[37] Is it honest to concoct events that seem to be spontaneous but are actually carefully contrived for ulterior purposes? Or to use "false front" "third party" techniques? These are all questions which public relations men and society must examine.

One of the legacies of public relations has been a pervasive cynicism concerning any public statements. American society is one in which "'salesmanship'—in the sense of selling through deft pretense of concern with the other fellow—has run riot." For those salesmen who can overcome the reputation for manipulation and convince the public that their concern is genuine, the potential rewards are great indeed.[38] It is ironic and perhaps fitting that Ivy Lee should have become a victim of this atmosphere of suspicion. During the 1920s, he developed independent positions on important issues. However, he encountered

> the greatest difficulty in getting people to take anything I say as an independent expression of opinion. I am always merely a propagandist. . . . Sometimes in my low moments I have thought of throwing the whole thing overboard and taking a minor job as a newspaper editor. Even then I wonder if I would not still be suspect; whether I have not been so thoroughly tainted as a propagandist that people would always suspect that there was an angel in the closet telling me what to say and think.[39]

One of the first uses of the term "confidence man" in print is said to have occurred in New York City in 1849 when one Thomas MacDonald was arrested for exploiting his ability to convey an image of honesty in order to swindle trusting citizens out of their possessions. Newspapers applauded his apprehension, but also asserted that his success had its beneficial implications for the "confidence of man in man shows that all virtue and humanity of nature is not entirely extinct. . . . It is a good thing, and speaks well for human nature, that . . . in spite of all the hardening of civilization . . . man *can be swindled*."[40] Few can afford today to give the Thomas MacDonalds the benefit of the doubt, for there are too many of them, too many promotion men who hold that ". . . the most effective way to get a man is to get him sort of off his guard, get him from an unexpected source."[41] Another legacy not only of public relations but of the whole constellation of forces trying to sell the citizen has been a "hardening of civilization," a retreat from the Arcadian ideal of innocence.

Counselors have been assailed not only for their failure to be ombudsmen but for what some have viewed as their too great success. One educator is said to have opposed the presence of counselors at any university board meetings because their advice could frighten administrators away from doing the right but unpopular things.[42] Excessive concern for the public could result in executives being "palsied by the will of [their] constituents." In describing the classic bipolarity between inner- and other-directedness, David Riesman wrote that the "control equipment" for the one could be likened to a gyroscope while that for the other was radar.[43] The radarlike character of public relations, with its polls and its constant insistence that the public's desires be discovered and made use of, is obvious.

Public relations men have indeed been ferocious adjusters, fighting for harmony and professing a spirit of compromise. They have been willing to accept human nature, by which they mean the irrational peculiarities of their fellow men, for what it is and turn it to the advantage of their client. "This adjustment, these motives mixed beyond any hope of untangling, the disbelief in the ability of truth, talent, or merit to win out alone," this surrender to "the facts of life" has constituted a weighty indictment.[44] Never did a philosophy call upon a man to be less a "fighter against his times." It is this willingness and ability to deal with the average man on his own terms which, according to one promotion expert, is the real reason behind the enmity of what he bitterly labels "the intellectual huckster baiter." These elitists, he claims, object to "any forms of communication that appeal to the masses."[45]

IV

We thus conclude our study of public relations on an ambiguous note. Has the vocation increased the sales of companies which have employed it? Sometimes, but that has hardly been its most important role. Has it increased the popularity of individual corporations and of the business system as a whole? To a limited extent, yes—but only when public relations activity has been accompanied by genuine achievement. Mere puffery has not availed for long. When public relations attempts to counteract palpable reality, as the NAM campaigns of the '30s did, the results are not likely to be convincing to many citizens. Despite all the talk of mass mind control, hidden persuasion, etc., the results of the campaigns which have been recounted dispel the fear that public relations men can turn public opinion off and on "like a faucet."

Some public relations men have influenced corporate policy by instituting specific reforms, transforming the style of corporate communications with the public, and making the corporation conscious of the impact of its actions on the public. They have usually not acted as ombudsmen, for they almost always identify too completely with their employers' interest. On the other hand, they have rarely behaved as hucksters.[46] For the most part, they seem to believe in what they do.

One of the most instructive aspects of a study of corporate public relations is what it reveals about America's business elite. The first lesson is that businessmen are insecure in the power they possess. This insecurity was marginally justified during the Progressive era and certainly understandable during the Depression. Yet even when business was good and polls favorable, executives tended to find danger in the future. This is because Americans believe in equality, and the businessman's wealth and power set him above the average.

Secondly, we have seen how businessmen themselves, on the whole, accept the fairness of being judged by public opinion, even when the public supports politicians whom the business community overwhelmingly opposes. This trait puts the twentieth-century businessman squarely in the tradition of his forebears.

It could be argued that though he may respect its power, the executive shows contempt for public opinion by endorsing manipulative stratagems designed to achieve the appearance, rather than the reality, of public support. This book has pointed out examples of such tactics, and no intelligent person would want to excuse them. One service which a study like this can perform is that for which critics have always asked—to keep the public aware of the cheap manipulation which has existed in the past and will in the future.

Yet it is, I think, an encouraging fact that many leading corporations show some respect for the public. It seems to me better to have the A&P, for example, appealing to the public, as it did through Carl Byoir, than bribing legislators or worse. Surely the Byoir campaign had distasteful aspects, but as one looks around the world one sees many nations with elites acting a good deal less responsibly. Once again, this is no effort to excuse wrongdoing, but rather to put it in perspective. Looked at this way, public relations—the commitment to talk rather than antilabor or antidemocratic violence—is not a sign of the deep disease which Mark Van Doren feared. Rather, it is an indication of the health of American democracy.

NOTES

1. "Some Considerations in Dealing with Public Opinion" (New York, 1950), p. 14.

2. "The Arts and Uses of Public Relations," *Time,* July 7, 1967.

3. "Public Relations in Industry—1946," *PO Index,* n.p.

4. Nugent Wedding, *Public Relations in Business* (Urbana: University of Illinois Bureau of Economic and Business Research, Bull. 71, 1950), p. 19.

5. U.S. House of Representatives, 86th Cong., 1st sess., Special Subcommittee on Legislative Oversight of the Interstate and Foreign Commerce Committee, *Investigation of Television Quiz Shows, Hearings* (Washington, D.C., 1960), pp. 1045, 1048, 1105–1108.

6. Meyer Weinberg, *TV in America* (New York, 1962), pp. 197–214; Eric Barnouw, *The Image Empire* (New York, 1970), pp. 68–69, 125.

7. Raucher, *Public Relations*, p. 113; Bernays, *Idea*, pp. 372–400; Gunther, *Flood*, pp. 163–169; Hiebert, *Courtier*, pp. 179–181.

8. Charles M. Pritzker to Lichtenburg, February 3, 1936, Vol. 15, Lichtenburg papers.

9. Gunther, *Flood*, pp. 154–155.

10. Lewis, "Henry Ford," pp. 381–404; Fairfax M. Cone, *With All Its Faults* (Boston, 1969), pp. 243–261; and see John Brooks, *The Fate of the Edsel and Other Business Adventures* (New York, 1963), pp. 17–75.

11. "Some day," moaned Stanley Walker as the twenties drew to a close, "newspaper editors are going to become weary of Reindeer Week, Thrift Week, Stone Mountain Memorial campaigns, cathedral drives, lip-reading tournaments, optimistic statements by Charlie Schwab's press agent, statistics from the Y.M.C.A., and synthetic interviews with bad actresses. . . ." "Men of Vision," clipping in Box 46, Lee papers.

12. See Cutlip and Center, *Public Relations*.

13. Swinehart to David R. Palmer, March 9, 1953, Box 1, Swinehart papers, State Historical Society of Wisconsin, Madison. Promotion man Nicholas Samstag also enunciated this thesis in his definition of public relations as "the process of making known to those whose good will is important to a company the facts about the company's history, personality, and standards, its good works in the public interest, and its popular attitudes toward public questions in order to create and maintain for it a climate favorable to selling." *Persuasion for Profit* (Norman, Okla., 1957), p. 4.

14. Lewis, "Henry Ford," pp. 521, 314–315. Of course it is possible that Ford would have had even a lower market share if it had been "unloved."

15. For the role of publicity and "gossip" in the motion picture business, see Robert Sklar, *Movie-Made America* (New York, 1975), pp. 233–236.

16. Alfred D. Chandler, Jr., *Strategy and Structure* (Cambridge, Mass., 1962), pp. 108–109; 273–274.

17. *Public Image*, p. 11.

18. Raymond W. Miller, "Keepers of the Corporate Conscience" (New York, 1946), *passim*.

19. In an otherwise deeply flawed study, Jacques Ellul has rightly insisted that the impact of this kind of propaganda cannot be accurately measured. *Propaganda* (New York, 1965), p. 287.

20. Barnouw, *Web*, p. 90.

21. Brayman is the author of an astute study, *Corporate Management in a World of Politics* (New York, 1967).

22. Golden, *Consent*, pp. 235–326. This incident illustrates how criticism can heighten the importance of public relations without necessarily being its cause. Du Pont had a rudimentary public relations apparatus long before Nye and maintained its more sophisticated descendant long after the "merchants of death" label had worn off.

23. Golden, *Consent*, pp. 235–326; Brayman, *Management*, p. 49; Brayman, Interview.

24. Lewis, "Henry Ford," p. 420.

25. Hiebert, *Courtier,* pp. 90–91.

26. Galambos, *Public Image,* pp. 27, 246–249, 260; Hofstadter, "Anti-trust," pp. 223–224. Galambos's book is an important contribution to this topic, but its value would have been enhanced by some attention to businessmen's evaluation of their image and their attempts to improve it. Galambos does not deal with the possibility that corporate public relations, either actively through the use of advertising pressure or covertly through contrived news stories, could have influenced treatment of big business in the journals whose content he analyzes. If it did, his sources may more closely reflect corporate skill at press manipulation than the opinion of the readership. More likely than not, the papers he used were relatively free from this kind of taint, but its possibility should have been considered. See Galambos, *Public Image,* pp. 32–40, 128–129. For acknowledgment of possible effectiveness of corporate publicity campaigns in the South, see ibid., pp. 212 and 236.

27. The ORC asked its 100-company sample in 1950 what trade associations had accomplished through efforts at economic education. The results: a great deal—24 percent; little if anything—40 percent; some have done well—7 percent; nothing at all—10 percent; no opinion—19 percent. *PO Index,* "Industry's Communications System, 1950," p. A-19.

28. Robert Heilbroner, "The View from the Top," in Cheit, ed., *Business,* p. 30.

29. Friedman, *Capitalism,* p. 133.

30. "Exit a Symbol," *The Saturday Review* 42 (November 21, 1959), p. 59. For the quiz shows, see Richard S. Tedlow, "Intellect on Television," *American Quarterly* 28, No. 4 (Fall 1976), pp. 483–495.

31. *New York Times,* April 29, 1973: July 31, 1973.

32. "Letter to an American," *Yale Revview* 47 (Summer 1958), p. 635.

33. Boorstin, *Image,* p. 10.

34. "The Self-Deceivers," *Esquire,* September 1959, p. 59.

35. Sedgwick to Bernays, March 12, 1934, Bernays papers.

36. "Struggle for Ethics in Public Relations," *Harvard Business Review* 37, No. 1 (January–February 1959), p. 56.

37. In 1937, Bernays orchestrated the launching of a new refrigerator line for Kelvinator. Dealers from all over the country were invited to witness its unveiling at a New York theater. Bernays arranged to have Senator Royal S. Copeland, an M.D. and former New York City health commissioner, as speaker and prepared a speech for him on the advantages of electric refrigeration. "When he came to deliver it before a full audience he started with, 'And now I will read you the speech the public relations counsel has prepared for me.' I never lived that down with Kelvinator." Bernays, *Idea,* p. 585. Wrote Alan Harrington: "The great man ascends to the platform—he calls for action! He lifts his hand to his brow and surveys the horizon; surely we are in the presence of a man of vision. The resounding phrases roll. In one superb address he proves to the world—that he can read." "Deceivers," p. 63.

38. Robert K. Merton, *Mass Persuasion* (New York, 1946), p. 10. Kate Smith's remarkable success as a war-bond salesperson resulted, according to Merton,

from her ability to establish her sincerity with her listeners. They felt estranged from pervasive commercialism. Once Smith won their confidence, she fell heir to the "craving for reassurance [and the] acute need to believe" which people normally must suppress to avoid being taken. Charles Schwab is said to have prefaced speeches thusly: "Gentlemen, before I came here tonight I had three written speeches to deliver. One of them I wrote myself, another Judge Gary wrote, and the third was written by my friend here [Lee]. But I am going to throw them all away and speak to you from the heart." He would then deliver Lee's speech. Here is an example of a man recognizing his sincerity would be doubted and therefore taking an extra step to fool his audience. So many steps have been taken in this direction that any protestation of sincerity must be suspect. Hiebert, *Courtier*, p. 163.

39. Hiebert, *Courtier*, p. 307.

40. Harris, *Humbug*, pp. 224–225; Warwick Wadlington, *The Confidence Game in American Literature* (Princeton, 1975), pp. 8–36.

41. Remark of Harold J. Seymour in "Semi-Annual Conference of the Staff . . . ," August 9, 1924, p. 281, John Price Jones papers.

42. David Finn, "The Price of Corporate Vanity," *Harvard Business Review* 39 (July-August 1961), p. 139.

43. Riesman, *The Lonely Crowd* (New Haven, 1969), p. 25.

44. Marvin Barrett, "Cart Before the Horse," *Reporter*, December 30, 1965, p. 44.

45. Samstag, *Persuasion*, p. 175; and see Raucher, *Public Relations*, p. 156.

46. John Gunther has described a huckster as one who promotes a product, cause, or idea he does not believe in. *Flood*, p. 173. Such men certainly exist (see, for example, Hacker, "Pressure Politics," p. 343), but they are not a major factor in modern corporate public realtions.

Bibliography

Bibliographical Note

Certain items in the following bibliography were particularly noteworthy and should be singled out.

The place to start for students of public relations is the Cutlip and Center textbook, *Effective Public Relations*. This volume contains a lengthy discussion of the history of the field, sensitive comments about ethical implications and dilemmas, an international survey, a helpful bibliography, and also photographs of pioneer counselors. Professor Cutlip, now at the University of Georgia, was formerly a professor of journalism at the University of Wisconsin, where he directed four useful master's essays (by Bennett, Goodman, Hamel, and Knight) and assembled the papers of many counselors. The interview which he kindly granted me was influential in my outlook.

The only published scholarly biography of a corporate public relations counselor is Hiebert's book on Ivy Lee. This study contains numerous enlightening incidents from Lee's career, but the author does not construct a satisfying analysis of them. [See John A. Garraty's review in the *Columbia Journalism Review* 5 (Winter 1966–1967) pp. 41–42.] Raucher's study of public relations from 1900 to 1930 was also an important aid, but for my criticism see notes 52 and 63, Chapter VII.

The treatment of public relations by Funigiello and Martin makes very interesting reading. The former supplies fascinating details about opinion manipulation in the thirties but is, I believe, somewhat naive about government propaganda (see Chapter IV, note 37). Martin adopts the novel approach of taking Ivy Lee at his word. The railroads needed the rate hikes the ICC denied them as Lee and others rightly insisted, Martin believes. The failure of the roads to convince the public that it had to pay for what it got, despite the most sophisticated public relations program of the time, has implications for the private enterprise system as a whole. Perhaps, as Schumpeter thought, capitalism will decline because, among other things, it is inexplicable.

The writings of Daniel J. Boorstin are rich with speculations about the role of persuasion and image making in America. Neil Harris's biography of Barnum is an engaging exploration of these same issues.

Among the unpublished works, Daniel A. Pope's superb dissertation on advertising is essential. Sydney Stahl Weinberg's study of wartime propaganda is comprehensive and astute.

I. MANUSCRIPT COLLECTIONS

William Henry Baldwin papers. State Historical Society of Wisconsin, Madison.
Bruce Barton papers. State Historical Society of Wisconsin, Madison.
Freddie Benham papers. State Historical Society of Wisconsin, Madison.
Edward L. Bernays papers. His possession. Cambridge, Mass.
Harry A. Bruno papers. State Historical Society of Wisconsin, Madison.
Charles W. Eliot papers. Pusey Library, Harvard University.
John W. Hill papers. State Historical Society of Wisconsin, Madison.
John Price Jones papers. Baker Library, Harvard University Business School.
Ivy L. Lee papers. Princeton University.
National Association of Manufacturers papers. Eleutherian Mills Historical Library, Wilmington, Delaware.
National Association of Manufacturers papers. Minutes of meetings of the board of directors, 1932–1934. NAM offices, New York, N.Y.
National Industrial Conference Board. Transcripts of meetings. Eleutherian Mills Historical Library, Wilmington, Del.
Arthur W. Page papers. State Historical Society of Wisconsin, Madison.
Public Relations Society of America, Definition file, PRSA Office, New York, N.Y.
Joseph M. Shaw papers. State Historical Society of Wisconsin, Madison.
Gerry Swinehart papers. State Historical Society of Wisconsin, Madison.
Henry Villard papers. Baker Library, Harvard University Business School.
George Woodbridge (Michaelis) file. Baker Library, Harvard University Business School.

COLUMBIA ORAL HISTORY COLLECTION

Lasker, Albert D., "Reminiscences."
Page, Arthur W., "Reminiscences."

II. PUBLIC DOCUMENTS

U.S. Circuit Court, Ninth Circuit. *United States* v. *the New York Great Atlantic and Pacific Tea Company,* 173 Federal Reporter, 2nd Series, 79.

U.S. *Congressional Record.* 63rd Cong., 2nd sess., Vol. 51, pp. 7736ff.
U.S. District Court. Eastern District, Illinois. *United States* v. *the New York Great Atlantic and Pacific Tea Company,* 67 Federal Supplement, 626.
U.S. District Court. Eastern District, Pennsylvania. *Noerr Motor Freight et al.* v. *Eastern Railroad Presidents Conference et al.,* 155 Federal Supplement 768.
U.S. House of Representatives. Special Subcommittee on Legislative Oversight of the Interstate and Foreign Commerce Committee, *Investigation of Television Quiz shows, Hearings,* 86th Cong., 1st sess. (1959).
————. Subcommittee of the Special Committee on Un-American Activities. *Investigation of Nazi Propaganda Activities and Certain Other Propaganda Activities,* 73rd Cong., 2nd sess. (1934).
U.S. Senate. Committee on Education and Labor. *Labor Policies of Employers Associations,* 76th Cong., 1st sess. (1939).
————. *Industrial Relations:* Final Report and Testimony Submitted to Congress by the Commission on Industrial Relations Created by the Act of August 13, 1912. 64th Cong., 1st sess. (1916).
————. Special Committee to Investigate Lobbying Activities. *Hearings* Pursuant to S. Res. 165 and S. Res. 184, 74th Cong., 1st sess. (1935).
————. Subcommittee of the Committee on Education and Labor. *Hearings* Pursuant to S. Res. 266, *Violations of Free Speech and Rights of Labor,* 74th-76th Congs. (1936-1940).

III. BIBLIOGRAPHIC GUIDES
Cutlip, Scott. *A Public Relations Bibliography.* Madison: University of Wisconsin Press, 1965.
Public Relations, Edward L. Bernays, and the American Scene. Boston: F. W. Faxon, 1950.

IV. BOOKS
Adams, Graham, Jr. (1966), *Age of Industrial Violence.* New York: Columbia University Press.
Adelman, M. A. (1959), *A&P: A Study in Price Cost Behavior and Public Policy.* Cambridge: Harvard University Press.
Alinsky, Saul D. (1949), *John L. Lewis.* New York: Putnam's.
Allen, Frederick Lewis (1959), *Only Yesterday.* New York: Bantam.
Andrews, Wayne (1941), *The Vanderbilt Legend.* New York: Harcourt, Brace.
Arnold, Thurman (1938), *The Folklore of Capitalism.* New Haven: Yale University Press.
Auerbach, Jerold S. (1966), *Labor and Liberty.* Indianapolis: Bobbs-Merrill.
Bailyn, Bernard (1964), *The New England Merchants in the Seventeenth Century.* New York: Harper and Row.
Baker, Ray Stannard (1945), *American Chronicle.* New York: Scribner's.
Bakke, E. Wight; Clark Kerr; and Charles W. Anrod, eds. (1960), *Unions, Management, and the Public.* New York: Harcourt, Brace.
Barbash, Jack (1956), *The Practice of Unionism.* New York: Harper.
Baritz, Loren (1960), *The Servants of Power.* Middletown, Conn.: Wesleyan University Press.

Barnouw, Eric (1968), *The Golden Web*. New York: Oxford University Press.
—— (1970), *The Image Empire*. New York: Oxford University Press.
—— (1966), *A Tower in Babel*. New York: Oxford University Press.
Batchelor, Bronson (1938), *Profitable Public Relations*. New York: Harper.
Bell, Daniel (1975), *The Cultural Contradictions of Capitalism*. New York: Free Press.
—— (1962), *The End of Ideology*. New York: Free Press.
Benson, Lee (1955), *Merchants, Farmers, and Railroads*. Cambridge, Mass.: Harvard University Press.
Berger, Meyer (1951), *The Story of the New York Times*. New York: Simon and Schuster.
Bernays, Edward L. (1965), *Biography of an Idea*. New York: Simon and Schuster.
—— (1923), *Crystallizing Public Opinion*. New York: Boni and Liveright.
—— (1928), *Propaganda*. New York: Liveright.
—— (1952), *Public Relations*. Norman: University of Oklahoma Press.
—— (1961), *Your Future in Public Relations*. New York: Richard Rosen Press.
——, ed. (1955), *The Engineering of Consent*. Norman: University of Oklahoma Press.
——, ed. (1927), *An Outline of Careers*. New York: Doran.
Bernstein, Barton, J., ed. (1969), *Towards a New Past*. New York: Random House.
Bernstein, Irving (1966), *The Lean Years*. Baltimore: Penguin.
—— (1969), *Turbulent Years*. Boston: Houghton Mifflin.
Bonnett, Clarence (1922), *Employers Associations in the United States*. New York: Macmillan.
Boorstin, Daniel J. (1960), *America and the Image of Europe*. New York: Meridian Books.
—— (1974), *The Americans: The Democratic Experience*. New York: Vintage.
—— (1965), *The Americans: The National Experience*. New York: Vintage.
—— (1969), *The Decline of Radicalism*. New York: Random House.
—— (1974), *Democracy and Its Discontents*. New York: Random House.
—— (1971), *The Image*. New York: Atheneum.
Brady, Robert A. (1943), *Business as a System of Power*. New York: Columbia University Press.
Braeman, John; Robert H. Bremner; and Everett Walters (1964), *Change and Continuity in Twentieth Century America*. Columbus: Ohio State University Press.
Brayman, Harold (1967), *Corporate Management in a World of Politics*. New York: McGraw-Hill.
Brandeis, Louis D. (1967), *Other People's Money*. New York: Harper and Row.
Brandes, Stuart D. (1976), *American Welfare Capitalism*. Chicago: University of Chicago Press.
Brecher, Jeremy (1974), *Strike!* Greenwich, Conn.: Fawcett.
Brody, David (1960), *Steelworkers in America*. New York: Harper and Row.
Broesamle, John J. (1973), *William Gibbs McAdoo*. Port Washington, N.Y.: Kennikat.
Brooks, John (1963), *The Fate of the Edsel and Other Business Adventures*. New York: Harper and Row.

—— (1970), *Once in Golconda*. New York: Harper and Row.

Bryce, James (1901), *The American Commonwealth*. New York: Macmillan.

Buchanan, A. Russell (1964), *The United States and World War II*. New York: Harper and Row.

Burns, James MacGregor (1956), *Roosevelt: The Lion and the Fox*. New York: Harcourt, Brace and World.

—— (1970), *Roosevelt: The Soldier of Freedom*. New York: Harcourt Brace Jovanovich.

Calkins, Ernest Elmo (1928), *Business the Civilizer*. Boston: Little, Brown.

Carey, Henry C. (1856), *The Harmony of Interests*. New York: M. Finch.

Caro, Robert A. (1975), *The Power Broker*. New York: Vintage.

Chaffee, Zechariah, Jr. (1947), *Government and Mass Communications*. Chicago: University of Chicago Press.

Chalmers, David M. (1964), *The Social and Political Ideas of the Muckrakers*. New York: Citadel.

Chamberlain, Neil W. (1973), *The Limits of Corporate Responsibility*. New York: Basic Books.

Chandler, Alfred D., Jr. (1956), *Henry Varnum Poor*. Cambridge, Mass.: Harvard University Press.

—— (1970), *Strategy and Structure*. Cambridge: Massachusetts Institute of Technology Press.

——, ed. (1965), *The Railroads: The Nation's First Big Business*. New York: Harcourt, Brace and World.

Cheit, Earl F., ed. (1964), *The Business Establishment*. New York: John Wiley.

Childs, Harwood L. (1965), *Public Opinion: Nature, Formation and Role*. Princeton, N.J.: Van Nostrand.

—— (1934), *A Reference Guide to Public Opinion*. Princeton, N.J.: Princeton University Press.

Clarke, Joseph I. C. (1925), *My Life and Memories*. New York: Dodd, Mead.

Cochran, Thomas C. (1962), *The American Business System*. New York: Harper and Row.

—— (1968), *Basic History of American Business*. Princeton, N.J.: Van Nostrand.

—— (1972), *Business in American Life*. New York: McGraw-Hill.

——. (1948), *The Pabst Brewing Company*. New York: New York University Press.

——. (1953), *Railroad Leaders*. Cambridge, Mass.: Harvard University Press.

Cole, Arthur H. (1959), *Business Enterprise in Its Social Setting*. Cambridge, Mass.: Harvard University Press.

Collins, Orvis, and David G. Moore (1970), *The Organization Makers*. New York: Appleton-Century-Crofts.

Cone, Fairfax M. (1969), *With All Its Faults*. Boston: Little, Brown.

Creel, George (1920), *How We Advertised America*. New York: Harper.

Cuff, Robert D. (1973). *The War Industries Board*. Baltimore, Md.: Johns Hopkins University Press.

Cutlip, Scott (1965), *Fund Raising in America*. New Brunswick, N.J.: Rutgers University Press.

——— and Allen H. Center (1971), *Effective Public Relations*. Englewood Cliffs, N.J.: Prentice-Hall.

Danielian, N. R. (1939), *AT&T*. New York: Vanguard.

Davie, Maurice, ed. (1940), *Sumner Today*. New Haven: Yale University Press.

Davis, Elmer (1921), *History of the New York Times*. New York: New York Times

De Caux, Len (1970), *Labor Radical*. Boston: Beacon.

Degler, Carl (1970), *Out of Our Past*. New York: Harper and Row.

Derber, Milton, and Edward Young, eds. (1957), *Labor and the New Deal*. Madison: University of Wisconsin Press.

Dewey, John (1930), *Individualism Old and New*. New York: Minton, Balch.

Diamond, Sigmund (1955), *The Reputation of the American Businessman*. Cambridge, Mass.: Harvard University Press.

Doob, Leonard (1935), *Propaganda*. New York: Henry Holt.

Dorfman, Joseph (1946), *The Economic Mind in American Civilization*, Vol. II. New York: Viking Press.

Dos Passos, John (1952), *The 42nd Parallel*. New York: Cardinal.

Dubofsky, Melvyn (1975), *Industrialism and the American Worker, 1865–1920*. New York: T. Y. Crowell.

——— and Warren Van Tine (1977), *John L. Lewis*. New York: Quadrangle.

Dunne, Finley Peter (1906), *Mr. Dooley's Philosophy*. New York: Harper.

Elias, Robert H., ed. (1966), *Chapters of Erie*. Ithaca, N.Y.: Cornell University Press.

Ellul, Jacques (1965), *Propaganda*. New York: Vintage.

Emery, Edwin (1950), *History of the American Newspaper Publishers Association*. Minneapolis: University of Minnesota Press.

Epstein, Edward Jay (1975), *Between Fact and Fiction*. New York: Vintage.

Ewen, Stuart (1976), *Captains of Consciousness*. New York: McGraw-Hill.

Filler, Louis (1961), *Crusaders for American Liberalism*. Yellow Springs, Ohio: Antioch Press.

Fine, Sidney (1969), *Sit Down*. Ann Arbor: University of Michigan Press.

Finn, David (1960), *Public Relations and Management*. New York: Reinhold.

Fishbein, Martin, ed. (1967), *Readings in Attitude Theory and Management*. New York: John Wiley.

Fisher, Burton R., and Stephen B. Withey (1951), *Big Business as the People See It*. Ann Arbor: University of Michigan Press.

Fogel, Robert W. (1960), *The Union Pacific Railroad*. Baltimore, Md.: Johns Hopkins University Press.

Foner, Eric (1976), *Tom Paine and Revolutionary America*. New York: Oxford University Press.

Franklin, Benjamin (1976), *Autobiography*. New York: Collier.

Friedman, Milton (1962), *Capitalism and Freedom*. Chicago: University of Chicago Press.

Funigiello, Philip J. (1973), *Toward a National Power Policy*. Pittsburgh, Pa.: University of Pittsburgh Press.

Galambos, Louis (1966), *Competition and Cooperation*. Baltimore, Md.: Johns Hopkins University Press.

———. (1975), *The Public Image of Big Business in America, 1880–1940*. Baltimore: Johns Hopkins University Press.

Galbraith, John K. (1952), *American Capitalism: The Concept of Countervailing Power*. Boston: Houghton Mifflin.

Gallup, George (1972), *The Gallup Poll*. New York: Random House.

Garraty, John A., ed. (1977), *Dictionary of American Biography*, Supplement 5. New York: Scribner's.

——— and Jerome Sternstein, eds. (1974), *Encyclopedia of American Biography*. New York: Harper and Row.

Gibb, George F., and Evelyn H. Knowlton, (1956), *The Resurgent Years*. New York: Harper and Row.

Gibson, W. B. (1939), *The Annual Report*. Cincinnati: Mead.

Girdler, Tom M. (1943), *Boot Straps*. New York: Scribner's.

Golden, L. L. L. (1968), *Only by Public Consent*. New York: Hawthorn.

Goldman, Eric F. (1960), *Rendezvous with Destiny*. New York: Vintage.

———. (1948), *Two-Way Street*. Boston: Bellman.

Graham, Otis L., Jr. (1976), *Toward a Planned Society*. New York: Oxford University Press.

Green, Arnold W. (1951), *Henry Charles Carey*. Philadelphia: University of Pennsylvania Press.

Grodinski, Julius (1957), *Jay Gould*. Philadelphia: University of Pennsylvania Press.

Gruening, Ernest (1931), *The Public Pays*. New York: Vanguard.

Gunther, John. (1960), *Taken at the Flood*. New York: Harper.

Haber, Samuel (1964), *Efficiency and Uplift*. Chicago: University of Chicago Press.

Hardman, J. B. S., ed. (1968), *American Labor Dynamics*. New York: Russell and Russell.

——— and Maurice Neufeld, eds. (1951) *The House of Labor*. Englewood Cliffs, N.J.: Prentice-Hall.

Harlow, Rex F., and Melvin Black (1952), *Profitable Public Relations*. New York: Harper.

Harris, Neil (1973), *Humbug*. Boston: Little, Brown.

Heald, Morrell (1970), *The Social Responsibilities of Business*. Cleveland: The Press of Case-Western Reserve University.

Hidy, Ralph, and Muriel Hidy (1955), *Pioneering in Big Business*. New York: Harper.

Hiebert, Ray E. (1966) *Courtier to the Crowd*. Ames, Iowa: Iowa State University Press.

Hill, John W. (1958), *Corporate Public Relations*. New York: Harper.

———. (1963), *The Making of a Public Relations Man*. New York: David McKay.

Hofstadter, Richard (1955) *The Age of Reform*. New York: Vintage.

———. (1963), *Anti-Intellectualism in American Life*. New York: Vintage.

———. (1967), *The Paranoid Style in American Politics and Other Essays*. New York: Vintage.

Hower, Ralph M. (1949), *The History of an Advertising Agency.* Cambridge, Mass.: Harvard University Press.

Interchurch World Movement, Commission of Inquiry (1921), *Public Opinion and the Steel Strike.* New York: Harcourt, Brace, and Howe.

Irwin, Will (1936) *Propaganda and the News or What Makes You Think So?* New York: McGraw-Hill.

Johnson, Malcolm; Thomas Kendre; and Will Yolen, eds. (1968), *Current Thoughts on Public Relations.* New York: M. W. Lads.

Jones, John Price, and David McClaren Church (1939), *At the Bar of Public Opinion.* New York: Inter-River Press.

Josephson, Matthew (1962), *The Robber Barons.* New York: Harcourt, Brace and World.

Kaplan, Justin (1974), *Lincoln Steffens.* New York: Simon and Schuster.

———. (1969), *Mr. Clemens and Mark Twain.* New York: Simon and Schuster.

Keller, Morton (1963), *The Life Insurance Enterprise.* Cambridge, Mass.: Belknap Press.

Kelley, Stanley, Jr. (1956), *Professional Public Relations and Political Power.* Baltimore, Md.: Johns Hopkins University Press.

Kirkland, Edward C. (1956), *Dream and Thought in the Business Community.* Ithaca: Cornell University Press.

———. (1961) *Industry Comes of Age.* Chicago: Quadrangle.

Kolko, Gabriel (1970), *Railroads and Regulation.* New York: Norton.

———. (1963), *The Triumph of Conservatism.* New York: Free Press.

Komarovsky, Mirra, ed. (1957). *Common Frontiers of the Social Sciences.* Glencoe, Ill.: Free Press.

Kornhauser, Arthur W.; Robert Dubin; and Arthur W. Ross, eds. (1954), *Industrial Conflict.* New York: McGraw-Hill.

Kronenberger, Louis (1954), *Company Manners,* Indianapolis: Bobbs-Merrill.

Krooss, Herman (1970), *Executive Opinion.* Garden City, N.Y.: Doubleday.

Larson, Henrietta A. (1948), *Guide to Business History.* Cambridge, Mass.: Harvard University Press.

———. (1968) *Jay Cooke,* Westport, Conn.: Greenwood Press.

Lasswell, Harold D.; Ralph D. Casey; and Bruce L. Smith (1969), *Propaganda and Promotional Activities: An Annotated Bibliography.* Chicago: University of Chicago Press.

Leab, Daniel (1970) *A Union of Individuals.* New York: Columbia University Press.

Lee, Alfred McClung (1937), *The Daily Newspaper in America.* New York: Macmillan.

Lee, Ivy L. (1915), *Human Nature and Railroads.* Philadelphia: E. S. Nash.

———. (1925), *Publicity.* New York: Industries Publishing Company.

Lesley, Philip, ed. (1950), *Public Relations Handbook.* Englewood Cliffs, N.J.: Prentice-Hall.

Leuchtenburg, William E. (1963), *Franklin D. Roosevelt and the New Deal.* New York: Harper.

————. (1958), *The Perils of Prosperity*. Chicago: University of Chicago Press.

Liebling, A. J. (1965) *The Press*. New York: Ballantine.

Lindsey, Almont (1942), *The Pullman Strike*. Chicago: University of Chicago Press.

Lindsay, Robert (1956), *This High Name: Public Relations and the U.S. Marine Corps*. Madison: University of Wisconsin Press.

Link, Arthur (1967), *American Epoch*. New York: Knopf.

Lippmann, Walter (1925), *The Phantom Public*. New York: Harcourt, Brace.

————. (1965), *Public Opinion*. New York: Free Press.

Lloyd, Craig (1973), *Aggressive Introvert: Herbert Hoover and Public Relations Management, 1912–1932*. Columbus: Ohio State University Press.

Malone, Dumas, ed. (1936), *Dictionary of American Biography*, Vol. XIX. New York: Scribner's.

Manchester, William (1974), *The Glory and the Dream*. Boston: Little, Brown.

Marston, John E. (1963), *The Nature of Public Relations*. New York: McGraw-Hill.

Martin, Albro (1971), *Enterprise Denied*. New York: Columbia University Press.

McAdoo, William Gibbs (1931), *Crowded Years*. Boston: Houghton Mifflin.

McCamy, James L. (1939), *Government Publicity*. Chicago: University of Chicago Press.

McCloskey, Robert G. (1964), *American Conservatism in the Age of Enterprise*. New York: Harper.

Meyers, Marvin (1960), *The Jacksonian Persuasion*. Stanford, Calif.: Stanford University Press.

Merton, Robert K. (1949), *Mass Persuasion*. New York: Harper.

Miller, William E., ed. (1962), *Men in Business*. New York: Harper.

Millis, Harry A., and Emily Clark Brown (1950), *From the Wagner Act to Taft-Hartley*. Chicago: University of Chicago Press.

Mittelberger, Gottlieb (1960), *Journey to Pennsylvania*. Cambridge, Mass.: Harvard University Press.

Mock, James, and Cedric Larson (1931), *Words that Won the War*. Princeton, N.J.: Princeton University Press.

Morgan, H. Wayne, ed. (1963), *The Gilded Age. A Reappraisal*. Syracuse, N.Y.: Syracuse University Press.

Morris, Richard B. (1946), *Government and Labor in Early America*. New York: Columbia University Press.

Mott, Frank Luther (1962), *American Journalism*. New York: Macmillan.

Mowry, George E., (1962), *The Era of Theodore Roosevelt*. New York: Harper.

Nevins, Allan (1922), *The Evening Post*. New York: Boni and Liveright.

———— and Frank E. Hill (1954), *Ford: The Times, the Man, the Company*. New York: Scribner's.

Nichols, Beverley (1928), *The Star Spangled Manner*. Garden City, N.Y.: Doubleday.

Packard, Vance (1976), *The Hidden Persuaders*. New York: Pocket Books, 1976.

Page, Arthur W. (1941), *The Bell Telephone System*. New York: Harper.

Paine, Albert Bigelow (1921), *In One Man's Life*. New York: Harper.

Pease, Otis (1958) *The Responsibilities of American Advertising*. New Haven: Yale University Press.

Persons, Stow (1958), *American Minds: A History of Ideas*. New York: Henry Holt.

Pimlot, J. A. R. (1951), *Public Relations and American Democracy*. Princeton, N.J.: Princeton University Press.

Polenberg, Richard (1972), *War and Society*. Philadelphia: Lippincott.

Porter, Glenn (1973), *The Rise of Big Business, 1860–1910*. New York: T. Y. Crowell.

Potter, David M. (1958), *People of Plenty*. Chicago: University of Chicago Press.

Prothro, James W. (1954), *Dollar Decade*. Baton Rouge: Louisiana State University Press.

Raucher, Alan (1968), *Public Relations and Business, 1900–1929*. Baltimore, Md.: Johns Hopkins University Press.

Rayback, Joseph G. (1966), *A History of American Labor*. New York: Free Press.

Reichenbach, Harry, and Donald Freedman (1931), *Phantom Fame*. New York: Simon and Schuster.

Remini, Robert V. (1963), *The Election of Andrew Jackson*. Philadelphia: Lippincott.

Riddle, Donald H. (1964), *The Truman Committee*. New Brunswick, N.J.: Rutgers University Press.

Riesman, David (1969), *The Lonely Crowd*. New Haven: Yale University Press.

Rollins, Alfred B., Jr. (1962), *Roosevelt and Howe*. New York: Knopf.

Ross, Davis R. B. (1969), *Preparing for Ulysses*. New York: Columbia University Press.

Ross, Irwin (1959), *The Image Merchants*. Garden City, N.Y.: Doubleday.

Salmon, Lucy Maynard (1923), *The Newspaper and the Historian*. New York: Oxford University Press.

Samstag, Nicholas (1957), *Persuasion for Profit*. Norman: University of Oklahoma Press.

Schoenfeld, Clarence A. (1963), *Publicity Media and Methods: Their Role in Modern Public Relations*. New York: Macmillan.

Schlesinger, Arthur M., Jr. (1958), *The Coming of the New Deal*. Boston: Houghton Mifflin.

———— (1957), *The Crisis of the Old Order*. Boston: Houghton Mifflin.

———— (1968), *The Politics of Upheaval*. Boston: Houghton Mifflin.

Schriftgiesser, Karl (1967), *Business and Public Policy*. Englewood Cliffs, N.J.: Prentice-Hall.

Seitz, Don C. (1928), *The James Gordon Bennetts*. Indianapolis: Bobbs-Merrill.

Sethi, S. Prakash (1977), *Advocacy Advertising and Large Corporations*. Lexington, Mass.: D. C. Heath.

Sinclair, Upton (1919), *The Brass Check*. Pasadena, Calif.: The Author.

Sklar, Robert (1975), *Movie-Made America*. New York: Vintage.

Smith, Adam (1937), *The Wealth of Nations*. New York: Random House.

Stiegerwalt, Albert K. (1964), *The National Association of Manufacturers, 1895–1914*. Grand Rapids: Bureau of Business Research, University of Michigan Press, 1964.

Steffens, Lincoln (1931), *Autobiography*. New York: Harcourt, Brace.

Steinberg, Charles (1972), *Mass Media and Communications.* New York: Hastings House.

Sutherland, Edwin H. (1949), *White Collar Crime.* New York: Holt, Rinehart and Winston.

Sutton, Francis X.; Seymour E. Harris; Carl Kaysen; and James Tobin (1956) *The American Business Creed.* New York: Schocken.

Tarbell, Ida M. (1925), *The Life of Elbert H. Gary.* New York: Appleton.

Taylor, Albion G. (1928), *Labor Policies of the National Association of Manufacturers.* Urbana: University of Illinois Press.

Thelen, David (1972), *The New Citizenship.* Columbia: University of Missouri Press.

Tolles, Frederick B. (1963), *Meeting House and Counting House.* New York: Norton.

Utley, S. Wells (1936), *The American System.* Detroit, Mich.: Speaker-Hines Press.

Wadlington, Warwick (1975), *The Confidence Game in American Literature.* Princeton, N.J.: Princeton University Press.

Walker, Strother H., and Paul Sklar (1938), *Business Finds Its Voice.* New York: Harper and Brothers.

Wedding, Nugent (1950), *Public Relations in Business.* Urbana: University of Illinois Press.

Weinberg, Arthur, and Lila Weinberg, eds. (1961), *The Muckrakers.* New York: Simon and Schuster.

Weinberg, Meyer (1962), *TV in America.* New York: Ballantine.

Weisberger, Bernard A. (1961), *The American Newspaperman.* Chicago: University of Chicago Press.

Westin, Alan F., ed. (1962), *The Uses of Power.* New York: Harcourt, Brace and World.

White, Leonard D., ed. (1956) *The State of the Social Sciences.* Chicago: University of Chicago Press.

Whyte, William H. (1952), *Is Anybody Listening?* New York: Simon and Schuster.

Wilder, R. H., and K. L. Buell (1923) *Publicity.* New York: Ronald Press.

Wiebe, Robert H. (1968), *Businessman and Reform.* Chicago: Quadrangle.

———. (1967), *The Search for Order.* New York: Hill and Wang.

Williams, Raymond (1975), *Television: Technology and Cultural Form.* New York: Schocken.

Winter, Ella, and Granville Hicks, eds. (1938) *The Letters of Lincoln Steffens.* New York: Harcourt, Brace.

Wolfskill, George (1962), *The Revolt of the Conservatives.* Boston: Houghton Mifflin.

Wright, Milton (1939), *Public Relations for Business.* New York: McGraw-Hill.

Young, James Harvey (1967), *The Medical Messiahs.* Princeton, N.J.: Princeton University Press.

V. UNPUBLISHED MASTER'S ESSAYS AND PH.D. DISSERTATIONS

Bennett, Robert James (1968), "Carl Byoir: Public Relations Pioneer," master's essay, University of Wisconsin.

Brown, Linda Keller (1972), "Challenge and Response: The American Business Community and the New Deal, 1932–1934," Ph.D. dissertation, University of Pennsylvania.

D'Emilio, John (1975), "The Committee for Economic Development," master's essay, Columbia University.

Goodman, Felice M. (1967), "Origins of a Continuing Conflict," master's essay, University of Wisconsin.

Greyser, Stephen A. (1965), "Businessmen View Advertising," Ph.D. dissertation, Harvard Business School.

Hamel, George Felix (1966), "John W. Hill, Public Relations Pioneer," master's essay, University of Wisconsin.

Henry, Kenneth (1969), "The Large Corporation Public Relations Manager," Ph.D. dissertation, New York University.

Hessen, Robert A. (1969) "A Biography of Chalres M. Schwab, Steel Industrialist" (since published as *Steel Titan*. New York: Oxford University Press, 1975). Ph.D. dissertation, Columbia University.

Heubner, Lee W. (1968), "The Discovery of Propaganda: Changing Attitudes toward Public Communication in America, 1900–1930," Ph.D. dissertation, Harvard University.

Knight, Harry Donald (1953), "Press Criticism of the Public Relations Function in Government," master's essay, University of Wisconsin.

Kolbe, Richard (1962), "Public Relations and American Administration," Ph.D. dissertation, Princeton University.

Leotta, Louis, Jr. (1960), "The Republic Steel Corporation in the Steel Strike of 1937," master's essay, Columbia University.

Lewis, David L. (1959), "Henry Ford: A Study in Public Relations (1896–1932)" (since published as *The Public Image of Henry Ford*. Detroit: Wayne State University Press, 1976), Ph.D. dissertation, University of Michigan.

Longin, Thomas (1970), "The Search for Security," Ph.D. dissertation, University of Nebraska.

Pope, Daniel Andrew (1973), "The Development of National Advertising, 1865–1920," Ph.D. dissertation, Columbia University.

Shapiro, Stephen R. (1969), "The Big Sell," Ph.D. dissertation, University of Wisconsin.

Stalker, John N. (1950), "The National Association of Manufacturers," Ph.D. dissertation, University of Wisconsin.

Sussman, Leila Aline (1947), "The Public Relations Movement," master's essay. University of Chicago.

Tedlow, Richard S. (1971), "An American Autocrat: Charles Revson and the Rise of Revlon, Inc." master's essay, Columbia University.

Tillman, Lee R. (1966), "The American Business Community and the Death of the New Deal," Ph.D. dissertation, University of Arizona.

Weinberg, Sydney Stahl (1969), "Wartime Propaganda in a Democracy: America's Twentieth Century Information Agencies," Ph.D. dissertation, Columbia University.

Wells, Lloyd (1955), "The Defense of Big Business," Ph.D. dissertation, Princeton University.

Wengert, Egbert S. (1936), "The Public Relations of Selected Federal Administrative Agencies," Ph.D. dissertation, University of Wisconsin.

VI. CONVENTION PROCEEDINGS

American Federation of Labor (1881), *Proceedings* of the 1st Convention.
——— (1942) *Proceedings* of the 62nd Convention.
American Petroleum Institute (1941), *Proceedings* of the 20th Annual Meeting, Vol. 20.
——— (1946), *Proceedings* of the 26th Annual Meeting, Vol. 26.
Business Public Relations Executives. Annual National Meetings held under the auspices of the National Association of Manufacturers and a special Sponsoring Committee:
Convention I (1942): Convention II (1943); Convention III (1945); Convention IV (1947); Convention V (1948); Convention VI (1949).
Business Public Relations Executives. Regional Meetings held under the auspices of the National Association of Manufacturers and local sponsoring committees: Philadelphia (1943); Cleveland (1943); Salt Lake City (1944); Los Angeles (1944); San Francisco (1946).
A complete set of the above transcripts, which constitute an invaluable source for the study of corporate public relations in the 1940s, are contained in the papers of the National Association of Manufacturers.
National Association of Manufacturers. *Proceedings* of annual conventions 1–38 (1896–1933) and 39-44 (1934–1939). The former set of convention transactions is published. The latter is available in manuscript in the NAM papers.

VII. MAGAZINES

This dissertation has been informed by a reading of hundreds of articles in the trade, technical and general business press; of scores of periodicals with a general readership; and of a few in scholarly journals. An enumeration of each article would be hopelessly lengthy. Citations for those to which specific reference is made may be found in the notes. What follows is a list of periodicals consulted.
Business periodicals: *Advanced Management, Advertising Age, Advertising and Selling, Advertising Club News, Banking, Barrons, Bell Telephone Magazine, Business Week, Columbia Journalism Review, Commercial and Financial Chronicle, Dun's Review, Eastern Underwriter, Economic Forum, Editor & Publisher, Electric Railway Journal, Electrical World, Factory Management and Maintenance, Fortune, The Fourth Estate, Harvard Business Review, Heating and Ventilating Magazine, Industrial Marketing, Industry, Michigan Business Review, Magazine of Wall Street, Management Review, Nation's Business, Printers' Ink, Public Relations Journal, Public Utilities Fortnightly, Public Relations Quarterly, Railroad Gazette, Railway Age Gazette, Sales Management, Steel, Textile World, Trusts and Estates, Wall Street Journal, Weekly Underwriter.*
General Circulation periodicals: *American Magazine, American Mercury, Atlantic, Arena, Book Week, Collier's, Esquire, Forum and Century, Harper's, Independent,*

Literary Digest, McClure's, The Nation, The New Republic, The New Yorker, North American Review, Reporter, The Saturday Review, Time.
Scholarly Journals: *American Bar Association Journal, American Historical Review, American Journal of Sociology, American Quarterly, American Scholar, Annals* of the American Academy of Political and Social Science, *Antioch Review, Business History Review, Harvard Law Review, Journal of American History, Journal of the History of the Behavioral Sciences, Journalism Quarterly, Industrial and Labor Relations Review, Labor History, Public Opinion Quarterly, Public Relations Review, Reviews in American History, Yale Review.*
Miscellaneous: *Infantry Journal, Labor and Nation.*

VIII. NEWSPAPERS
New York *Herald-Tribune.*
New York Times.

IX. INTERVIEWS
Edward L. Bernays, Summer, 1973.
Harold Brayman, June, 1974.
Scott Cutlip, November, 1973.

X. CORRESPONDENCE
Robert L. Barbour, Edward L. Bernays, Paul Garrett, Denny Griswold, Ernest Gruening, Frederick Teahan.

XI. PAMPHLETS, SPEECHES, AND MISCELLANEOUS MATERIAL
American Council on Public Relations (1939), "The Short Course in Public Relations at Stanford."
——— (1939), "The Short Course in Public Relations at the University of Washington."
American Trade Association Executives (1945), "Trade Association Executives and Public Relations," Washington, D.C.; Public Relations Committee of the American Trade Association Executives.
Bernays, Edward L. (1930), "Mass Psychology and the Consumer." Speech to the Boston Conference on Distribution.
Byoir, Carl (1930), "What is Big Business?" Speech to the Boston Conference on Distribution.
Cheape, Charles (1974), "The 1907 Contract; Or How Philadelphia Learned to Live with the Traction Monopoly," unpublished paper delivered at the Brandeis University Graduate School Colloquium on American Business History (April 30).
Engle, Nathaniel H. (1955), "Public Relations in Large Corporations," Seattle: Bureau of Business Research, University of Washington.
Garrett, Paul (1938), "Public Relations—Industry's No. 1 Job," speech to the American Association of Advertising Agencies (April 22).
Goldman, Eric (1965), "Public Relations and the Progressive Surge, 1898–1917." New York: Foundation for Public Relations Research and Education.

Hebb, Richard D. (1930), "Fundamentals of Company Publicity." New York: American Management Association, General Management Series, No. 111.

Institute for Propaganda Analysis (1937–1938), *Propaganda Analysis*. Vol. I.

Market Research Corporation of America [1937(?)], "Industrial Relations, Public Relations, Economic Research, Market Research."

Metropolitan Life Insurance Company (1928), "Functions of a Public Relations Council." New York: Policyholders Service Bureau.

Miller, Raymond W. (1945), "Keepers of the Corporate Conscience." New York: American Council on Public Relations.

National Association of Manufacturers (1947), *The NAM and Its Leaders*.

National Industrial Conference Board (1945), *Business Record*, Vol. 2, No. 3 (March).

————. (1946), *Studies in Business Policy*, No. 20.

Neely, Paul (1970) "Catering to the Trade: A Critical Analysis of *Editor & Publisher*," Columbia University School of Journalism Major Paper (May).

Newsom, Earl (1950), "Some Considerations in Dealing with Public Opinion," speech delivered at the New School for Social Research, New York City (April 12).

Opinion Research Corporation (1946–1952), *Public Opinion Index for Industry*. Vols. 4–10.

Riegle, Donald W. (1966), "Hill and Knowlton, Inc." Harvard Business School Case Study.

Ross, Thomas J. (1950), "Some Comments on Public Relations Today and Tomorrow," speech delivered at the New School for Social Research, New York City (May 30).

Sharpe, Lynn (1972) "Black Public Relations," Columbia University School of Journalism Major Paper (May).

Index